The Henry Luce Foundation

Henry R. Luce

THE
Henry Luce
FOUNDATION

A HISTORY: 1936–1986

BY WALTER GUZZARDI JR.

THE UNIVERSITY OF NORTH CAROLINA PRESS

CHAPEL HILL & LONDON

The paper in this book meets the guidelines
for permanence and durability of the Committee on Production
Guidelines for Book Longevity of the Council on Library Resources.

Printed in the United States of America

92 91 90 89 88   5 4 3 2 1

Library of Congress Cataloging-in-Publication Data

Guzzardi, Walter.

The Henry Luce Foundation.

Includes index.

1. Henry Luce Foundation—History. I. Title

LC243.H45G89   1988   001.4'4   88-40182

ISBN 0-8078-1816-X

To the memory of Henry R. Luce

Contents

Foreword

Walter Guzzardi Jr. is a journalist. He has written countless articles for *Fortune* and *Time*, as well as other magazines. His *Fortune* stories have won him two Gavel Awards from the American Bar Association and the Gerald Loeb Award from the University of California's Graduate School of Business Administration. In 1983–84 he took leave from *Fortune*'s Board of Editors to accept the Ferris Fellowship at Princeton University, where he taught an undergraduate course about the press. He is the author of *The Young Executives*, a book about young managers in big corporations, and the editor of *A View from the Street*, by Donald T. Regan, the former White House chief of staff. For this present volume, which I commissioned, Guzzardi did his own reporting, and in it he expresses his own views. They may not be the views of the Luce Foundation.

Henry Luce III
President
The Henry Luce Foundation

Preface

Henry R. Luce had strong ideas about almost everything. I remember standing by his side thirty-five years ago in front of a statue of John Calvin that commands a park in Geneva. After staring at the statue intently for a few minutes, as he always did when he confronted a work of art even though he had seen it many times before, Harry turned to me and asked what I thought of Calvin. I answered that my knowledge was pretty scanty but that I thought of him as one of history's towering figures, who worked on and was moved by complex forces. I said that I was often unable to pass judgments on such giants; I was satisfied if I could learn something about them.

In that odd way he had, Harry raised his eyebrows, looked shocked, and delivered one of his famous lectures. He told me that I had a responsibility not only to know more than I did (I agreed with that and can apply the maxim to just about everything today as then) but also to make up my mind what I thought, to be for or against. I had to decide, Harry said, whether I believed that Calvin was a force for good or for bad in history. Then he went on to tell me his views—of course, he was very knowledgeable, and he had strong opinions about Calvin.

Harry's interests, both in their extraordinary range and their burning intensity, have been important determinants at the Luce Foundation for fifty years. Henry Luce III—Harry's son Hank—has been president and chief executive officer of the foundation for thirty years, and since Harry's death in 1967 the leading interpreter of what Harry would think and how he would apply his ideas to the sweep of current issues that not Harry or anyone else could have foreseen. And Harry's sister Mrs. Maurice T. Moore—Hank's Aunt Beth—has also been a perceptive guiding force at the foundation, clear in her opinions and vivid in her cheerful recollections of her brother: "Oh, Harry would have loved this," Beth is fond of saying.

I like to think that Beth is right and that if Harry were around, he would be just as enthusiastic as Beth is about what the foundation has been doing. It seems to me that Hank has strong views about the directions the foundation should be taking—strong ideas about what it can do in the world, which are clearly and consistently and pragmatically applied. Around the foundation for a year or so, I heard very little rhetoric about a better world, and a great deal of good sense about what would work and what wouldn't. It would be extraordinary, of course, if Harry were to like everything going on at the foundation today. I doubt very much that he would, because liking everything just wasn't Harry's style. But I think he would like most of what has been going on, and he would be especially pleased by its keen sense of perspective.

W.G.

Acknowledgments

First, I wish to thank Henry Luce III, who commissioned me to do this work. He was a sound and readily available source of information about the history of the foundation, both because of his nearly thirty-year association with it and his familial connections. He made no effort to control my reporting or my judgments and showed remarkable forbearance when the project, originally planned to take six months, stretched out to over a year-and-a-half. Since his father died, Henry Luce III has been the major motivating force at the foundation.

The entire project also was enormously helped by Robert E. Armstrong, the executive director of the foundation, who was unstinting in his help and guidance, as well as kind in his judgment about my judgment. After Henry Luce III, Armstrong and his predecessor, Martha Wallace, have been the important shapers of the foundation's directions. I also want to thank the entire staff of the Luce Foundation, especially Mary Jane Crook and Terrill E. Lautz, who were always willing to interrupt their busy day to lend me a hand. Melissa Topping arranged for and chose the photographs. Every member of the Luce Board of Directors spent time with me; my own view of the foundation's work would surely have been less accurate without their insights. Elisabeth Luce Moore spoke with great good cheer of the foundation's work as well as of its early years. One of the highlights for me was the couple of hours we spent together.

My thanks also go to the people working on Luce grants whom I interviewed. All were forthcoming and helpful. They range from bright-burning intellects such as Leon Kass at the University of Chicago to confined spirits such as inmates of Sing Sing prison. Without all of them, the book could not have been written.

I received help in the early phase of research from Angela Haines and from Helen Howard. More prolonged assistance came from Eleanor Schwartz. All were colleagues of mine at *Fortune*, and all performed in accordance with the high professional standards of that magazine. But I take responsibility for errors in the text—factual as well as judgmental.

My thanks also go to the patient people at the University of North Carolina Press: Matthew Hodgson, the director of the Press; Sandra Eisdorfer, the managing editor; and Trudie Calvert, whom the Press pressed into service as my copy editor. Robert Lubar, for many years my editor at *Fortune*, was kind enough to read this manuscript and make many helpful suggestions. An old friend and *Fortune* colleague, Wyndham Robertson, who is now vice-president for communications at the University of North Carolina General Administration, encouraged me to send the manuscript to the University of North Carolina Press, and even spoke a kind word to me about the text. I am grateful to her on both counts.

W.G.

The Henry Luce Foundation

I

The Founder

When I first went to work for him in Rome in 1953, Henry R. Luce was already rich, famous, and powerful. Cofounder of *Time* magazine, founder of *Fortune* and *Life*, and soon to found *Sports Illustrated*, Luce then was at the height of his celebrity as the most successful and the most contentious editor in the country. He had long since become accustomed to being called "king of a publishing empire," usually in critiques that were invidious in tone and illustrated by a symbolic octopus with round-the-globe tentacles. The magazines that Luce controlled were indeed worldwide in reach and influence. *Time* magazine in 1953 had a circulation approaching 1,800,000, and its foreign circulation of 377,000 gave it an important voice abroad. *Life's* weekly circulation was 5,473,000; in addition, *Life International* in English had a circulation of 285,000, and *Life en Español*, new that year, reached 210,000. *Fortune*, the elegant and authoritative business monthly that Luce with his courage and superb editorial intuition had started in the Depression year of 1930—and had nervily priced at one dollar an issue—was nearing 250,000. Rounding out the empire were *House & Home* and *Architectural Forum*, both glossy and classy monthlies for the housing industry and the architecture professions. All the magazines were leaders in their fields: *Time* magazine had twice the circulation of its nearest competitor, *Newsweek*, in 1952; *Life* soon became bigger and better than *Look*, a picture biweekly founded shortly before *Life* appeared; *Fortune*, although competitive with other business magazines, was nevertheless in a class by itself in urbanity of style and elegance of presentation.

Time Inc., the publishing company that Luce ran, was fast becoming a giant. The magazines brought in revenues of over $125 million in 1953, with advertisers from more than thirty countries buying space. The company, of which Luce was by far the largest shareholder, showed a net profit of $8,144,000 in 1953, with revenue exceeding $170 million. Those were big numbers for any company at that time: in 1955, when *Fortune* published its first "Fortune 500"— a list of the largest industrial corporations in the United States— Time Inc. ranked 176th. Thirty-three years later, in 1986, Time Inc. ranked 114th, with revenue of $3.4 billion, net income of $200 million, and over $3 billion in assets. In 1987 its revenue was $4,193,000,000. All four Luce-founded magazines—*Time, Life, Fortune,* and *Sports Illustrated*—remain among the company's most valued properties. The house that Luce built has become one of the world's largest publishing companies and a giant in the cable TV industry.

But Luce, so successful as a businessman, always thought of himself first and foremost as a journalist. Early he chose for himself the title of editor-in-chief of all the magazines, although he was in every respect except the titular one the company's chief executive officer, and he kept the editor's title until he retired. Editors do not usually make news, but Luce, with his dogged views and original cast of mind, was an exception there too. A legend in his lifetime, he held important dialogues with four presidents—Franklin D. Roosevelt, Harry S. Truman, Dwight D. Eisenhower, and John F. Kennedy—and had associations of varying degrees of closeness with nearly all the famous names of his era: Alcide de Gasperi, Konrad Adenauer, Chiang Kai-shek, Winston Churchill, Douglas MacArthur, Gamal Abdel Nasser, Pope Pius XII, and countless others. He knew titans of business from a dozen countries. Especially after his marriage to Clare Boothe Luce, he was regarded by his brethren in the press to be at least as interesting and newsworthy as many of the people he was covering in his magazines.

A man of iron will, Luce could be surprisingly flexible at times. When he addressed his editors, Luce unabashedly called himself "Your Boss," and he sometimes reminded them that he could fire any man in the place. (They often referred to Luce as "the Proprietor"—but so far as I know never in his presence.) But in 1953, in Rome, Luce was not cast as director of the show; he was playing a supporting role. He was there simply as the husband of the American ambassador to Rome. Mrs. Luce was appointed to that post by President Eisenhower, who had been helped to the presidency not only by the favorable coverage he received from Time Inc. publications but also by the considerable talents of the Time Inc. people whom Luce had loaned to Eisenhower's campaign. Clare Luce was, of course, a personage in her own right—she had been successful as editor, playwright, and congresswoman—but many observers attributed her appointment as ambassador to the money and power of her husband. Given that situation, it was not hard to find evidence for the view that Harry Luce would be uncomfortable in Rome—that he could never learn to play second fiddle.

But it turned out that subordination by protocol did not in the least cramp the style of the "Mr. Luce" half of "the Ambassador and Mr. Luce" team. He joined Mrs. Luce in presiding at diplomatic functions with charm and grace. He also made it obvious that he was pleased with and proud of how well Mrs. Luce was performing as ambassador. He had good reason for his pleasure: her presence in Italy brought that country more attention from the American public and the U.S. State Department, and more coverage by the media, than it ever had before or has ever had since. She handled beautifully the issue of Trieste—a hot spot for the United States, Britain, Italy, and Yugoslavia in those years—and made marvelously timed gestures of confidence: immediately after an Italian airliner crashed, Mrs. Luce switched her tickets from an American airline and flew Alitalia to New York. Italy soon became very fond of her. As for Henry Luce, he discharged his embassy-related social chores in good spirit. And despite their burden, from his office at 19 Corso d'Italia—just a few blocks from the American embassy on the other side of Hadrian's Wall—Harry Luce ran Time Inc. just as though he were still settled in his corner office on the thirty-third floor of the Time & Life Building in Rockefeller Center, to which he made frequent trips.

My job as Luce's assistant in the Corso d'Italia office—a two-line footnote to Harry's life but a major chapter, as well as a critical turning point, in mine—came about through coincidence, followed by misunderstanding. A couple of years before, as a twenty-nine-year-old Foreign Service officer, I had started on my first diplomatic assignment, which took me to the American embassy in Djakarta, Indonesia. In mid-1952, Luce came through Djakarta on one of his famous and, for *Time* foreign correspondents, much dreaded whirlwind tours around the world. The U.S. ambassador to Indonesia at the time was H. Merle Cochran, a blimp of a man whose bland Santa Claus smile concealed one of the shrewdest minds—and one always alert for intrigue—in the professional diplomatic corps. Cochran later became deputy managing director of the International Monetary Fund, which I have no doubt enlarged considerably the field that his paranoia, as well as his formidable abilities, required for full expression.

When he found out about Luce's visit, Cochran saw trouble coming. For moral and religious reasons, as well as because of his judgments about where American interests lay, Luce was always a determined anti-communist, but he never in his life held that counter-dogma more rigidly than in the early 1950s. President Ronald Reagan's description thirty years later of the USSR as an "evil empire" would have gotten Luce's instant agreement. He believed that every country not with us in the battle against communism was against us. He strongly disapproved of the policies of President Truman and Secretary of State Dean Acheson, neither of whom, Luce thought, recognized the true nature of the Soviet threat—especially in the Far East. Luce held Acheson responsible for the loss of China to the communist armies, which a couple of years before had driven the Nationalist government of Chiang Kai-shek off the mainland to Taiwan. These were the years when Senator Joseph McCarthy was making headlines around the world with his demagoguery about communists in the State Department. In his magazines, Luce condemned McCarthy, but that came too late to suit some of Luce's critics, who suspected that he was tolerating McCarthy's witchhunt because Luce hated communists so much. Luce's anti-communist views were well known in foreign offices around the world; after all, they found expression in millions of copies of his magazines.

The very issues that at the time swirled around the person of Luce were also hot topics in Indonesia. Under the leadership of Sukarno, a flamboyant politician then called "the George Washington of his country," Indonesia had only recently rid itself of the occupying forces of Japan and won its independence from the Netherlands. After freedom—Merdeka! it was called in Indonesian, always with an exclamation point—Indonesians expressed a flurry of warm feeling for America as a nation that had revolted successfully against colonial power. But the admiration was short-lived: a sadly mistaken U.S. policy killed it off.

Through aid programs and other means, the United States was constantly pressing Indonesia to align itself openly on the side of the West. With his country so recently freed of colonial subjection and foreign occupation, Sukarno was skeptical of the intentions of all the great powers. The more the United States tried to persuade Indonesia to join the "free world," the more aid programs swelled the numbers of Americans swarming around the Indonesian countryside, the more dedicated Sukarno became to a policy of neutrality. He was forever playing hard to get, declaring that Indonesia would accept American assistance—but only "with no strings attached." The epic lunacy of American insistence on aid programs and high visibility in Indonesia continued until the Sukarno government—and at least as much, its political opposition—finally tilted to the belief that the United States was a greater threat to Indonesian independence than the distant and disdainful Soviet Union. Suspicion of U.S. intentions was the first tenet of Indonesian foreign policy.

Ambassador Cochran at the time was arguing hard for a change. His view, which then and now I believe to have been correct, was that the United States should adopt a strategy of "hands off." Cochran thought we should leave the Indonesians alone and give up urging our aid upon them, which was only costing us millions, embroiling us in Indonesian internal affairs, and stirring up their hostility. The best policy, Cochran kept telling his superiors in the State Department, would be to stay aloof, save our dollars, and wait for opportunities. Cochran's persistence in this unpopular view was making him more and more disliked in the State Department and in the administration of the aid program back home, and occasional rumors were floated in Washington about his dismissal. Of course the rumors reached Djakarta.

On that diplomatic hot seat, the last thing in the world that Cochran wanted was to have an American VIP on the scene passionately trying to convince the Indonesians of the evils of communism. Unable to prevent the Luce visit, he decided to distance himself from it—and promptly left for consultation in Washington. The chargé d'affaires in Cochran's absence was a cautious, semi-articulate man wanting nothing to do with Luce, whose approach he regarded with the same pleasure that a bait fish takes watching a circling piranha.

To organize a schedule and to escort Luce around Indonesia therefore fell to me—an obscure embassy staff member too junior in rank to lead Luce to the highest-ranking Indonesian officials. I worked out a full itinerary for Luce, introducing him to American businessmen (in the oil companies, of course), but mostly taking him on visits to Indonesian journalists and a few politicians and second-tier officials with whom I had become friendly. My wife and I also had a couple of dinners for Luce in our tiny house in Djakarta; among my fond memories of Harry is the vision of him cross-questioning all of us about this or that (stabbing at the food with his forefinger) exotic Indonesian dish, prepared by our marvelous cook.

We filled our house on those nights with bright young Indonesians. Luce was always deeply interested in interesting people, more so if they had ideas different from his own. He was especially impressed with Koko Soedjatmoko, a putative socialist, who could articulate his intelligent and informed views with great effect. Searching for his meaning in English, Soedjatmoko would pause for a moment—and then, much to Harry's admiration, produce precisely the right word or phrase. (Many years later, Soedjatmoko became Indonesian ambassador to Washington.) With Soedjatmoko, Luce at first stood angrily anti-socialist, furious at the thought that anyone could contemplate neutrality—or worse—in the cold war. But characteristically he ended by admitting that there was more on Koko's side than he had thought. And Luce also had long exchanges with Mochtar Lubis, an editor who later was to spend several years under house arrest for violating government restrictions on press freedom—but by then Sukarno was no longer George Washington, but just another tin-horn dictator.

Luce cared a lot less, however, for the few officials in the ruling Masjumi party whom I managed to reach. To Luce, they were small potatoes in the first place. I couldn't get him to the heights of officialdom to which he was accustomed: to the foreign minister or the prime minister or Sukarno. What's more, a couple of low-ranking bureaucrats kept Luce waiting for a long time in the bare, hot anterooms of their offices. One scheduled interview never came off at all: fed up with waiting for an assistant minister for something or other, Luce stalked out of the Foreign Office, with me a couple of nervous steps behind. To fill the gap, I improvised an afternoon in the countryside. Harry enjoyed the drive from the frying heat of Djakarta to the cool hill town of Megamendung, dotted with lovely villas built by the Dutch. On the round trip he asked me every conceivable question about the region, few of which I was able to answer. I found out later that he was famous among *Time* correspondents for asking the impossible: where does that staircase go, why are they digging that big hole, why is it called Smith Street?

On the whole, Luce found his Djakarta trip disappointing. The big-shot solons wouldn't see him; the American ambassador wasn't even in town. To make matters worse, Luce was staying at the Hotel des Indes, which, when the Dutch ran it, was often compared to the Raffles in Singapore. But now in Indonesian hands it was oppressive and run-down. In the morning the place was crowded with Dutchmen in pajamas having breakfasts of raw bacon and rich cheese, and the dining room did not exactly exude chic. Full of the spirit of Merdeka!, the Indonesian staff had no desire to give much in the way of service. Moreover, what sleep one could get on those humid nights in

Djakarta was often interrupted by gunfire. Luce's eagerness as a reporter would have made at least that a pleasure—if anyone could have explained to him who was shooting at whom. But unfortunately no one knew the answer to that question either. Luce left Djakarta having concluded that the country was a hopeless case, an opinion that he passed on to his editors with some force when he got back home. As far as I know, he never visited the place again.

Luce's annoyance at Indonesia, however, evidently did not extend to me, and he must have made a note at some point that I might be worth hiring. He never discussed the matter personally with me. But a few months later, as my tour of duty in Indonesia was ending, I heard from Allen Grover, a gracious and influential vice-president of Time Inc., one of whose responsibilities was said to be "vice-president in charge of Harry." At Luce's request, Grover first looked me over and then offered me the job of assistant to Luce in the office in Rome, which was just then being set up. The misunderstanding that I mentioned earlier—and that I didn't learn about until years afterward—was that since my name was Guzzardi, Luce somehow thought that I spoke Italian. I didn't, and one of the first jobs I had was to learn the language quicker than Luce himself was learning it. I was able to do that in part because, of course, he immediately wanted to use the language to express complex ideas—he never seemed to have any other kind—while I was willing to settle for the ability to cope with everyday needs. Then, too, Luce was absent in New York for long periods, and I had plenty of time to study while he was away. If Luce was disappointed when he found that I didn't speak Italian from the beginning, he never said so. In his last months there I was able to interpret for him on occasion, which he seemed to enjoy.

While he was in Italy, Luce never lost his interest in the language, and he never forgot that he and I had started out together to learn it from ground zero. Once when we were in a hotel in Milan on business together, he twisted his ankle slightly. I used the phone in his sitting room to call the *portiere* and asked for an Ace bandage for "Mr. Luce's ankle," using the Italian words. Overhearing, Harry turned to me with sudden surprise and a touch of envy: "Walter, do you know all the parts of the body in Italian?" Somehow, that was typical of the way he approached learning the language.

Those years in the early 1950s were surely as interesting and exciting as any in Luce's fascinating life. In 1953, he was fifty-six years old, in full possession of his remarkable talents and at the height of his corporate power. He was a strongly handsome man, with the commanding presence that befit his station. He dressed elegantly, although I suspect that he was never especially aware of what he was wearing or how he looked; I believe he was thinking of more important things. Italian neckties were the height of fashion in those years, and like the rest of us Luce wore them; on special occasions he would make me a present of one, and I would do the same for him. But once when I visited him in New York, I gave him a couple of neckties, and when I saw him the next day, he gave them back to me, along with a bunch of others I had given him in the past. "This necktie business has gone far enough," he said gruffly. Only a very poor spirit could have been offended.

Luce was an important man, and he acted like one. Modesty would not have become him, and he did not affect it, any more than he affected the role of blowhard. Leading a tightly organized life, he was always checking the time, in a characteristic gesture pulling out his gold pocket watch with a sudden jerk, glaring at it, and then shoving it back into his pocket again. He never expected to wait, and of course he was very seldom kept waiting. When we called together on Alcide de Gasperi, the prime minister who set postwar Italy on its democratic path and who came as close as anyone since Garibaldi and Cavour to being a great Italian patriot, de Gasperi was already waiting for Harry. Once *Life* did a picture spread of Pope Pius XII in a Vatican garden visiting crowds of little children. The pictures were superb, and Harry decided to make Pope Pius a present of an album of them. The album was put together; the audience was fixed; Harry invited the office staff to go along to meet the Pope. We arrived on the minute and were seated in one of the Vatican's frescoed anterooms.

But the Pope was late, and then later still. Harry kept yanking out that watch in exasperation. Finally, he turned to me: "Walter, where the hell is the Pope?"

I had just asked him whether he really thought the Pope's tardiness was my fault—we knew each other well enough for that kind of retort by then—when, while Harry was still steaming, the Pope came in. The change was instantaneous: Luce became so charming and attractive that the Pope was captivated. We all stayed later than scheduled, while Harry engaged the Pope in a discussion about world affairs. He showed no reluctance to interrupt His Holiness to make his points. If the Pope was shocked, he didn't show it: he listened to Harry attentively through all the interruptions. Harry then talked a bit about the power of religion in the world: he believed it was great but not as great as it ought to have been. With what I can only assume was great sincerity, the Pope expressed his agreement. The Pope then blessed the group from the office whom Harry had brought along—I don't recall that he muttered any prayers over Harry—and the audience broke up with great good feelings on both sides. That was typical of Harry—to go quickly from an expression of annoyance to the pleasure of intent discussion, the annoyance forgotten. Issues, ideas, broad questions, important matters—they were what Harry liked.

Luce's propensity to interrupt frequently came from his interest in substantive discussion. He had no facility for small talk, a shortcoming that led many to think him rude. But that deficiency, so awkward and obvious on some social occasions, was usually forgotten when Luce himself began to talk and when he started to question people who might be around him at the dinner table. Intensely interested in any topic that others cared about, he often left them with a pleasant sense of their own importance. That quality of Luce's was ignored by one biographer, who dwelled excessively on his "cold blue eyes" (which in fact had a temperature well within normal range) and his "haughty manner" (which in fact came from his impatience with trivia and a conviction that if trivia could be pushed aside, something better would take its place). Indeed, that biographer, a writer of great skill, seems to me to have been cruel and hostile to Luce, denigrating both the man and his accomplishments. Those of us who knew Harry hope someday for a fairer evaluation of him.

My association with Luce remained close until his Roman adventure ended with Mrs. Luce's resignation. By that time we had held many discussions on many subjects; besides, I had been present at countless lunches and dinners at which Harry held forth in company of celebrated guests both Italian and American, and I had occasionally risked a comment or two. Over the two and a half years or so, he must have decided that my interests were journalistic, not managerial, although I had never been a journalist. He asked me once whether I had ever written anything journalistic in tone, and I fished out a "Letter from Djakarta" that I had done a year or so before and had never gotten around to submitting anywhere. Harry never commented on the letter, and I forgot about the matter. Then, quite suddenly, almost on the eve of his departure, he told me that he had decided to make me chief of the Time-Life Bureau in Rome.

The uproar from *Time*'s editors and the chief of *Time* correspondents in New York was audible to *Time* correspondents around the world. Communications from the editors that Harry casually dropped on my desk argued vigorously against the appointment: "Don't do this, Harry," ran one note, with the expectable addition: "It isn't fair to Walter." Rome was a very desirable post, and correspondents were supposed to sweat somewhere else for years to get it. The notion held by those who think of themselves as hard-bitten reporters that no one could be a good journalist without first covering high school basketball games may never die; it lives along with the cherished myth that journalism is a profession (it isn't: it's a trade). Anyway, Harry settled the matter in a one-line cable to New York: "Have hired Guzzardi as bureau chief for a six-month trial." When he came through Rome a few months later, Harry said, "You seem to be doing fine," and I gathered the trial period was over. I like to think that the episode reveals Harry's special willingness to make guesses and take risks with people—to break out of the conventional modes, into which he himself never fitted. Some of the editors who at first opposed my appointment later became good friends and colleagues.

During my five-year stint as bureau chief in Rome, I saw Harry only now and then. Although his interest in Italy was fading, he made a trip to Rome occasionally; when I was in New York, I called on him in the office, and once in a while we had a private lunch together. That sporadic association continued after I left *Time* magazine and went to *Fortune* in New York as a writer. When I went to see Harry to tell him that I was being promoted to editor at *Fortune*, he gave a pleased grunt. But we saw each other very little from then on. I was astonished and saddened when I walked into my *Fortune* office on March 1, 1967, to hear the news that Harry Luce was dead, just a month before his sixty-ninth birthday.

THE FOUNDATION'S PROVENANCE

Henry Robinson Luce was born in Tengchow, China, on April 3, 1898, the first of four children. His father, Henry Winters Luce, was a tireless Presbyterian missionary, a worker in the vineyard unflagging in his faith through all adversity. His mother, Elizabeth Root Luce, was the prototype of the courageous, devoted missionary wife—a woman of character. Thus three powerful forces— China, church, character—were part of Henry Luce's birthright. They shaped his life, and on their account, in a way, Luce through his magazines helped to shape his times.

Of that remarkable boyhood in China, which he left in 1912 to attend school in the United States, Luce said later: "In some ways that background endowed me with special qualifications to be editor-in-chief of great American publications . . . in some ways, it disqualified me. I probably gained too romantic, too idealistic a view of America. Missionaries have their faults, but their faults are comparatively trivial. I had no experience with evil in terms of Americans . . . it marks, I think, some grave fault in me that I was never disillusioned

Courtesy of Henry R. Luce Estate

Henry Winters Luce, the father of Henry R. Luce, died in 1941 at the age of 73. A graduate of Yale and the Princeton Theological Seminary, he taught for 30 years at missionary colleges in China, where his two sons and two daughters were born.

with or by America, but I was, from my earliest manhood, dissatisfied with America. America was not being as great and as good as I knew she could be, as I believed with every nerve and fiber God Himself had intended her to be." That frame of mind—never disillusioned, always dissatisfied—may be a clue: had Harry been disillusioned, or had he been satisfied, he might never have started the foundation that bears his name.

At Hotchkiss and Yale, Luce distinguished himself as a student and as a budding journalist, editing campus papers and writing vigorous editorials. Although he was the impoverished son of a missionary family, his striking qualities and abilities, as well as the associations formed at school and college, soon led him into the company of people with money and connections. He and a college friend, Briton Hadden, used those connections to raise enough capital—$86,000— to start *Time* magazine, whose first issue was dated March 3, 1923. Success came to the magazine quickly, and Luce became its boss after Hadden died in 1929. In 1930 Luce, convinced that business was "the prime determinant of society," started *Fortune* magazine, a business monthly, which hired such famous writers as Archibald MacLeish, Ernest Hemingway, James Agee, and Dwight Macdonald. *Time* and *Fortune* were new editorial genres, and Luce followed them with yet a third, *Life*, in 1936, a picture weekly started, as Luce said, "to see life; to see the world; to eyewitness great events; to watch the faces of the poor and the gestures of the proud." *Life* in its best days was the most successful magazine in history. Luce's final success in publishing was *Sports Illustrated*, which he began in 1954 and which took longer than its sisters to reach profitability, but later became the fourth largest magazine in the United States in revenue generated.

Over the forty years between the time he founded *Time* magazine and his retirement in 1964 as editor-in-chief of Time Inc., Luce showed his talents as a forward-looking chief executive. Besides start-ing the magazines that became leaders in their fields, he approved decisions that put Time Inc. into the forest products business and into book publishing, and prepared the way for the company's strong presence in television. I don't know how much he would have ap-

Courtesy of Henry R. Luce Estate

Elizabeth Root Luce, Henry R. Luce's mother, sailed for China as a missionary's wife in 1897. Home leaves included holidays in New Hampshire, where this photo was taken when she was in her early 40s. Elizabeth Luce was 77 years old at her death in 1948.

proved the use of words like "multimedia"—I suspect he would not have liked it—but he laid the groundwork, just the same, for Time Inc.'s prominent position as a media giant. Always, though, the magazines had first call on his interests.

Not the magazines, however, but the power and tenacity of Luce's mind, for which the magazines were only the medium, explain his fame. Despite occasional very direct reminders from him to his editors about who was boss, Luce ruled the magazines not by command but by force of argument, often grinding down opposition with his resolve and remarkable ability to retrieve facts. He wanted to convince, not to give orders, and he sometimes won debates just because he wanted to convince so badly: he was willing to wage a debate almost endlessly, and with notable fervor. The debate was Luce's special kind of ex-post-facto method of editing—expressing disagreement with what one magazine or the other had said the week before. Luce was forever floating great ideas: about the American Century, the American Proposition, the national purpose, the rule of law, the anti-communist Christian crusade, free trade and capitalism, and the survival of the race. He was insatiably curious, and when he got on a favorite topic, he could talk at great length, associating ideas, making historical references, and running on until his listeners were exhausted—as one put it, "intellectually black and blue."

Through the spreading influence of the magazines, Luce associated with the great and then became one of them in a way that no other editor ever approached. The list of people in high places with whom he conducted dialogues reads like a catalog of those in power around the world during Luce's lifetime. The examples, in part enumerated earlier, are endless. *Life* ran Churchill's memoirs; Luce met and banged heads with Churchill. *Time* ran covers on Nasser of Egypt; Luce spent hours with him ("I am for Nasser," he cabled his editors). For *Time*'s fortieth birthday, Luce gave a huge dinner to which the famous flocked; included were 284 people who had been *Time* cover subjects. All came more for Harry Luce than for *Time*. "Never in our experience have as many titans and titanesses of industry, sports, music, theater, philanthropy, politics, publishing, finance, science, medicine, government, advertising and religion taken spotlighted bows in one place," remarked Geoffrey Hellman of *The New Yorker*—the ridicule that magazine had directed at Luce in a famous parody years before long since forgotten. Wired President John F. Kennedy on that occasion: "Every great magazine is the lengthened shadow of its editor, and this is particularly the case with *Time*. *Time* has instructed, entertained, confused and infuriated its readers for nearly half a century. Like most Americans, I do not always agree with *Time*, but I nearly always read it." Wrote one of Luce's associates after his death: "His life served its sovereign and precise purpose: to make some difference in history."

If the suspicion about foundations is that they are the compliment that vice pays to virtue, the charge can be quickly dismissed in the case of Henry Luce and the foundation he started in 1936. He was no enormously rich plunderer pouring his fortune into philanthropy as a deathbed atonement. In that year, Luce was thirty-eight years old, still approaching the apex of his fame and power. *Time*, *Life*, and *Fortune* were all growing and prospering, with Luce's editorial talent and business acumen showing the way, and there was the promise of much more to come. Luce still had the major part of his career, the greatest successes of his life, and the long period of celebrity before him. He was just becoming what he was to remain for the next thirty years: America's most successful journalist.

There is no evidence that a single urge or purpose impelled Luce to start the foundation. Luce was curious about everything, and every idea attracted his interest, but private philanthropy does not appear to have had any important place in the wide range of his thinking: evidently he never spoke or wrote on the subject. His sister Elisabeth Luce Moore does not recall that Luce displayed any intensity about the foundation or its aims. "I don't think Harry was thinking about the foundation in important terms," remarks Mrs. Moore. Henry Luce III, whose tenure as the foundation's president and chief executive officer includes the last ten years of his father's life, does not think so either: "I have the impression that Dad was not at all articulate or particularly focused on what the objectives of the foundation ought to be," Henry Luce III says today.

Still, Henry R. Luce's general motivations are clear enough. As his wealth grew, he was more and more importuned to give to charities and causes. Certainly he wanted to be rid of the burden, both financial and administrative, of passing judgment on that stream of requests. A foundation offered just such relief, holding out the prospect of an orderly handling of the flow of entreaties without heavy invasions into the time of Luce and his staff. Those advantages, Elisabeth Luce Moore recalls, were emphasized to Luce by her late husband, Maurice T. Moore, a senior partner of the prominent New York law firm of Cravath, Swaine and Moore, which was to become longtime counsel to the foundation. Moore also urged Luce to establish a foundation for tax purposes, a reason Moore foresaw was to become more and more important over the years. And although Luce does not seem to have made the point explicit anywhere, it seems obvious that he liked the idea of a foundation as a vehicle for action—a way of attaching real-world consequences to his many ideas about good causes.

Besides all that, as a practicing Christian sensitive to society's needs, Luce surely wanted to be certain that he did not neglect the Christian virtue of charity. A long list of the charitable donations he made before the foundation began, and continued independently of the foundation later, testifies to that desire. Even after the foundation was in full swing, Luce contributed his own time and money to various philanthropic endeavors. As the narrative that follows relates, he was a trustee of the Metropolitan Museum of Art, and a generous donor to Yale University. In the last year of his life, Luce traveled extensively around the country and addressed church groups on behalf of the Presbyterian Church's $50 Million Fund, much of whose ultimate success was attributable to Luce's willingness to exhaust himself for the good of the church. Finally, slowly over the years, there emerged what was to become the most important reason of all for Luce's ever more generous contributions to the foundation and for the large endowment he willed it when he died. The reason, seldom mentioned in earlier years, evidently grew steadily in Luce's mind and has been given appropriate prominence by Henry Luce III: to dedicate the foundation as a tribute to Henry Winters Luce and Elizabeth Root Luce, Henry R. Luce's parents.

2

The Foundation in Formation

The Henry Luce Foundation was born on December 24, 1936, when the certificate of incorporation was filed in the office of New York's Secretary of State. At that time the corporation paid its first bill: a $40 filing fee. Five people subscribed to the certificate, all of them close to Henry R. Luce: Elisabeth Luce Moore and her husband, Maurice T. Moore; Clare Boothe Luce, Henry R. Luce's wife; and Luce's two closest business associates, Charles Stillman, the chief financial officer of Time Inc., and Roy Larsen, three years later to become Time Inc.'s president. Three of those five—Clare Luce and Maurice Moore were absent, as they often were to be—held the foundation's first meeting two days later on December 26. "None of us took it terribly seriously, it was just a friendly meeting," says Mrs. Moore. As members of the corporation, the quorum of three elected the foundation's first Board of Directors, made up of four of the five (Maurice Moore did not become a director). Stillman was elected president, who then as now was also the chief executive—two posts that he was to hold for twenty-two years. Larsen became the foundation's vice-president.

At their first meeting, the directors accepted the foundation's first contribution—from Henry R. Luce, who with two exceptions was to be the sole contributor to the foundation for the next thirty years until his death in 1967; there was to be no other contributor after 1967 except for the huge gift left to the foundation by Clare Boothe Luce (see "A Look Ahead," page 189). (The two exceptions before 1967 were Henry Luce III, who shortly after becoming foundation president set up a trust, and Claire McGill Luce, his late wife, who gave the foundation $6,000 in 1965.) Henry R. Luce gave the foundation on that day of its founding 38 shares of the common stock of General Publishing Company, a personal holding company that held Luce's

The Foundation in Formation

Ken Haas

Henry Luce III

Time Inc. stock. Two years later, in December 1938, as a result of changes in the tax laws, General Publishing was liquidated, and in place of its shares the foundation received 557 shares of Time Inc. common stock, with a market value of $56,224, along with $2,679 in cash. Since the General Publishing shares were carried on the books of the foundation at $89,851, the foundation suffered a decline of assets with the swap that followed General Publishing's liquidation. If that can be looked on as an unfortunate financial experience, it was a rare event, happening on only one other occasion in the foundation's history. The remarkable growth of the value of the stock of Time Inc. donated by Henry R. Luce over the years and left to the foundation in trusts and in his will has taken the foundation to its present level of assets. At the end of fifty years they stood in excess of $225 million and made possible foundation commitments in 1986 for grants totaling $14.6 million.

The letter from Henry R. Luce to the foundation announcing his contribution of thirty-eight shares of General Publishing included a suggestion from the founder to the directors of the new corporation that the dividends from General Publishing should be donated to Yenching University in Peking. Yenching, a missionary-founded academic institution of international repute, had achieved its preeminence partly because of the labors of Henry Winters Luce, who had been a leader in its establishment. Honoring his work there, the principals of Yenching had built a pavilion located on an island in Unnamed Lake on the campus, and christened it the Henry Winters Luce Pavilion. Then, in 1935, one year before he founded the foundation, Henry R. Luce gave $50,000 to Yenching as part of an endowment to honor his father.

Henry R. Luce's gift to Yenching at that time stands as an antecedent to his creation of the foundation, as well as a signpost indicating the convergence of interests that have come to distinguish the foundation. That gift and a subsequent $1,500 grant from the foundation to Yenching, following Luce's request, set several enduring patterns in motion. Henry Winters Luce was honored, as Henry R. Luce wished him to be—a gesture that was to be repeated many times over the years; the foundation's connections with China and its significant presence in Chinese-American relations were declared and were to be thereafter reinforced; and the foundation's goal of furthering higher education was made evident and was to continue. Thus were the early guiding principles of the Henry Luce Foundation defined.

For a number of years after its founding, the Luce Foundation led a quiet life. Its assets slowly grew as a result of continuing contributions from the founder of steadily rising stock. Grants made by the foundation took expectable directions. Elisabeth Luce Moore remembers that even though Luce was not a participant in the foundation's discussions—"Tex Moore said to Harry, 'Now listen, you have to stay out of this, it's either a foundation or it isn't,' " Mrs. Moore remembers—its directors knew his interests. "We all knew what Harry wanted," as Elisabeth Luce Moore puts it today. The foundation therefore distributed its donations much as Luce would have made them if he had been responding personally to requests made to him. The grants also reflected the interests of Elisabeth Luce Moore. She was working, as she still is today, in the cause of Christian colleges in China and for the Young Women's Christian Association (YWCA), of which she is a trustee; her sister Emmavail also worked for and supported the YWCA. Samplings of the foundation's gifts of the early years demonstrate the point:

1937	Federal Council of Churches \$250
	Bowery Branch of the YMCA 250
	International YMCA 500
1938	Associated Boards of the China Christian Colleges, at the request of Henry Winters Luce 500
1939	Associated Boards of the China Christian Colleges. 1,000
	Associated Boards of the China Christian Colleges (for the endowment fund of Yenching College for Women). 2,150

Federal Council of the Churches of Christ
in America 250
National Board of the YWCA
(for work in China). 100

To approve these grants, the board met once or twice a year, in those "friendly little meetings." In a couple of Decembers, however, some board members must have been away for Christmas: in December 1939 only Roy Larsen showed up for the meeting that was to have taken place in his own office; in December 1943 Charles Stillman, the president, found himself alone at the foundation's meeting and in the absence of a quorum promptly gave himself leave to adjourn.

Meanwhile, Henry Luce's contributions to the foundation continued. In 1941 Luce took out two life insurance policies, making the foundation the beneficiary. The foundation paid the premiums until his death. (Total premiums paid by the foundation over twenty-six years came to $143,754; the proceeds paid to the foundation totaled $308,014.) Just before the end of 1941, immediately after both the Japanese attack on Pearl Harbor and the death of his father, Luce made one of his rare cash gifts to the foundation: $9,500. In a move that was probably related, the foundation contributed $5,000 to United China Relief, of which Henry R. Luce was the driving force. Luce also gave twenty-two hundred shares of Time Inc. stock to the foundation the following year.

During this time no one around the foundation was worrying much about long-range planning. In 1942 Elisabeth Luce Moore suggested that perhaps more planning was in order, and it should be geared to the interests of "the principal donor" while continuing the charitable interests of his and her parents. A breakdown of the grants made by the foundation from 1936 to 1945 shows that Asian affairs received the largest share—$82,782 for that period. Of that sum, $73,332 went to the China Institute of America. U.S. religious institutions were the next largest beneficiaries: grants to them totaled $59,950. Next came Christian higher education in Asia, with the

Ken Haas

Directors Elisabeth Luce Moore and the late Charles L. Stillman,
who died in 1986.

Associated Board of Christian Colleges in China receiving $11,650. In 1945, four years after Henry Winters Luce's death, the foundation made its biggest single grant to date: $50,000 to the Union Theological Seminary, of which Henry R. Luce was to become a director, to establish the Henry Winters Luce Visiting Professorship in World Christianity. Income from a Henry R. Luce trust and foundation grants supported that chair and increased its endowment until 1967, when the foundation made its final grant of $125,000. The foundation's total funding of that Luce chair came to $275,000.

These early years—the first phase of the foundation's history, when some form of help to China was its major concern—ended with the fall of the bamboo curtain in 1949. Having driven the Nationalist government of Chiang Kai-shek to exile in Taiwan, the Chinese Communists took command of the mainland and began rooting out the pernicious U.S. influence—especially the influence of American missionaries and educators. The Chinese Communist authorities closed Christian schools and colleges run by missionaries and expelled Americans. Many American and European missionaries were jailed. United China Relief was compelled to end its efforts in China.

For more than twenty years afterward, the Luce Foundation, like the United States, was forced to end its activities on the mainland of China. The foundation then moved in two directions. First, it went to work elsewhere in East Asia, supporting and building educational and religious institutions. "After the conquest of Mainland China by anti-western and anti-Christian communism," Henry Luce III wrote in 1969, "when the movement known as the China Christian Colleges turned its attention and support to a group of universities in the countries of the East Asian perimeter, these became logical subjects of the Foundation's interest." (As a demonstration of the continuity of the foundation's interests, those same "logical subjects" were to receive special foundation attention in 1987; see Chapter 8.) Second, as part of a careful plan that grew into one of the foundation's most important policies, the foundation embarked on a program of grants to American organizations—especially but not solely educational institutions—that were principally concerned with East Asia.

The move to the periphery of China took concrete form with the foundation's first building programs. The foundation underwrote five major construction projects at important educational institutions in East Asia. One building was constructed at each of the universities that were at that time the primary and traditional affiliates of the United Board for Christian Higher Education in Asia.

• A new Christian college named Tunghai University was established at Taichung in central Taiwan in 1955. The foundation pledged $50,000 to the United Board for Christian Higher Education in Asia for the construction of the Henry W. Luce Chapel at Tunghai. I. M. Pei was the architect. Engagement with the construction of the chapel turned out to be longer, more complex, more detailed, and sometimes more maddening than anyone on the board had foreseen. Henry Luce III, who in 1958 had become a member of the foundation's board, was the principal actor in the affair. Because of an unrealistically low budget set by the board before he was elected to it, he plunged into details about estimates, working drawings, and construction materials—"the new design using less hinoki [wood] but adding copper roofing, comes out to about $25,000 less," he told board members in September 1958. (It ended up with neither material, the exterior being entirely ceramic tile.) Finally, total grants from the foundation for the chapel ran around $166,000. The splendid structure was then in place. When in 1963 Elisabeth Luce Moore and Roy Larsen visited the chapel, they found it "the most striking piece of architecture in Taiwan, and a great monument to the foundation's work." In September 1968 Henry Luce III presided over an observance of his grandfather's centennial in the chapel.

• To Chung Chi College in Hong Kong, now part of the Chinese University of Hong Kong, the foundation in 1970 gave $250,000 toward the cost of badly needed library resources. The new facility, called the Elisabeth Luce Moore Library, was dedicated in 1971. "This important new addition," the foundation reported, "represents a significant expansion of the academic resources available to the Chung Chi faculty and the rapidly expanding Chinese University."

• Setting a general pattern that it was to support later elsewhere, the foundation made a grant of $100,000 for a new University Center at Satya Wacana Christian University in Salatiga, Indonesia. As with Chung Chi, the center opened in the autumn of 1971. The center, which includes a new auditorium, has served as a focus for the cultural life of central Java. It also has provided the student body with facilities such as a broadcasting station and bookstore—amenities not readily found in Java.

• The foundation in 1968 committed $300,000 to Silliman University, in the province of Negros Oriental, four hundred miles south of Manila in the Philippines, to construct a cultural center on the campus. Since its founding, Silliman University has been noted for its commitment to the liberal arts and for stimulating culture and the arts in the more remote rural areas of the Philippines. The university raised matching grants to build the center, the first time such a device was used in Asia. Completed in the mid-1970s, it includes an auditorium, recital hall, and exhibition areas. The center is named for Claire Isabel McGill Luce, Henry Luce III's wife, who died in 1971.

• In 1971 the foundation approved a $200,000 grant to Yonsei University, on the outskirts of Seoul, Korea, for the design and construction of a university chapel. One of the oldest Christian institutions in the Far East, Yonsei had never had a chapel that could also serve as a center for its church-related programs. The five-hundred-seat chapel, named the Henry Winters and Elizabeth Root Luce Chapel, is more than a place where religious services are conducted: it also has accommodations for counseling and numerous student activities. The chapel has become a model for church architects in Korea, using a design that successfully connects Christian traditions and the contemporary life of that country. The chapel was dedicated by Henry Luce III in 1974 (the year he also dedicated the Luce Auditorium at Silliman University in the Philippines).

The foundation's building program went into abeyance for a while but it was revived some years later, and the foundation remains receptive to building proposals today. In 1980 the foundation was approached by the United Board for Christian Higher Education in Asia with a request on behalf of Payap College, a liberal arts college in

Thailand founded by the Church of Christ there six years earlier. The college at the time was building a new campus near Chiang Mai, 360 miles north of Bangkok, and, in the words of the United Board, wanted funding for a chapel that will "occupy a prominent place on the new campus, symbolizing the strong spiritual foundations of the institution. The building will serve as an outstanding example of Thai architecture, and at the same time be thoroughly functional, accommodating 500 but designed so that the seating can be expanded for special events." In response, the foundation contributed $300,000 to the $400,000 project; Payap raised the balance from other sources. Ed Sue, an architect from San Francisco who lived for three years in Thailand as a representative of the United Presbyterian church, was commissioned to do the work, which was completed in 1984.

In 1985 and 1986, the board of the foundation committed a total of $60,000 to restore the Henry W. Luce Pavilion, which had been built on the campus of Yenching more than fifty years before. These funds put the Luce Pavilion back into operation as a social and recreational center for the faculty of Peking University, which now includes what was once Yenching. Peking University authorities said just before the restoration that the newly refurbished pavilion would commemorate once more "the Luce family's contribution to Chinese education and culture."

Most of the foundation's building program took place after Henry R. Luce's death. But he saw some part of it begun and saw his son carry on the program. Surely the building phase, and his son's role in it, were among the works he intended the foundation to accomplish.

When the foundation seemed to wander from his interests, though —when "the people who knew what Harry wanted" seemed forgetful—Luce made clear that he was troubled. After the foundation had made a grant to St. Bernard's, a secondary school in Gladstone, New Jersey, of which Henry Luce III was president, Henry R. Luce and Henry Luce III had an interesting exchange of ideas in 1962, just a few years after young Luce had taken over as foundation president. Probably because he regarded such a grant as largely irrelevant to his main concerns, Henry R. Luce expressed his displeasure, which he

Peter Charlesworth

The Elisabeth Luce Moore Library at Chung Chi College, Chinese University of Hong Kong, was dedicated in 1971. The foundation awarded a grant of $250,000 toward the cost of the library. Money for the land was raised locally.

was always able to do with considerable clarity. In response, his son, the initiator of the grant, wrote his father a rather plaintive letter. "For many years this office was held by Charlie Stillman," ran the letter. "It is my impression that he regarded his role as one of financial stewardship on your behalf . . . when I took over this office, it seemed to me implicit that my assignment was two-fold: 1) to carry out certain intentions which had already been set in motion, and to fulfill others which might arise from you . . . and 2) to assume a degree of responsibility which had not previously reposed in me before I was president . . . nor in the Foundation when it was smaller than it was yet to become." Evidently Henry R. Luce shared his son's judgment about the importance of his assignment: although Henry Luce III suggested other candidates to his father, the outcome of the affair was that Henry Luce III continued as foundation president—

The Luce Chapel, at Payap University in Chiang Mai, Thailand, was designed by Ed Sue, a San Francisco architect who had worked in Thailand for several years. A symbol of Payap's strong religious foundations, the chapel was completed in 1984.

continued, as he said, "to carry out certain intentions which had already been set in motion" and assumed new responsibilities as well.

Some years later, in the foundation's first published annual report in 1969, Henry Luce III described the "intentions already set in motion." Wrote he: "Seventy-two years ago my grandparents, Henry Winters Luce and Elizabeth Root Luce, embarked for China to take up their life work as missionaries in the Church Universal. This Foundation is in a very direct sense a continuation of the work they began. . . . The Reverend Dr. Luce was a man of lifelong curiosity about the human condition and of deep concern for all human needs. It is safe to say that whatever may loom today or henceforth as a pressing social issue would also be a subject of great interest to him. . . . Even more explicitly can this concern be ascribed to my father."

Despite that philosophy of continuity, however, the foundation at

The Luce Student/Community Center at Satya Wacana Christian University in Salatiga, Indonesia, was formally opened in 1971. The center has provided space for student assemblies and theatrical productions while serving as a focus for cultural life in central Java.

the time those words were written was going through its first period of dramatic change. While its endowment had grown, the foundation's character had not altered much over the preceding thirty years. Even though Henry Luce III had taken on more independence than his predecessor as he assumed "new responsibilities," the foundation essentially remained an expression of the will of Henry R. Luce as interpreted by his son, his sister, other members of the family, and a couple of close associates. And despite Henry R. Luce's generosity, the foundation remained a small player in the philanthropic field.

When Henry R. Luce died suddenly in February 1967, however, all that changed. Luce's bequests not only more than quadrupled the assets of the foundation, they also laid the ground for enormous future growth. As a result of that multiplication of assets, the foundation immediately confronted an array of new tasks, the most impor-

Hyunwong Kang

The Henry Winters and Elizabeth Root Luce Chapel is at Yonsei University on the outskirts of Seoul, Korea. One of the oldest Christian institutions in the Far East, Yonsei planned the chapel to include facilities for counseling and student-related activities as well as for Sunday and daily services.

tant of which was vastly to increase its role as grant giver. Not only did such an increase accord with the desires of Henry Luce III and the board, but changes in federal laws mandated it. The foundation thus faced new requirements: it needed to acquire a larger professional staff, to formalize its procedures, and to engage in more long-range planning. In this new phase, Henry Luce III continued to be the guiding force; Elisabeth Luce Moore remained influential on the board; the board remained remarkably stable, with only four changes from 1936 to 1976 (see Appendix A). Despite the homily that "every foundation in the long run loses the spirit of its origin," at the Luce Foundation the steering by the ideas of three generations of the Luce family was still resolutely adhered to. Yet the notion of the foundation as an expression of family, and some of the accompanying familial intimacy that characterized it, had to fade. In the years

Peter Charlesworth

The Luce Chapel at Tunghai University in Taichung, central Taiwan, was named for the Reverend Dr. Henry Winters Luce. The striking design, by the Chinese-American architect, I. M. Pei, gives the chapel its great distinction.

after Henry R. Luce's death, Henry Luce III and the directors undertook to build a new foundation—one that could take its place in a new world.

At the time of his death in 1967, Henry R. Luce owned 1,012,575 shares of Time Inc., or about 15 percent of the company's outstanding stock. His estate had a total value of $103,014,000 before federal and state taxes totaling $10,338,000 were paid. In his will, drawn in 1964, Luce named his son Henry Luce III, his brother Sheldon R. Luce, and his brother-in-law Maurice Moore as co-executors. Luce left to the foundation a big bundle of 145,040 shares of Time stock, valued at the time of Luce's death at $14,449,610. At the same time the foundation acquired 540,000 shares valued at $53,797,300 under

Melvin Calderon

The Claire Isabel McGill Luce Cultural Center at Silliman University in Dumaguete City, Negros Oriental, the Philippines, includes an auditorium, recital hall, and exhibition areas. The Center has been widely hailed as the foremost such facility in the Philippines' Visayan Island group.

the terms of a trust that Luce had set up on June 9, 1961, of which he and Moore were trustees.

When Luce died, the foundation already owned 191,029 shares, given by Luce over the thirty years that had gone by since he made the first donation of the shares of General Publishing. In only three years over that long stretch had Luce failed to give stock to the foundation: 1940, 1941, and 1959. In the latter year, rather than make a gift of stock, he set up his first trust for the benefit of the foundation, the Henry R. Luce (Settlor) Trust, which provided that the income from 10,000 shares of Time stock was to go to the foundation for the lifetime of his son, Henry Luce III. During Henry R. Luce's lifetime only two sales of Time stock were made by the foundation. Both were

Forrest Anderson

The Luce Pavilion at Peking University in China was built in 1930 in honor of Henry R. Luce's father, the Reverend Dr. Henry Winters Luce. In the mid-1980s the foundation funded the restoration of the pavilion to encourage its use as a social and recreational center.

very small: 448 shares were sold in 1944 and 250 shares in 1949. After Luce died, therefore, the foundation owned a total of 876,069 shares of Time Inc., or about 12.7 percent of the outstanding shares. The 876,069 shares made up virtually the entire assets of the Luce Foundation at the time.

Accounting practices then came into play. The value of the stock on the foundation's books was figured until 1966 on what was called the "fair market value" of the shares, that is, the price of the shares on the day that they were turned over to the foundation. This carrying value was far below the real value as the price of Time stock climbed—the higher the climb, the greater the spread between the two measures. On the day of Luce's death, the value on the books for the 191,029 shares the foundation owned stood at $4.5 million. The true market value—the actual amount that owners could realize by a sale—of those shares on the last day of 1966 totaled $18,960,000. One year later, when the foundation owned 879,069 shares, Time Inc. was quoted on the New York Stock Exchange at 97⅜. So the value of the foundation's stock, by the true value measure, came to $85,307,000, or about four and a half times more than it had been the year before—and nineteen times greater than the amount shown on the foundation's books on the day Luce died.

After it put on so much muscle, the foundation barely resembled its former self. It became a much more significant figure in the foundation world. And that world was already in turmoil when the foundation joined it. The turmoil was to have lasting effects on the finances and methods of the foundation, although its purposes remained the same.

The high visibility and wealth of a few big foundations, which were assumed to be having a dramatic impact on American life, were attracting public resentment and hostility in the late 1960s. The visibility came partly from the move of prominent officials, including Dean Rusk and McGeorge Bundy, from positions of power in government to top jobs with top pay in the foundation world, and the other way. The Ford and Rockefeller foundations especially seemed to be bursting with money; to their critics they appeared to be the beneficiaries of favorable tax treatment while remaining secretive about and unaccountable for their actions. The spreading notion that foundations were abusing their tax status led to congressional hearings. The well-publicized arrogance of some heads of foundations when they appeared before a committee of the House of Representatives added to the resentment of many lawmakers. The hearings became hotter still because of political divisions within Congress: southern conservatives resented the funding by foundations of drives to register black voters, and northern politicians disliked foundation grants to inner-city organizers. Waldemar Nielsen's important book, *The Big Foundations*, made the argument that foundations became implicated in a current curious explanation of the nation's ills: that the very rich were banding together with the very poor to rob everybody else. Hearings and investigations led to the conclusion, as Henry Luce III wrote in the foundation's 1969 annual report, that "some foundations have engaged in practices which are generally agreed to be corruptions of their charitable intent or abuses of their tax-free status."

Punitive laws resulted from the furor. Congress wrote new tax laws that in effect obliged foundations to pay out to qualified charities 6 percent of their assets or all of their annual income, whichever was greater. (That figure was later effectively lowered to 5 percent, where it remains.) At the same time, the angry Congress levied a 4 percent excise tax on foundations for the purpose of paying the cost of auditing their records. That tax led Henry Luce III to explode in the same annual report: "The conception of this tax suffers from so many debilities in equity, in the national interest, in philosophical principle, and in future implication that it is difficult to imagine a worse one." Agreement with that sentiment was evidently widespread enough that Congress later changed its mind. The excise tax on foundations was lowered and now stands at 1 percent; it is 2 percent for foundations that fail to meet their pay-out requirements in any single year.

Thus, even if the increase in the Luce Foundation's assets had not fueled the desire of its directors to expand the foundation's activities, the legal obligation to do so would have been imposed on the foundation anyway. A couple of examples give the dimension of the consequent increases. In the first period of its life, the ten years from 1936 to 1945, the foundation made grants totaling about $158,000— around $15,000 a year. Over the later decade, from 1956 to 1965, the foundation's grants reached a total of $2.5 million—an average annual outlay of nearly $250,000. That increase in dollar amounts, however, was modest when compared with what ensued after 1967.

At that time, under the twin spurs of new inheritance taxes and new regulation, the foundation entered the middle period of its fifty-year life. Grants between 1967 and 1974 ran between $1.1 million and $2.9 million a year; in some of those years they came to more for a single year than they had for all the years from 1936 to 1966. In every year but one since 1979, the foundation's grants came to an amount larger than their cumulative total from the date of the foundation's beginning to the date of its founder's death. It was indeed a new world.

But in that middle period from 1967 to 1974, very little expansion took place from year to year. That was the grim time of collapsing markets and collapsing houses on Wall Street, and nearly all common stocks came under pressure: the Dow Jones Industrial Average, very close to 1,000 in December 1968, stood at 631 in May 1970. From the alluring price of 97⅜ in December 1967, the Time stock dropped in what seemed like a free fall: it closed at 24⅞ on the last trading day of 1974, down 75 percent over the seven-year span. The assets of the foundation, of course, decreased in correlation with that decline. At the end of the miserable market year of 1974, the true, realizable value of the foundation's Time Inc. stock, which had stood at $85,307,000 at the end of 1967, had dwindled to $19,802,216.

All that may not have been as unfortunate as it then appeared. When Henry R. Luce traveled around the world, interesting events always seemed to happen someplace where he landed. *Time*'s foreign correspondents used to joke about "Luce luck," and they figured that Harry and a revolution were likely to visit their country about the same time. Bad news, in a way, was good news: all the correspondents wanted Harry to be pleased, and nothing could have pleased Harry more than a splendid revolution. In a way, the foundation in the 1970s seems to have inherited some Luce luck: stagnation and worse in money markets at that time was bad news, bringing the foundation's assets down by 76 percent.

But that decline provided time to adjust to the new era and to organize more formally for the future. Martha Redfield Wallace, who began her association with the foundation in 1967, became first a vice-president and program director of the foundation and then its first executive director. In 1972 she was elected to the Board of Directors—the first addition, except for foundation president Henry Luce III, since 1936. Robert E. Armstrong, who in 1970 came from the Rockefeller Brothers Fund to the foundation as program director, succeeded Wallace as executive director and board member in 1983.

Melissa S. Topping

Shigeru Kaneshiro was the first member of the Henry Luce Foundation staff to have served for twenty years. The foundation's business manager and assistant treasurer, he retired in 1982.

Managerial continuity on the operational level was established, as it should be in a sizable corporation. Administrative expenses reflect the larger staff that larger assets had to bring: in 1960 they ran $256.11. At the outset of the middle period, in 1968, they came to $65,918. In 1985, net administrative expenses came to almost $1 million—but by then, the years of declining assets were far behind, and the foundation had become a giant relative to its position in 1974.

Still, for all the advantages that a period of consolidation afforded, back in the early 1970s it must have seemed as though that shocking drop in the value of Time stock, and so of foundation assets, would go on forever. The foundation made its first substantial sale of Time stock in April 1972, when it sold 80,000 shares at 55¼. Made in part because of the "prudent man" rule that in effect requires directors to diversify the assets of which they are custodians, and in part because of market judgment, the sale looked brilliant two years later, when the New York Stock Exchange finally closed its books on 1974 and Time Inc. could be had for $24.87 a share. But measured by the rule of the free market, and not the rule of the prudent man, the sale came to look less than brilliant in ensuing years. That is far more true of a transaction made in 1976, when the foundation sold 40,000 shares whose cost exceeded the then current market value, resulting in a loss of $860,931.

But the years of drought did not, after all, last forever. Finally, the stock of Time Inc. began to climb, taking the foundation's assets to new heights. With the stock selling at 47⅛, the assets reached about $70 million in 1979, a big increase over 1974 but still below the level at the time of Henry Luce's death. Then after an earlier two-for-one split, the stock went in 1980 to 62⅝, carrying the assets for the first time over $100 million. They stood at $156 million, another record, in 1982, with the stock, after another two-for-one split, selling at year end at 52⅛. By 1985 the assets had doubled over what they were in 1980: the stock then sold at 62⅛ at year end, and the value of the assets came to $205 million.

Ken Haas

*Henry Luce III, president of the foundation, and Robert E.
Armstrong, its vice president and executive director.*

Acting as prudent directors must, and selling on the way up, the
Luce board sold 75,600 shares in 1979. These sales followed:

1980 75,000 shares at 57 to 57¼
1983 200,000 shares at 49 to 50¾ (following a two-for-one
      stock split)
1984 200,000 shares at 38 to 38⅞
1986 100,000 shares at 72½ to 73½

Those sales had the effect of accelerating the foundation's move
away from its dependence on the stock of Time Inc. As we have seen,
virtually all of the foundation's assets were in Time Inc. stock immediately after Henry R. Luce died: only around 3 percent of the assets

Executive director Robert E. Armstrong with associate director Melissa S. Topping.

Ken Haas

Robert E. Armstrong with administrative assistant Kimberly S. Melton (left) and grants manager Suzanne W. Wagoner.

were invested elsewhere, mostly in short-term money-market instruments. By 1974, with assets down to a bare excess over $24 million, $4.3 million, or 18 percent, was invested in securities other than Time Inc. stock. In 1975, with assets more than doubled over the level of the previous year, the balance had tilted again: the value of Time stock increased, and it accounted for 90 percent of the foundation's total assets. The portion of assets invested elsewhere went up once more, to 13 percent, in 1976, following that sale of 40,000 shares.

Subsequent to those sales listed above, the ratio of Time stock to the total assets of the foundation began a slow and steady decline. Time Inc. stock came to 88 percent of the total in 1977, 88 percent in 1981, 84 percent in 1982, and 80 percent in 1983. In 1984 Time Inc. spun off to its shareholders 90 percent of Temple-Inland, its large forest products subsidiary; at the end of that year, Time's stock came

Ken Haas

The foundation's controller, Irwin Skolnick, and administrative assistant Margaret Werner.

down to 57.5 percent of the foundation's total assets. With subsequent appreciation greater than the appreciation of the diversified portfolio, the ratio of Time stock rose again to 64 percent in 1985. Slowly over the years, therefore, the foundation has diversified its holdings—as the definition of prudence dictates—while its assets grew to make it, if not a giant, at least a full-grown member of the foundation world.

Grants have moved up apace with asset growth. As we have seen, the law requires that foundations must distribute to qualified charities each year either all of their annual income or 5 percent of the average market value of their assets, whichever is greater. The 5 percent rule has usually governed in the case of the Luce Foundation, since the 5 percent each year has consistently amounted to more than annual income. The annual pay-out of 5 percent of assets averaged over each year brought the total of approved grants to $6.4 million in

Ken Haas

*Directors Charles C. Tillinghast, Jr., John C. Evans, and
David V. Ragone.*

1982, $6.9 million in 1983, $9 million in 1984, and $8.4 million in 1985. When added together, grants and administrative expenses—the total annual outlays of the foundation—have substantially exceeded income in recent years. The excess came to $4.859 million in 1983, $5.869 million in 1984, and $3.879 million in 1985. Although the dimensions are greater, however, the pattern is not new. In 1968, when administrative expenses stood at $65,918, grants and expenses exceeded income by $773,760. Those numbers demonstrate what is obvious to the slowest member of the arithmetic class: if assets grow annually at more than 5 percent, the institution that owns them can pay out 5 percent, do a lot of good work to help good causes, and get bigger forever.

Immediately after Henry R. Luce died, his family and close associates at Time Inc. began groping for a suitable "memorial to Harry." Ideas about that memorial flowed to Henry Luce III—by then president of the foundation for nearly ten years. At that time he was also chief of the Time-Life Bureau in London, but keeping in close touch with the affairs of the foundation during his frequent trips to New York and in discussions with Martha Redfield Wallace and board members. From Roy E. Larsen came the suggestion that the foundation might explore what private philanthropy and American business should be expected to contribute to social welfare; Larsen went on to propose a study of the needs of higher education over the next twenty years, examining questions such as where the funds would come from and what the government and private roles should be in providing them. Elisabeth Luce Moore expressed some interest in a foundation program that would send visiting professors to six colleges in East Asia and provide funds for a local professor at those colleges as well. Board members agreed that medical and scientific projects had long been excluded from foundation activities because the federal government was so deeply committed in those areas, and, as Martha Wallace noted, "no one seemed disposed to change this informal situation." Journalism was ruled out in principle as a possible beneficiary of the foundation.

Some interesting thoughts also came from people outside the foundation's walls. The late John K. Jessup, who had been an editor of *Fortune*, chief editorial writer for *Life*, and a valued colleague of Henry R. Luce, held a discussion of "a suitable memorial to H.R.L. in the field of higher education" with Paul Weiss, a professor of philosophy at Catholic University. In his letter to Henry Luce III describing the discussion, Jessup explained that he had reminded Weiss of "H.R.L.'s belief in what John Murray called 'the unity of truth'—his way of seeing continuity and consistency between one field of knowledge and the next, from theology and political philosophy down to sports and fashions." In an intriguing response that indicated the temper of the times, Weiss told Jessup that "the Yale Divinity School is not now nor likely to become a source of intellectual light and leadership . . . the Divinity students make their Christian affirmation by practicing the social gospel in the ghettos, while the faculty, all too ready to argue whether God is dead, turn for support and guidance to the Philosophy Department. But the philosophers are running scared—scared of anything that might be challenged by findings of Science."

Then Weiss suggested to Jessup a way of countering "the trend toward increased specialization and compartmentalization of knowledge," which stood in opposition to Luce's idea of the unity of truth. "Weiss's idea," explained Jessup in his letter to Henry Luce III,

> is that every bright college senior about to plunge into graduate work in economics or biology or physics or law or whatever should be given an inducement to look around before he leaps. Weiss would offer a clutch of one-year fellowships to such seniors, giving them a year of graduate study in a field totally alien to their intended specialty. The economics major would study Egyptology for a year, the biologist philosophy, the lawyer Greek or history. . . . The general objective is to leaven the lump of the American academic intelligentsia with scholars who have some sense of the range and diversity of human knowledge and therefore are more likely to ponder its interconnectedness. Weiss's somewhat jocular name for the recipients of these fellowships is "Luce Cultural Mutants." They would as individuals punch a few holes and let air and light through the walls of overspecialization.

In the end, the foundation itself became "the memorial to Harry," in turn dedicated to his parents. None of these specific ideas developed into direct foundation commitments, but traces of all of them can be found in programs the foundation later funded. Although the particulars of Elisabeth Luce Moore's idea never materialized, higher education in East Asia has remained a major foundation concern. No "Luce Cultural Mutants" ever lived and breathed, but the notion of countering specialization by interdisciplinary teaching survived in one of the principal undertakings the foundation supported following the death of Henry R. Luce: the Luce Professorship Program. The foundation also entered the field of social welfare, which Roy E. Larsen had focused on, although it was not Larsen's early interest but the times, and the concern of Henry Luce III, that provided the incentive. For an account of the foundation's movement in that direction, see Chapter 7.

3

The Professors

When at the age of eighteen Henry R. Luce headed with grim determination toward a career in journalism, part of his drive came from his conviction that journalism afforded the broadest possible education. He chose it as his trade, he said then, because he could "by that way come nearest to the heart of the world," and he accepted with eagerness the breadth of the learning he would have to acquire: "Journalism means that my interests must include everything from Beethoven to labor strikes," he declared. An early *Time* magazine slogan, "De omni re scibili et quibusdam aliis"—"concerning everything knowable and various other things besides" has been called by John K. Jessup in his book *The Ideas of Henry Luce* "the inventory of Luce's mind." Luce was fascinated by grand concepts, which he unhesitatingly enunciated; the sudden revelation of linkage between apparently unrelated grand ideas stimulated him enormously, and he filed them away in his remarkable memory to produce them later for the stimulation of others.

Henry R. Luce's interest in such connections is apparent from the nature of a gift he made to Yale University in 1955. At that time, when his wife was the American ambassador to Italy, Luce's busy life was divided between Rome and New York, and one might assume that Yale and the interplay between academic disciplines would be far from his mind, but not so. In the summer of 1955 Luce gave Yale 957 shares of Time Inc. stock, along with the income for a period of thirty years from another 957 shares that Luce gave in trust to one of his granddaughters. The stock at the time was traded over the counter and was selling at around $52 per share. The purpose of the grant was to establish a professorship of jurisprudence at Yale Law School and so to further not only Luce's interest in Yale but also his persisting interest in the law (a phrase he frequently capitalized). "Our leadership can succeed," Luce said in a speech he gave in the summer of 1952, "only if we formulate a rational idea of order—giving meaning to our phrase 'Liberty under Law.'" And he came back to the theme in 1959: "The U.S. needs excellence . . . the basic proposition is the advancement of the rule of law."

Most interesting in all this is the letter of acceptance that Yale President A. Whitney Griswold sent on June 24, 1955, describing the nature of the professorship. "This arrangement represents a bridge-building operation in which I have long been interested," Griswold wrote. "The H.R.L. Professor would be a regular member of the Law School Faculty, with regular half-time assignment to upperclass teaching in Yale College under the auspices of either the Department of History or the Department of Political Science (or both). The H.R.L. Professor should be a man of such character, personality, cultural breadth and teaching ability as will ensure his success as an undergraduate teacher."

An amusing footnote to that episode remains to be told. In his letter, Griswold said he would like to call this "the Henry R. Luce Professorship of Jurisprudence, and hope Harry will let me, though of course I'd defer to his wishes." In his graceful reply that began "Dear Whit," Luce remarked that "your letter admirably states the purposes of the Professorship, and our hopes for it." Added Luce: "I am honored by the suggestion that the Professorship should be named for me and offhand am unable to summon up enough modesty to decline."

In the intervening years, there have been only two Luce Professors of Jurisprudence at Yale. The first, Charles Black, has since become a professor at the Columbia University Law School in New York. (His wife, Barbara A. Black, is now the dean there.) The present occupant of the Luce chair at Yale, like Black "a man of character, personality, cultural breadth and teaching ability," is Leon Lipson, who has held the Luce chair for ten years. Besides being a lawyer of note—he was an editor of the *Harvard Law Review* and practiced with a top New

York firm—Lipson is also a specialist on the legal institutions of the Soviet Union, and was retained as a consultant by *U.S. News and World Report* in 1986, when Nicholas Daniloff, its Moscow correspondent, was under arrest in the USSR for thirteen days. As the holder of the Luce chair, Lipson also teaches in the philosophy and political science departments at Yale.

In a recent seminar for undergraduates at Yale, Lipson held forth on dialectical materialism. Asked how that topic related to jurisprudence, he replied that arguments are something on which undergraduates and budding lawyers ought to sharpen their minds. From his classroom (and classic) analysis of the dialectic as expounded by Hegel and Marx, Lipson proceeded to question the idea of quantity and quality—concepts that partake of dialectic opposites—and pressed his students on the question whether quantity might ever become a function of quality. Among the mind-stretching examples with which Lipson challenged his students was the difference between a boy just getting hair on his face and a man who had a beard—is the difference only one of quantity? What about the oyster and the pearl, Coca-Cola versus new Coke—what kind of metamorphoses are they? He mentioned the impostor who pretended he was a flight attendant and did such a good job that passengers called in their compliments, leading to his exposure—things are so good they're bad? He then asked whether any in the class of around fifteen students recalled Engels's analysis of the French campaign in Egypt against the Mamelukes in 1798. The following dialogue with a student ensued:

> *Student*: Engels said that one on one, the Mamelukes were superior to the French forces. But the French forces were better organized. With three Frenchmen on two Mamelukes, the Mamelukes would still definitely win. Then he went on to something about three hundred versus three hundred. . . .
> *Lipson*: Yes. Two Mamelukes were undoubtedly more than a match for three Frenchmen. One hundred Mamelukes were equal to one hundred Frenchmen. Three hundred Frenchmen

could usually beat three hundred Mamelukes. And a thousand Frenchmen could invariably defeat fifteen hundred Mamelukes.

Student: What happens is you have this quantitative change and then you have a qualitative difference. Even though you are not changing the proportions the Frenchmen become better, which is a qualitative change.

Lipson: But you have changed the proportions.

Student: Yes, but it doesn't matter. One on one the Mamelukes win; one thousand on one thousand, the French win.

Lipson: Yes. So even if we set them up as equal, which is not the way Napoleon did it, the relative quality of the forces changes.

It was a seminar that Henry Luce would have loved to attend.

Today, to select from the foundation's many activities a few that would be closest to Luce's heart—in their willingness to innovate, perhaps, or in their perception of the value of change—is no easy task. But surely the Henry R. Luce Professorship program would have to be one of the choices. That program expresses the foundation's commitment to intellectual experimentation on the campuses of privately funded colleges and universities—a program, as Henry Luce III put it when the foundation made the commitment, "specifically dedicated to encouraging a great intellectual adventure in higher education." And the nature of the adventure is to encourage the establishment of professorships that cut across academic disciplines, and bring to undergraduates new insights into the cross-currents between one discipline and the other in the humanities and social sciences.

Both the temper of the times and the beliefs of Henry Luce III were key elements in the initiation of the program. In the late 1960s, the major foundations, hearing the roar from the ghettos, were addressing their attention to social questions and to "problem solving." The Luce Foundation responded to those circumstances. But Henry Luce III also feared that what he called the "intellectual excitement" in higher education was in danger of dying down. He believed that the traditional modes of academic expression, housed and sheltered in departmental structures in universities, were too neat and rigid. They were tilted toward specialization too soon in the education of under-graduates: the "liberal" side of a liberal education was being lost in the name of "relevance." Wrote Luce in 1971: "In such a time of turmoil as we are experiencing, it is important for the universities to concern themselves less with social fashion, and more with their fundamental responsibility as carriers of civilization's accumulating and lasting wisdom." And he added that "ultimate questions"—the kind his father loved to raise and argue about—were being neither adequately posed nor sufficiently debated in the undergraduate's academic world.

At its meeting in December 1968—a critical moment in the foundation's history, as it began to assess the role that its greatly increased assets, willed to the foundation by Henry R. Luce in 1967, permitted it to play—Henry Luce III put before the board one of the most important proposals of his long tenure. He asked the board to make a commitment to fund a number of Luce professors at private four-year colleges or universities in the United States. His purpose was to be accomplished by the unusual characteristics of the chairs—they would express the dynamic quality that Henry R. Luce would have applauded.

To win funding, applying universities would have to propose chairs that cut across traditional boundaries of the academic disciplines, merging two or more departments in some integrative and imaginative way. The new synthesis, Henry Luce III hoped, would revive discussions of "ultimate questions" as it revealed unsuspected associations between the disciplines. The Luce professors, he said, "would seek to wrest from a combination of insights some greater truth than is contained in any of the parts." To help in their search for that greater truth, Luce and the Board of Directors established a committee, with two university presidents and other high-ranking academics as members, to help them choose among the flood of proposals that they anticipated—and got—from dozens of universities across the country.

The Professors

In 1987 the walls between the academic departments at American universities still stand, as solid as ever. But the Luce professors—the thirty-eight chairs established between 1969 and 1986 are listed in Appendix G—have helped undergraduates here and there to scale the walls. Luce professors have also provided a good deal of the missing "intellectual excitement" as some of them pressed the "ultimate questions" at thirty-three colleges and universities. And the excitement is likely to continue.

Several important policies govern the award of these professorships. One is that faculty members already present at the university applying for a grant are not eligible to fill the chair, so that the foundation does not find itself underwriting an ongoing program at the university in some other guise. Another is that the chairs are approved by the Luce board before the university goes about recruiting the person to fill them—discouraging the practice of using grants simply to attract a celebrated performer whose principal contribution might be to the university's prestige, not to undergraduate enlightenment. On the financial side, the foundation took the unusual step of deciding simply to pay the costs of the chair for a limited number of years—first a maximum of ten, now a maximum of eight years: at present, a first grant of five years and a possible renewal for three more years—instead of endowing the chair. The directors, explains Robert Armstrong, executive director of the foundation, "had a sense of skittishness about endowing the chairs. They felt that by limiting the time period of the chair, universities would be much more willing to bring us high-risk proposals, because they would know that they won't be stuck with a named chair for all time. If we wind up with something that doesn't work, it's easier for them and for us to cut bait." The directors originally voted a $42,500 annual grant for Luce professors, including some nonstipend expenses. In 1982 the annual award was increased to $60,000, and it now stands at $90,000.

The First Two

The first two Luce professors turned out to be men of some celebrity who generated public controversy as well as intellectual excitement. One was Franklin A. Long, whom President Richard Nixon in 1969 planned to appoint as director of the National Science Foundation. But the political reaction to Nixon's soundings about the nomination of Long turned out to be hostile: Senator Everett Dirksen and others opposed Long because he had argued against President Lyndon Johnson's antiballistic missile defense system. Nixon then withdrew Long's name from consideration; later, however, confronted by an angry scientific community, Nixon in a rare moment confessed he had been wrong. Disinclined to reenter the political arena, Long on July 1, 1970, became Henry R. Luce Professor in Science and Society at Cornell University, where he had been vice-president for research and advanced studies. He also took over as director of Cornell's new Science, Technology and Society Program.

Applying the candor that sometimes is missing from the reports that the Luce professors submit annually to the foundation, Long described his first year—the first year of a Luce professor anywhere—as "exciting, vigorous, and often confusing." Long taught two very popular undergraduate courses at Cornell: Biology and Society and The Social Implications of Technology. Characteristically, however, he thought that some of the popularity of the courses in 1970 might be "slightly faddist," resulting from the novelty of his presence at Cornell and the tumultuous cries for "relevance" rather than from the courses' merits. As it turned out, the undergraduate concern with the impact of technology on society was no fad: in his final report, ten years later, Long confessed to personal gratification with the continued enthusiasm of undergraduates for his courses and for the larger program of which he was a part. With the understatement of the scientist, Long concluded: "We remain pleased with our work with undergraduates."

The second controversial man to become a Luce professor was Irving Kristol, one of the fathers of the neoconservative movement.

With Daniel Bell, professor of social sciences at Harvard, Kristol is a founder of *The Public Interest*, an influential quarterly noted for its scholarly treatment of public issues. Later he founded *The National Interest*, another quarterly that promotes neoconservative views on American foreign policy. The proposal for the chair that went to Kristol came from James Hester, then president of New York University and now an adviser to the foundation on the professorship program. NYU, said Hester, had strong professional schools, including a school of social work, dealing with the usual scourge of urban problems: "traffic, sanitation, communication, the nourishment and feeding of millions." Needed, Hester added, was a professorship that would pull together these elements into a single course, cutting across the specialties and teaching philosophically about the values of urban society.

Kristol's main courses were called The Culture of Cities and The Urban Intellectual. Rioting on the streets and on campuses was hitting the headlines, and the courses were addressing hot current issues. Kristol's analysis, as he explained it, took the following form: "The counter-culture was anti-urban: the environmental thrust was anti-urban, the anti-scientific and anti-technological thrust was anti-urban. It was a kind of romanticism. But still urban values permeated the culture as a whole, largely as a consequence of the mass media, television above all, and the spread of higher education." A skilled teacher teaching about the day's most emotional issues in a newly designed course had to be successful, and Kristol was.

A Luce professor for nine years, Kristol later drifted away somewhat from the multidepartmental concept with which his courses began. The drift came about, he says, because "at the beginning there was a whole program of metropolitan studies. The students were fascinated, they were majoring in urban affairs. By 1976, my students were no longer so interested, and the urban studies courses began slowly to melt away. No one was passionately excited about it any more. The urban crisis went away. Nothing changed, but the crisis went away." In his latter-day teaching, Kristol switched to Adam Smith and what is right about capitalism—"he taught about the things that were important to Irving," one critic says. But as an early Luce professor, Kristol added both substance and glitter to the foundation's effort.

Kindling at Chicago

When they are most successful, grants to Luce professors carry kindling to universities—they start intellectual fires that burn long after the foundation's support has ended. Although a gifted teacher is the principal agent, other elements also fuel the flames: a merger of disciplines in the humanities hitherto ignored, a university congenial to such mergers, students receptive to liberal arts. Just such a fusion has taken place at the University of Chicago, where the Luce Professor of the Liberal Arts of Human Biology for eight years was Leon Kass, whose academic achievements are among the most unusual in America. Kass holds an undergraduate degree from the University of Chicago, an M.D. from that university's medical school, and a Ph.D. in biochemistry from Harvard. He has written on a wide range of subjects; for example, he followed his piece in a medical journal titled "B-Hydroxydecanoyl-Thioester Dehydrase from *Escherichia coli*" with an article in *The Public Interest* (the magazine edited by Irving Kristol) called "Making Babies—The New Biology and the 'Old' Morality." Leon Kass would have been recognized as a Renaissance man even in the Renaissance.

A mark of Kass's success is the work he is doing now, five years after his eight-year tenure as Luce professor ended. He continues to teach the distinctive and oversubscribed courses that he began with Luce sponsorship. The University of Chicago has installed a program of study with Kass's courses at its core, and students are responding with growing enthusiasm to this rare curriculum. Speaking of the students, Kass says, "If you spread a good table for them, you'll find they are hungry."

The design for the table that Kass was soon to spread came to the foundation in March 1974 in the form of a proposal from the University of Chicago. University President Edward H. Levi, (later U.S.

Dr. Leon M. Kass, former Henry R. Luce Professor in the Liberal Arts of Human Biology at the University of Chicago, teaches courses there on such subjects as Aristotle's De Anima *and Rousseau's* Second Discourse on the Origins of Inequality.

attorney general) was troubled by "issues arising from the relation-ship of new discoveries in biology and society. . . . Problems concerning the biological and ethical definition of death, the right to live or die, and the ethics and psychological impact of organ transplantation, behavior modification, and genetic engineering became critical as the general inability on the part of the medical profession, the government, and indeed of the private citizen, to understand the dimensions of these issues becomes more evident." To Levi, these issues, which form one of the principal dilemmas of our time, called for "the creation of a new area of study" at the common frontiers of biology, the social sciences, and the humanities. The Luce board enthusiastically endorsed the idea and ultimately awarded $430,000 over an eight-year period to that "new area of study."

No account of what Leon Kass did in his first year at the University of Chicago tells more than the one Kass himself submitted, in accordance with the foundation's request for annual reports from all Luce professors, at the end of the academic year 1977. "What have I done in my first year?" Kass asked. "The simplest and truest answer is that I taught my classes—formal courses entitled 'Human Nature and Human Good: Aristotle's Nicomachean Ethics,' and 'The Human Passions' and 'Science and Society: Knowledge, Morals, and Power' and two reading courses with smaller groups of students, on 'Plato's Symposium' and on 'Plato's Theaetetus.' "

That would seem enough, but Kass went on to explain that his purpose as Luce Professor of the Liberal Arts of Human Biology was to respond to the challenge that

> modern scientific notions of nature and of man fail to provide any grounding for morals or any support for opinions regarding a worthy human life. Moreover, the very successes of the scientific concepts call into question the validity of the more traditional notions of nature and man . . . for example, the findings of molecular biology have encouraged those who believe nature is blind and dumb, and indifferent to good and evil, and studies in animal behavior have posed a sharp challenge to the importance,

if not the existence, of freedom of will. . . . We need critically to examine the traditional understandings of human nature and human good in the light of the findings of modern biology, psychology, and medicine.

Henry R. Luce would certainly have agreed with the need "to examine human nature and human good," although he approached the question from the viewpoint of science's conflict with religion rather than of its conflict with society. Characteristically, Luce viewed the conflict optimistically: "In recent years, the relation of science and religion has entered into a new phase of peaceful coexistence," Luce told the Princeton Theological Seminary in 1962.

From 1977 on, Kass enlarged the scope of his teaching as Luce Professor and later helped to lay the foundation for a new course of study at the university. His annual reports over the years show the enlargement of his fields as a teacher: "A graduate tutorial on the book of Genesis . . . a seminar on Rousseau's *Discourse on the Origins of Inequality* . . . coordination of a lecture series on 'Human Being and Citizen' . . . a seminar on 'Philosophy of Nature: Purpose and Form,' devoted largely to the question of teleology in living organisms and to the reading of Kant's *Critique of (Teleological) Judgment* . . . an undergraduate seminar on 'Science and Society: Knowledge, Morals and Power' . . . a tutorial on Descartes' *Rules for the Direction of the Mind.*" Kass accompanied all that with a spate of public lectures—for example, one called "The Case for Mortality" to a group of older people and another "On the End of Medicine" to Loyola Medical School. He also wrote articles for such publications as the *Journal of the American Medical Association* and *The American Scholar.* But Kass, who says, "I don't believe in false modesty about my talents," never loses his evaluative powers or his sense of true modesty. Commenting about the Human Being and Citizen course, he remarked: "The teaching went rather poorly. The class was small and the students both diffident and disengaged."

In the new program at the university, Kass is now chairman of a field of concentration called Fundamentals: Issues and Texts, which concentrates on fundamental questions of human existence and, Kass says, "certain fundamental books that articulate and speak to such questions." The "precise and thoughtful pursuit" of the fundamental questions is carried on by the acquisition of "the knowledge, approaches and skills of conventional disciplines—historical, philological, literary, scientific, political, and philosophical . . . offering an alternative to the more disciplinary and methodological emphases of other undergraduate programs." Undergraduates choose the "fundamental issue," which Kass says "is usually something of intense personal importance to them." Then they study intensively the classical books that "address or embellish or enlarge the issue."

Such studies, reminiscent of the Great Books program that Chancellor Robert Hutchins initiated at the University of Chicago, Kass believes are made possible by the very nature of that institution. "This place is very flexible when it comes to the crossing of boundaries. There are all types of interdisciplinary committees here, some of which actually grant degrees . . . and the place is, for lack of a better term, philosophical. The practice of philosophy without a license goes on everywhere around here." Students in Kass's classes—budding philosophers themselves, perhaps—are greatly attracted by the man: "He's the main event around here," said one. From the dean of the college comes this addendum: "His greatest contribution is to have taken the upsurge of popular student interest in biomedical ethics and informed it with a patient, rigorous, and inspiring investigation of the classical roots of Western science and humanism. The student response to this incredibly demanding ideal has been splendid."

In the tradition that must include Henry R. Luce—although his thought on the subject was never set out coherently in one place— Kass believes in "the strength of knowledge in the world, which gives us tremendous power to do things. . . . If science teaches us the truth about a world that has no room in it for moral insights, then maybe one has to reconsider what you mean by scientific truth. It may be inadequate because it is part of the truth masquerading as the whole. One needn't throw out the moral insights of the race just because science can't prove them to be true." Henry R. Luce himself could not have said it better.

Social Art at Tulane

Not every university is as congenial to humanistic study as the University of Chicago, not every proposal can match the one from there in originality, and not every professor can reach Kass's pitch of intellectual fervor. But in other ways Luce grants can make an imprint of demonstrable importance in environments very different from the University of Chicago.

After Tulane University's proposal for a Luce Professorship of Art, Culture, and Society was turned down by the Luce Board of Directors in 1979, Sheldon Hackney, president of Tulane (he has since been succeeded by Eamon M. Kelly) promptly ordered his troops to regroup. Consultation with foundation officers was followed by a rethinking and a redrafting of the earlier request. "The proposal as submitted," wrote Tulane's vice-president for academic affairs, "provided insufficiently firm links between the humanities and the professional schools." The new grant application corrected that omission: "The humanities are widely perceived by students as being somehow separate from the rest of life. . . . This perception has led to their being considered an ornament rather than a necessity for the educated person. The growing specialization within the humanities on the part of the faculty has only hastened this development." A suggested counterforce was a Luce professorship to teach architecture "as an integrative activity in the humanities. . . . Architecture, after all, is the most social of the arts, and is no less deeply involved with the religious, philosophic, and ideological spirit of an era."

Not a startling concept, that revised and improved proposal was good enough to win foundation approval for David Scott Slovic, an architect, and his wife, Ligia Slovic-Rave', a sociologist, as joint Luce Professors in Architecture and Society at Tulane's School of Architecture. The Slovics taught several courses over their five-year tenure, which was extended in June 1986 by the foundation. Most recently,

Ligia Rave' taught the Philosophy of Architecture, concentrating on "the continuum of thought" from Plato, Alberti, Wittgenstein, and Freud to Frank Lloyd Wright in connecting the ideas of a society to its environment. David Scott Slovic's course focused on architecture as "the making of private places in a public environment." And the Slovics recently organized a series of discussions with faculty members from the Departments of Political Science, Philosophy, History, and Sociology, culminating in public seminars with such titles as "The Post-Industrial Society—Now What?" and "Perspectives on Public Places."

In a neat overlap with the activity of a Luce Scholar about whom they knew nothing at all—his work will be described presently—the Slovics also sponsored a distinguished visitor program at Tulane. Their first lecturer was Kenya Maruyama, the principal architect of a major Tokyo firm. Maruyama's discussions at Tulane stressed a point that Luce Scholar Timur Galen became aware of during his work in a Tokyo architectural atelier in 1982–83: collaboration between Japanese architects, artists, industry, and craftsmen explains much of the success of many of their recent public buildings. Interest by artists and careful work by artisans make many Japanese buildings and public places attractive, efficient, and imaginative. In Maruyama's Auto Building, for example, cat-shaped accessories decorate the sales floor. In that workplace, such furnishings as screens and chairs are designed by architects.

Among the satisfactions that arise out of the Slovics' professorship is the linkage they have effected between Tulane University, a huge installation in a city that has waged its struggle against slow decline, and the community of New Orleans that surrounds the university. Besides sponsoring the public symposia, they have tried to bridge town and gown by fostering involvement by the university in changes in the physical environment of the city and in the city's proposals for urban development. Led by the Slovics, Tulane's School of Architecture has taken as projects for student work both New Orleans' design for a new public library of the arts in the city and the ideas for the development of the seedy and run-down New Orleans waterfront.

For a Luce professorship to bring such immediate and practical proposals is not usually part of the agenda. But the board seems unlikely to object: indeed, Henry Luce III says that "the Foundation has supported many projects that are pragmatic, and it is a great satisfaction to have been of such concrete service."

Leadership at Princeton

One of the nation's leading figures in the study of leadership is Fred I. Greenstein, who was a Luce professor at Princeton from 1973 to 1981. Greenstein, recently chairman of the Politics Department at Princeton University, specializes in leadership and the presidency. He examines the components of leadership, and how presidents exercise, or fail to exercise, that elusive quality. His writing on leadership goes back to an early book on the way young children perceive the political world. His next book asked whether clinical psychological insights are of much help in explaining political behavior.

Greenstein's Luce professorship came after Princeton University was turned down by the foundation in its search for funds to support a chair in public law. Woodrow Wilson had taught public law before he became president of Princeton, and William Bowen, newly appointed president of the university in 1972, was receptive to suggestions to revive that old interest. After the foundation decided against making a grant for that purpose, Princeton went back to the drawing board and took the kind of conceptual leap that the foundation likes to encourage. Definitions were broadened. Then Princeton proposed a Henry R. Luce Professorship in Politics, Law, and Society. After the foundation approved the professorship, the university offered the job to Greenstein, who at the time was perfectly happy with his job at Wesleyan University as chairman of the Department of Government. After a struggle with the decision, Greenstein took his talents to Princeton as a tenured professor.

Greenstein dates the modern presidency from the time when the White House became a house not just for presidents but for all the trappings of power: for burgeoning staffs, for the Office of Management and Budget, and for such recently embattled institutions as the National Security Council. Then he breaks down the process of presidential decision making in that enlarged environment, which began in the era of Franklin Roosevelt. From the time he arrived at Princeton, says Greenstein,

> I began teaching courses in the presidency which heavily emphasize the president as individual, the whole set of relationships between the president and his advisers, and the interplay between the advisers and the political context. I found students were not deeply interested in abstract academic issues about presidential leadership. It seemed to me what they could best use was some thinking about actual presidential actions, and an immediate sense of the ambience of serving in the west wing. This was something these young people might end up doing. Therefore every year I used the course so that there was some contact with former presidential aides.

To make that contact, Greenstein as a highlight of his Luce years staged at Princeton a conference called "Advising the President." That conference brought together some names famous in White House history: Clark Clifford (the dean of all White House advisers); the late Bryce Harlow (an adviser to Dwight Eisenhower, Richard Nixon, and Gerald Ford); Arthur Schlesinger, Jr. (who, besides his work as a historian, served as a special assistant to John F. Kennedy); and such latter-day public officials as Donald Rumsfeld, White House chief of staff and Secretary of Defense under Ford. Two years after that extremely successful conference in 1975—"in the afterglow of a great bash," Greenstein says—the foundation gave Princeton another grant to sponsor Greenstein for his second term, this one for three years, the maximum permissible under foundation rules. In a somewhat different afterglow, Greenstein brought out a book, *The Hidden Hand Presidency: Eisenhower as Leader*, which made partial use of the materials presented at the conference.

Although their formal service in that capacity comes to an end, it seems that once a Luce professor, always a Luce professor. As we have seen, that is in a sense true of Leon Kass at the University of Chicago; it is also true of Greenstein. Grants from the foundation to support his chair for eight years came to $375,000 for his salary and related program expenses. At Princeton Greenstein now teaches both undergraduates and graduate students and has carried the added burden of chairman of the Politics Department. But Greenstein notes wryly that the university has continued to bill him in brochures as "the Henry R. Luce Professor of Politics."

Nor has Greenstein's association with the foundation ended. Although his Luce tenure is over, the foundation awarded Greenstein a grant of $50,000 to stage another of his "great bashes" during the Constitution's bicentennial celebrations in 1987. Vice President George Bush addressed the conference, which took place at Princeton in April 1987. Greenstein organized the conference, whose topic was leadership in the modern presidency, so as to have one leading scholar on each of the nine presidents from Roosevelt to Reagan present a paper. Then one person who had been in the White House during each of the presidencies made comments and led a roundtable discussion. The Roosevelt scholar was William Leuchtenburg of the University of North Carolina; the commentator was Wilbur Cohen, then seventy-three, who worked on the Social Security legislation passed in the Roosevelt era and later became Lyndon Johnson's last Secretary of Health, Education and Welfare. "Cohen was great," says Greenstein, "and it was a poignant moment"—the more so because Cohen died six weeks later. Greenstein himself was the Eisenhower scholar, and the commentator was General Andrew Goodpaster, Eisenhower's defense liaison officer and staff secretary. Joan Hoff-Wilson, executive secretary of the Organization of American Historians, presented the paper on Nixon (she is at work on what Greenstein calls "the first scholarly Nixon biography") and H. R. Haldeman, who was White House chief of staff under Nixon and a villain of Watergate, led the discussions. Richard Nathan, a Princeton professor, who was Nixon's chief adviser on welfare reform and is a leading analyst of welfare programs, did one of the summations of the conference on its closing morning. Also present at the conference as a participant was a former Luce professor, John Roche, a professor of civilization and foreign affairs at the Fletcher School of Law and Diplomacy at Tufts University. He was a special consultant to the president between 1966 and 1968. And Greenstein's students from Princeton's Woodrow Wilson School of Public and International Affairs participated fully, helping to organize the affair; they attended sessions, and later wrote papers and theses on some aspect of what they observed.

"I like conferences that have some kind of outreach," remarks Greenstein. "The Luce chair enabled me to introduce interests that flop out of my department. And the university was encouraged to do something creative that it might not otherwise have done." Greenstein is now at work on a book analyzing the decisions on Vietnam from 1965, during the Johnson administration, to the end of the war under Nixon. He is comparing the way those decisions were made with the process of decision making during the Eisenhower administration after Dienbienphu in 1954, when Eisenhower kept the United States out of Vietnam.

Wheaton and Vanderbilt

In September 1986 one of the smallest institutions ever to be awarded a Luce professorship rolled out the mat for Joseph H. Pleck. A social scientist and academic administrator, Pleck is an expert on family studies and family sociology.

Wheaton College is a rarity: it is located in a rural setting in Massachusetts south of Boston, and its student body of eleven hundred is made up entirely of women (although it goes coed in the fall of 1988). Wheaton has traditionally offered a solid liberal arts program, and it has no professional schools. But it is strong in economics, and, as much as a liberal arts college can, it prepares its women for the job market. Many Wheaton graduates go into banking, brokerage, and insurance in the Boston area.

In September 1983, after Hannah Goldberg, the new provost,

came to Wheaton from Antioch College in Ohio, Wheaton started to introduce more material by and about women into its curriculum. The Departments of History, Psychology, Economics, and Sociology added new information about women in history, in society, and in the home. Soon after her arrival at Wheaton, Goldberg, a historian who had been academic dean at Antioch, began to discuss with professors from those departments some proposals that might bring a Luce professorship to Wheaton. Out of those talks came the basic notion that the radical changes in the family structure in the last couple of decades were not yet adequately reflected in undergraduate courses. Goldberg concluded that issues such as work and the family, the fragmentation of family life, and the changing role of children were not getting sufficient academic scrutiny. What courses there were on the subject seemed like remnants of old-line instruction in home economics and were not substantively connected to any discipline— much less to several. That governing idea about family life may not have a place on the most exciting level of learning, but it has obvious merit. Wheaton's proposal for a Luce Professorship in Families, Change, and Society was approved by the foundation's board in 1984.

Judgments are hard to pass after only one academic year. But Pleck, whose experience as research director of the Center of Research for Women at Wellesley obviously qualified him for the Wheaton assignment, seems to be getting a good response there. His seminar Work and the Family is well attended by upperclassmen, most of whom are economics majors. And he conducts a seminar on family studies for faculty members, which about one-third of Wheaton's faculty attends.

A somewhat similar course was taught at Vanderbilt University in Nashville, Tennessee, by John C. Masters, Luce Professor of Public Policy and the Family. In his course Masters, a child psychologist, stresses both the need and the difficulty of relating psychological research to responses to issues of public policy. In that respect, Masters' course has a relation with still another Luce professorship, the one conducted by Robert C. Wood at Wesleyan. Masters also teaches in Vanderbilt's Psychology Department; students who have finished his course in public policy are likely to sign up for his psychology courses.

A Sampling of Others

Many Luce professorships by now have a long history, and all cut across many of the chambered corridors of academe. Their diversity, and the different interests and purposes of those who have filled them, would make efforts to rank their success a challenge for Maecenas. But the following descriptions provide a sampling of some that have special attractions.

The Luce Professorship in Democratic Institutions and the Social Order at Wesleyan University in Middletown, Connecticut, designed to determine whether "liberal democracies are capable of coping with the problems that confront them in ways consistent with democratic norms and values," has been filled since its inception by a man with a rare background as an academic *cum* public servant. Robert C. Wood served as secretary of the Department of Housing and Urban Development, superintendent of the Boston Public Schools System during the crisis of desegregation, and chairman of the Massachusetts Bay Transportation Authority. He also found time to serve as president of the University of Massachusetts in Amherst.

From the agitation of public life, Wood has turned to agitating the minds of undergraduates at Wesleyan with such courses as The Political Economy of American Cities (echoes of Irving Kristol) and Education in Industrial Societies. In his teaching he also evaluates the efficacy and appropriateness of social science research in the shaping of public policy, a topic of especial interest to him (echoes of Fred Greenstein). Applause from all the worlds of Wood has accompanied his tenure at Wesleyan.

The Luce Professorship in Comparative Religious Ethics, begun in 1978 at Amherst College, has been distinguished in many ways, but the stroke of genius has come from its unusual structure. Generally, the foundation prefers to have one person appointed for the five years of its grant, believing that the special qualities of the chair require continuity. In this case, though, the chair has been filled by several people who surely make as interesting a cast of characters as can be found anywhere under the elms.

David Little, the first occupant, was a Harvard theologian and a professor of religion and sociology at the University of Virginia, to which he has since returned. (Little is also the only person to have occupied two Luce chairs; he filled in for a year in the chair of Ethics and the Professions at Haverford College.) His successor was Wande Abimbola, dean of the Faculty of Arts at the University of Ife in Nigeria. Abimbola is an authority on the traditional life and literature, including the religious beliefs, of the Yoruba. At Amherst, among other subjects, he taught about the interaction of Christianity and Islam with the traditional religions of Africa. After Abimbola came Lal Mani Joshi, at birth a Brahmin who converted to Buddhism; before he arrived at Amherst he was head of the Department of Religious Studies at Guru Gobind Singh Bhavan, Punjabi University—an interesting post for a man who had been Indian Buddhist delegate to the second session of the Asian Buddhist Peace Conference in Sri Lanka ten years before.

After Joshi came Yusuf Ibish, a Harvard Ph.D., who had been a professor at the University of Beirut. Among his works is *Al-Baqillani's Doctrine of the Imamate*. Many of Ibish's other books have not been translated from the Arabic. By the time Tara Tulku Khensur Rinpoche, a lama from Tibet, and Professor Veena Das, a sociologist from the University of New Delhi, arrived at Amherst, very little room remained for any surprises. To evaluate the program conservatively, it seems to offer undergraduates a chance to sample a good deal of original and alien thinking.

Before Frantisek Daniel, the Luce Professor of Creative Arts at Carleton College, in Northfield, Minnesota, came to Carleton, he was dean of the Center for Advanced Film Studies in Beverly Hills, California, a place farther from academia than Sri Lanka. But in his three years at Carleton, Daniel turned out to be a superb choice, undertaking, as he said, to "incorporate the new humanities—film and television—into the studies of the old humanities." He continued: "It has always been my conviction that cinema and TV, due to their corporate character, require categorically as broad an education as a liberal arts college can offer." Developing that thought, Daniel instructed Carleton undergraduates in script-writing and directing, as well as in the skills of using the camera for dramatic purposes. At the end of his first year, he reported proudly that his students wrote eleven half-hour comedies during the autumn. During Minnesota's winter, a new group wrote eight scripts, while the seasoned students from the earlier term wrote five feature-length original scripts and a full-length stage play. In a bravura performance, they also produced three half-hour comedies based on the best scripts of the fall, as well as eight documentary films. Engaging in the outside activities that so many Luce professors somehow find time for, Daniel also conducted a series of lectures at the Walker Art Center in Minneapolis.

Daniel's successor, John Schott, was a film historian who changed the direction set by Daniel. Schott put more emphasis on the traditions of filmmaking, especially documentary films, a field in which he is a recognized authority. And Schott also began what Carleton's president at the time, Robert Edwards, described as "a swirl of programs," bringing artists from Minneapolis and St. Paul to the Carleton campus and sending students to the Guthrie Theatre and the Walker Center. Summing up the impact of the two professors, Edwards remarked: "We have been beneficiaries to a degree I would not have anticipated—as an institution and in the lives of individual faculty members here."

Alterations in the relationship between man and the environment, and how changes in that relationship have changed the course of history, have set Yale historians to asking new questions. Answers presumably will be forthcoming when a new Luce professor, as yet unnamed, takes over the Luce Professorship in History and the Environment at Yale, the first that the foundation has supported there. The purpose of the chair will be to examine environmental history, an emerging field at Yale and across the nation. Yale expects that the course will also "forge permanent links between history and science, and through their interconnections encourage a richer understanding of the past and its influence"—expectations that should warm any historian's heart.

National policy and theology, two areas of interest to the Luce Foundation, are rarely seen together in public. But they have been brought together at Occidental College in southern California. Occidental was awarded the Luce Professorship in Religion, Power, and the Political Process after it applied for support for a chair "to explore the interrelationship between religious ideology and political change in other parts of the world." The Luce professor at Occidental is Margaret E. Crahan, a specialist in Latin American history.

One of Crahan's courses seems designed to explore that double-disciplined area in a way that perfectly fits the foundation's purposes. Called Religion and Power, it surveys the ways major religions respond to political pressures in various parts of the world, including Poland, the Middle East, the Indian subcontinent, and Latin America. Then Crahan narrows the focus to the Roman Catholic church— which serves, she says, as "a case study of a complex bureaucratic institution responding to pressures for internal democratization and societal change." Although religion and political power have been in contention through the ages, the course's contemporaneity is reflected in its reading lists: the earliest publication date of any book on the list is 1980. In the judgment of Occidental's president, Richard C. Gilman, Crahan "is a woman of tremendous talent and extraordinary energy." She is also a political activist and a zealous advocate of human rights; indeed, one of her courses, which may not cut across conventional academic disciplines, is called Human Rights and Basic Needs in the Americas.

At Harvard, the Luce Foundation sponsored a Professorship in Business, Ethics, and Public Policy, which Harvard housed at the John F. Kennedy School of Government. The distinguished professor was Winthrop Knowlton, investment banker, novelist, former assistant secretary of the U.S. Treasury Department, and for eleven years chief executive officer of the publishing firm of Harper & Row.

Knowlton's achievements over five years were considerable. He launched the newly established Harvard Center for Business and Government in the Kennedy School. He designed new courses at the Kennedy School that examined the relationships between business and government, two of which he taught himself and two of which were taught by a leading lawyer and philosopher of business, Ira Millstein. And Knowlton arranged an impressive series of seminars with leaders of the public and private sectors, with such cosponsors as the New York Stock Exchange, the State Street Bank of Boston, and the German Marshall Fund. A new course that Knowlton taught he called The Private Sector: Its History, Values, Practices, and Role in Society; material on that all-inclusive subject must be bursting out the doors of the Kennedy Center.

Commenting on Knowlton's activities, Harvard's President Derek Bok said: "While any one of Knowlton's efforts would represent a considerable achievement for someone new to academia (and collectively they speak for themselves) Dean Graham Allison's [dean of the Kennedy School] and my judgment of Professor Knowlton's 'greatest accomplishment' has to do with the sharpened awareness of all of us who have come into contact with him of the possibilities for developing new attitudes and formats to help us solve pressing social and economic problems."

Regarding the professorships as a whole, the principal officers at the Luce Foundation might feel some disappointment because the program has not gotten more national recognition. As we have seen, the program is one of the foundation's lasting commitments, begun in 1968 and still flourishing twenty years later. The foundation spent $11.2 million on the program from 1977 to 1986; its total cost since its beginning has been $17 million. The educational achievement has been considerable, and the direction in which the program seeks to move American education is unexceptionable. Furthermore, beneficiaries—universities, professors, students—and benisons abound. Universities get distinguished teachers who are unusually active, as Luce professors are, in the university community where they are domiciled. The books that the professors produce often add to their universities' repute: that is true of the publications of Kass at Chicago, Greenstein at Princeton, and many others. Garry Wills, Luce Professor of American Culture and Public Policy at Northwestern University, wrote the widely praised *Reagan's America: Innocents at Home*; Northwestern was mentioned in many of the extensive reviews. (Typical of the quality of the book was the remark about Reagan: "He is the opposite of a chameleon: environments adapt themselves to him.") The professors get an opportunity to structure courses with content that they have originated, and they work sometimes for years in refreshingly new academic environments. Students get a chance to study under people of unusual talents, who lead them to new educational discoveries. It is hard to find a loser in the picture.

Yet all that does not seem to get the foundation the public credit it deserves. Many of the books, papers, and seminars it sponsors carry no credit lines. Locally generated publicity on Luce professors seems all too rare. Perhaps that arises through oversight; but it also arises from the unprovable notion that sometimes it may come from the unattractive meanness of spirit that occasionally shows itself at academic institutions. Generally, the complaint about inadequate recognition is a common one throughout the foundation world, and it has its justifications. But foundations take consolation from the view that the accomplishments, and not the recognition, are what they seek. The Luce Foundation will continue to show zest for sponsoring professorships as long as the foundation's beliefs in the soundness of the program's precepts endure. The program has had its disappointments, but the successes have far outweighed them.

In 1984 Henry Luce III assembled in Princeton a couple of dozen former and present Luce professors. In his remarks to the gathering, Theodore Sizer—chairman of the Department of Education at Brown, former dean of the Harvard Graduate School of Education, headmaster of Phillips Academy at Andover, Massachusetts, and one of the advisers to the Luce Foundation on the Luce Professorships Program—said: "Isn't the Luce Professorship Program wonderful . . . it's obviously designed to upset the academic system totally. These professors all have helmets. They must wear them all the time at some universities. . . . They are mess-makers *par excellence*." Luce happily agreed: "He's obviously right, and I hope he is righter than he knows." Of course, since the Luce professorships were inaugurated in 1968, the walls of academe have not come tumbling down—in some places they remain better defended than the Berlin Wall. But dozens of Luce professors with their unique franchises are being heard, and more and more are seen to be making a difference. Luce charged the professors as they left the meeting: "Go back out there to your classrooms and your publications—and in some cases even to the moat of Congress—and see if you can achieve proper and beneficial change."

OTHER ACADEMIC ENTERPRISES

The Whitney Humanities Center at Yale, which opened in 1981, has also been the beneficiary of Luce largesse. This assistance, however, is not funded by the Luce Professorship Program but by other foundation funds directed to academia. The center, according to its director, Peter Brooks, was founded "to augment Yale's long, rich tradition in the humanities by bringing people in the field together in a new way exciting for the Yale community, and some sort of exemplar for the outside world." In 1981 the foundation awarded the center $500,000 to support a new undertaking: to bring Luce visiting scholars to the center for lectures and faculty seminars. The scholars were to be people of extraordinary distinction in the humanities—whether in scholarship or in the creative arts—who would teach an undergraduate or a graduate course and would also conduct seminars primarily, although not exclusively, for the Yale faculty. "The idea," says Brooks, "was that the Yale faculty spends a great deal of time teaching students in the classroom, but hasn't had an opportunity to teach each other—to benefit from the kind of cross-fertilization that comes from serious and intensive discussion groups."

The nearly missed opportunity is now being offered by foundation money, which has made it possible for the Whitney Center to attract as Luce Visiting Scholars in the Humanities and Social Thought some renowned humanists, whose courses have to rank among the most stimulating offerings in academe.

The first was Elie Wiesel, winner of the Nobel Peace Prize in 1986 and former chairman of the U.S. Holocaust Memorial Council. Wiesel was the visiting Luce scholar in 1982–83. A prisoner in Birkenau, Auschwitz, and Buchenwald concentration camps, Wiesel wrote his first book in 1958, a memoir of those experiences. At Yale he taught Literature and Memory with a reading list that began with prophetic memory such as Jeremiah and extended to the work of Sartre and Malraux. Wiesel also led a faculty seminar entitled Attitudes Toward Suffering, which took for its text the Book of Job and the Hasidic tale "The Seven Beggars." Press coverage indicates—if that were really necessary—the impact of man on institution: "Elie Wiesel Teaches the Lessons of Anguish" (*New York Times*); "Indifference is the Enemy to Elie Wiesel" (*New Haven Register*); "As Long as We Remember" (*Yale Daily News*); "Holocaust Tapes Make All Witnesses to Horror" (*New Haven Register*).

Also conducting sessions at the center that year was Stanley Cavell, professor of philosophy at Harvard, among whose provocative books is a collection of essays called *Must We Mean What We Say?* Cavell led the Yale faculty on an intellectual dance through Thoreau, Emerson, Coleridge's *Biographica Literaria*, and Shakespeare's *The Winter's Tale*—magically threading together authors and works of apparent diversity. He called his lectures "The Quest of the Ordinary."

In 1983–84, Yale reached to England to bring as visiting scholar to New Haven Juliet Mitchell, an English psychoanalyst and author, who brought together the study of psychoanalysis, literature, and social thought, which converged on the issues of femininity and gender differentiation. Lively discussions ensued, with plentiful debate between Mitchell and what Peter Brooks describes as "a psychoanalytic community here which is much more orthodox and Freudian than she was." A sentence from the *Yale College Programs of Study* outlines the nature of Mitchell's challenge: "an exploration of how changing psychoanalytic concepts of femininity not only reflect shifts in the social position of women but also affect the course of psycho-analytic theory itself."

For two of the following years, Brooks called the sixteenth century back to Yale. Carlo Ginzburg of the University of Bologna recounted the details of medieval trials for heresy of those accused of being werewolves and witches, thus introducing Yale audiences to a world more superstitious than New Haven. He also reconstructed the world view of those people who have been neglected in historical writing—the illiterate peasantry, whose beliefs and traditions so much influenced events. One of Ginzburg's books, *The Cheese and the Worms*, is based on an Inquisition trial of a miller who learned to read and write, and then constructed his own cosmology. He concluded that the world was made of rising cheese.

In the spring term of 1987, Brooks brought in Natalie Davis, professor of history at Princeton, whose archival work on sixteenth-century France led to a popular and fine motion picture called *The Return of Martin Guerre*. Davis uncovered in the archives this marvelous story of the village impostor who successfully took the place of a long-absent husband; she acted as a consultant during the filming, conferring on the film a rare degree of historical authenticity. At Yale, Davis taught both an undergraduate and a faculty seminar. For undergraduates, her course was Society and the Sexes in Early Modern Europe, a topic of such appeal that it is easy to accept her judgment during the semester that "we are having a splendid time in that class." For the faculty, she taught Shared Texts: History, Literature and Law, a cross-disciplinary voyage that explored the ways different fields "approach the same cultural object—the different criteria they use, what happens when they adapt each other's texts and methods of interpretation, and the limits to the advisability of borrowing each other's approaches." Among the texts were the autobiography of a seventeenth-century rabbi in Venice and the stories people told to get pardoned for homicide in sixteenth-century France. Part of the material for the tales of pardon came from Davis's new book *Fiction in the Archives: Pardon Tales and Their Tellers in Sixteenth Century France*.

For 1987–88, Brooks has reached abroad again. The Luce Visiting Scholar is Jack Goody, an internationally known professor of social anthropology at Cambridge University. Goody has done extensive work on writing as a form of social power in primitive societies, as well as on the general issue of literacy. Summing up the Luce program, Brooks says, "Every year a large number of my colleagues and our students look forward eagerly to the visit of the Luce Scholar as a major intellectual event."

The Luce professorships remain the foundation's principal commitment to integrative innovation, but they have been supplemented by a series of project grants. Sometimes these grants have been awarded after the foundation has considered a proposal of first quality for a professorship but has decided, perhaps because the cup containing first-rate proposals runneth over, not to fund a chair but to extend help of a different kind. The grants have also taken the form of direct, onetime transfusions, not related to previous applications for Luce professorships.

After having decided not to fund a chair in the field, the foundation in 1977 made a three-year grant of $75,000 to Connecticut College in New London for a program called Communication through Human Movement. The highly imaginative program involved faculty members from six departments of the college, including anthropology, theater, psychology, dance, child development, and religion. This diverse group taught courses that engaged such subjects as "the role of visible behavior in interaction, including spatial positions, posture, gesture, and facial expression" and "analysis of the role of visible movement in interaction." In 1981 the foundation contributed another $34,000 to help Connecticut integrate this new material into its regular curriculum.

A proposal from Stanford University in California for a Luce Professorship in Human Nutrition came from a group of teachers in the Schools of Humanities and Social Sciences and Medicine and the Food Research Institute. The board in 1976 found the proposal attractive, but at that time it had already settled on two new chairs for the year and the budget was stretched. Instead of turning down Stanford's application, the foundation drew on funds from its public affairs area, which, as discussed in a later chapter, can be used to fit many different circumstances. The foundation made a public affairs grant to Stanford directed toward the establishment of a program of undergraduate courses, workshops, and student projects dealing with human biology and nutrition, bringing together the varied academic fields that have an interest in those subjects. It awarded $90,000 for a three-year period, with the initial amount paid in December 1976. When the foundation's three-year grant expired, the university used its own money to reappoint the professor in charge of the program— a sure sign of success. And the foundation took similar action in other cases, for example, help for a program involving the humanities within the School of Health Services at Johns Hopkins and assistance to develop an undergraduate curriculum within the Institute for Values, Law, and the Professions at the University of Southern California.

Poetry and music, said Aristotle, share a salutary influence: they train and civilize the emotions. Yet the two beneficent forces rarely are joined in academia; departments of literature and of music live there in discrete worlds, in a friendly but distant divorce. From Fordham University in New York came a proposal for a Luce professorship in poetry and music, which was not approved by the board but was found sufficiently interesting that it invited Fordham to submit the idea as a self-standing project. In 1983 the board approved a $105,000 grant over three years to support Fordham's undergraduate program in poetry and music; in 1986 another $70,000 over two years was added.

The program at Fordham is being run by Father John Dzieglweicz, S.J., an accomplished pianist and occasional composer, who is also an assistant professor of English. Fordham pays Dzieglweicz, and the foundation foots the bill for all the other expenses of the program. Dzieglweicz's reading list, drawing from many classical sources, bursts with appeal missing from the course of Margaret Crahan. It includes such widely separated yet intimately conjoined works as John Hollander's *The Untuning of the Sky*, Henry James's *Turn of the Screw*, and Sophocles' Theban plays. In its discussion of the opera as drama, the course compares such play-and-opera works as *Macbeth, Othello,* and *Carmen.* Says Dzieglweicz: "We are explaining not so much the additioñ of music to a story line, but more the way one translates into the other. When Othello steps into Desdemona's bedroom, a single line of music tells us what will happen next in the drama."

In the fall of 1967, on the eve of his retirement as chairman of the Board of Trustees of Columbia University, the foundation honored Maurice T. Moore by establishing the Maurice T. Moore Professorship at Columbia Law School, with an award to Columbia of $400,000. The chair was dedicated to the study of the broadest aspects of the legal role of the corporation in public life, and it praised Moore, as Columbia President Grayson Kirk said at the time, "for his important contributions as a lawyer in the complex affairs of modern industry, for his public service as a legal adviser to his government, and for his charitable and educational activities." The Moores made contributions to the professorship in ensuing years so that the endowment in 1986 was calculated by Columbia to stand at just under $1 million. The occupant of the chair at the time was Albert J. Rosenthal, who had served as dean of the law school. The foundation rounded out the endowment to $1.5 million by making an additional payment of $500,000.

4

The Foundation in Asia

Since the Luce Foundation began, the United States has fought three major wars in East Asia. In the past fifty years American troops have battled the forces of Japan, fought a standstill land war against the armies of North Korea and China, and clashed in the jungles with the communists in Vietnam. The war in Korea and the long civil war on the mainland of China, in which the United States was deeply involved, estranged the two nations for nearly thirty years of hostile silence, broken only by public recrimination. Those historical convulsions vastly complicate the already imposing task of better understanding between East and West. But they also illustrate with bloody clarity the enormous importance of bringing the societies of each to a better comprehension of the norms and values of the other. That is the crucial concern to which the Luce Foundation, following the experiences and traditions of the Luce family, has long been dedicated and toward which it will continue for its lifetime to contribute.

The first major new commitment of the foundation in East Asia after the death of Henry R. Luce came in 1972. In that year, Henry Luce III began his report of the president of the foundation by quoting his father's words, spoken in 1965: "In the second half of the 20th century, we will test our leadership of the world by whether or not we can do our part in bringing East and West together in basic mutual understandings: intellectual, ethical and political." Then Henry Luce III went on to announce, "with a sense of transcending purpose, and yet at the same time with some trepidation," the Luce Scholars Program. Representing the long engagement—personal, political, religious, and intellectual—of Henry W. Luce, Henry R. Luce, and Elisabeth Luce Moore with China, and the Luce family's interest in all of East Asia, the program has central importance for Henry Luce III and for the foundation. Despite the early trepidation about the program, it has turned out to be unique in approach, varied in execution, and durable enough conceptually so that now in its fifteenth year the Luce Scholars Program still thrives and gives every sign that a long life span lies ahead.

Launched in 1974, the Luce Scholars Program provides a journey for a few to distant lands for intangible gain. The few are young Americans—by foundation policy, none over twenty-nine years of age—fifteen of whom are chosen annually to work in a professional internship in an East or Southeast Asian country for one year on grants made by the foundation. The purpose is to imbue them, Henry Luce III said, "with a firsthand familiarity with Asia at a time when they are flexible and receptive." And the deeper purpose goes back to the words of Henry R. Luce about "bringing East and West together in basic mutual understandings." That has been one of the goals to which Henry Luce III has committed the foundation during his presidency, and the Luce Scholars Program stands as an important part of that commitment.

Like the foundation's enterprises discussed elsewhere—the one that encourages museums to display and catalog American art, for example, or the one that encourages academia to bridge conventional academic disciplines—the Luce Scholars Program has a unique perspective, which differentiates it from the many exchange programs with East Asia recently so popular in the United States. To begin with, the foundation has barred as recipients of its Luce Scholar grants Americans who are experts on Asia. Luce Scholars are young people who have *not* had extensive study of or experience in the Orient and who have no intention of making their futures there, although a few of them may end up doing that. Rather, they usually have already settled on careers that will take them in directions other than Asian affairs—law, medicine, journalism, politics, or business in America. A guiding intention of the program, as the foundation has explained it, is that in later work, "the broadened insights of these young people into East Asia could have a significant impact on the course of our future

The Henry Luce Foundation

relations with Asia and on our own cultural, intellectual, and political development. . . . At the end of a year, they return to the U.S. not as Asian experts but as citizens and leaders whose perceptions—of Asia, of America, and of themselves—will have been sharpened as a result of their experience." Experience is the operating word: "No academic credit is involved and the participants normally do not enroll in academic institutions. The heart of the program lies in the internships and job placements that are arranged for each Scholar on the basis of his or her individual career interest, experience, training, and general background."

Luce Scholars are chosen by a rigorous process. They apply for a Luce scholarship through any one of sixty-six nominating institutions, which include the country's leading colleges and universities, where people on campus serve as liaison with the foundation. Besides the requirement that they be no more than twenty-nine years of age, the applicants must also be American citizens with at least a bachelor's degree. The nominating institutions submit the names of the applicants to the Luce Foundation, where five people, including the executive director, conduct interviews. Of all the Luce programs, this is the only one in which people who work at the foundation interview individual applicants directly. In 1987, for example, 142 young people were interviewed.

Generally, from a group of about that size, forty-five are selected for the next step. They appear before three regional selection panels made up of academics, politicians, business executives, which in the past have included Bill Bradley, now senator from New Jersey; Vernon Jordan, former president of the National Urban League; and W. H. Krome George, former chairman of Aluminum Company of America. Current members include Breene Kerr, chairman of Kerr Consolidated in Oklahoma City; Edwin Dodd, chairman emeritus of Owens-Illinois; and George R. Packard, dean of the School of Advanced International Studies at Johns Hopkins (for more, see Appendix H). By the middle of March, fifteen of the forty-five are named Luce scholars. They meet in the late summer at Princeton University for a week's orientation. Then they go to Hong Kong, where they spend another week in a series of seminars held at the Chinese University of Hong Kong. Finally, they move to the country where they will spend the year.

The Asia Foundation administers the program for the Luce Foundation in Asian countries. Its cadre of representatives in East and Southeast Asia has proved ideal for this purpose, with just the right blend of country knowledge and cordial hospitality, the Luce Foundation believes, "to make the Luce Scholars' adjustment to Asia both painless and productive." The Luce Foundation committed $450,000 to the Asia Foundation for the first five years of the scholars program; it paid $500,000 for the next five years. The current commitment stands at $750,000 over five more years.

The selection process—a key criterion is identifying young people with leadership potential—is extremely competitive. No one at the foundation would assert that every chosen scholar was clearly better than some who were turned down. For those selected, however, the internship in Asia becomes an experience that affects their whole lives. Nothing tells the story of the Luce scholars as well as their own words:

● Debra Knopman is a hydrologist in the U.S. Geological Survey in Virginia. Before that, she worked for four years as a staff member on a Senate subcommittee on water resources. A graduate of Wellesley College, she has a degree from MIT and got her Ph.D. from Johns Hopkins in 1986. She was a Luce scholar in 1978–79 and spent the year working with the Joint Commission on Rural Reconstruction in Taiwan.

Commenting about her experience in Taiwan, she says:

I am far more aware of Asian politics and culture than I was before my year in Taiwan, and more fascinated by the increasing connections between our economy and that of Asian countries. In America we have been rewarded all our lives for our productivity, for being "go getters." I came back from Asia anxious to participate in American political life. Nowhere did the Taiwan lesson in patience and respect for process pay off more than in my four years of work in the Senate. And in the field of hydrology, scientific exchange with the People's Republic is flourishing. My exposure to China as a Luce scholar has left me particularly well equipped to participate in these scientific exchanges.

● Timur Galen is an architect and a construction manager for Gerald Hines Interests with headquarters in Houston, Texas. Galen graduated from Haverford College and got his architectural and engineering degrees from the University of Pennsylvania. He later worked for the Philadelphia firm of Venturi, Rauch and Scott Brown. He was a Luce scholar in 1982–83, working in Tokyo in the architectural office of Fumihiko Maki, a well-known Japanese architect, and lecturing in the Department of Architecture in Tokyo University.

I got to Japan at the beginning of a whole reconsideration of Japanese architecture by American architects. We are at a time right now when there is a tremendous cross-current in U.S. and Japanese architecture. Maki was trained at the Cranbrook School in Michigan and at Harvard. He lectures widely in the United States, and has become a very potent force here representing Japanese architecture. He represents a sophisticated kind of cross-cultural influence taking place: not Western architecture going to Japan, but Japanese architecture coming to America. The Japanese digested outside influences, made them their own, and we now see them exporting those ideas.

Clichés were reexamined:

In Maki's office, I learned that most of the prejudices about the Japanese were indeed just prejudices. I was able to work in a small group of very individual, creative people. The common perception of the Japanese and the company mentality just did not exist at all. My counterpart in the office, who was trained in Japan, had the same desire I had to express himself individually and had the same creative impulses, but they manage them very

Ken Haas

Former Luce Scholars Susan Wallace (extreme left) and Timur Galen confer with associate director Melissa S. Topping and administrative assistant Catherine Baron Piazza (behind sofa).

differently than we do. The way Maki orchestrated his people was spectacular. His work is a synthesis of the minds of the people in his office, yet it is his synthesis. It is Maki's work, because he is the one who makes the judgments and balances the talents of all the people. The more time I spent there, the more I liked the idea of the leader of the orchestra. He is not the loudest voice, but he is the most sure voice.

Thus impressed, Galen now gives occasional lectures at the University of Pennsylvania on "the whole question of the last hundred years of architecture in America, and the role of the Far East." He adds: "Now you hardly meet a student at Penn who doesn't want to go to Japan."

Galen also has been doing part-time work as a partner in a two-man firm in Philadelphia. "All of our work is influenced by my Japanese experience. We have worked in suburban Philadelphia settings where the architectural tradition is principally English. Our small practice has involved additions and renovations to build wings, incorporating my Japanese experience: porches and verandas . . . an environment perfectly suited for both a spiritual and a formal kind of Japanese architecture."

Evidence of the cross-cultural influence that Galen speaks of with such passion is growing every day in the United States. The Museum of Contemporary Art in Los Angeles, housed in what one critic called "one of the most eagerly awaited buildings in the United States," recently opened to critical applause. And the Brooklyn Museum in New York has hired Arata Isozaki, the architect for the Los Angeles museum, to design a major renovation and expansion for its landmark Beaux-Arts building. Thus one of Japan's greatest architects is becoming a prominent designer of museums in the United States, with an important building on one coast and an important assignment on the other. And three Luce Scholars have worked with Isozaki in his Tokyo atelier. Galen's choice of profession and milieu seems almost prescient; so does his selection as a Luce Scholar.

● Carolyn Cantlay is a specialist in family planning, working for the

Enterprise Program of John Snow, Inc., in Arlington, Virginia. She is a graduate of Bryn Mawr College and took her Master of Science in Public Health at the University of North Carolina. She was a Luce scholar in 1983–84. Her assignment took her to Bangkok, where she worked with the Population and Community Development Association, a private Thai group active in family planning.

Thailand has been successful in recognizing and taking steps to address a very high population growth rate. Since the early 1970s the growth rate has decreased by more than half. Working there, I got used to talking about the mechanics of contraception without blushing. At the time I couldn't really believe I was doing anything for myself except making me unfit for polite company when I got back. But it was all directly relevant to what I am doing now, which is making an effort to assist family planning efforts worldwide. I've been to Senegal, Nigeria, Indonesia, gone back to Thailand twice, and now I'm off to Pakistan. In each place I am struck by the need to replicate the kind of enthusiasm and ingenuity I saw in Thailand. Countries like Nigeria and Senegal are not Thailand, but I know what works, and what has not been tried, and somewhere in between lies the challenge. I've learned what it is to be irredeemably and for a long time a foreigner and being looked on as a stranger in places as far away from home as you can imagine being.

• John Bussey is a reporter for the *Wall Street Journal* in Detroit. A graduate of Dartmouth, he was a Luce scholar in 1982–83. He worked that year for the *South China Morning Post* in Hong Kong.

You find when you get back that there is remarkable Asian dimension to things in the states. Three thousand workers just went on strike at a Ford plant in Hapeville, Georgia. The underlying issue was outsourcing—work that used to be done by the United Auto Workers is now being done in Korea and Japan. Ford is building a Mazda-engineered and designed car in Korea, and importing it to the United States. Our story had to include how workers and the industry in Asia are affecting the auto industry in the United States. So I find myself in Detroit writing in some measure about Asia.

He echoes the view of Debra Knopman, the hydrologist: "Asia leaves you a better observer. For a reporter, you can't come away with a better lesson. You learn to find your way more effectively in a city where you don't speak the language, in a place where you don't understand the social values. You become a quicker study."

• Lynda Sharp Paine is an assistant professor of business administration at Georgetown University. She has a B.A. from Smith, a D.Phil. from Oxford, and a doctorate in jurisprudence from Harvard. She was a Luce scholar in 1976–77 and taught at National Chengchi University in Taiwan.

Here are snippets from her comments on the occasion of the tenth anniversary of the Luce Scholars Program:

I certainly would not have found myself doing the Chinese plate dance before a distinguished assemblage of economists, philosophers, and biologists last summer if I had not studied Chinese dance during my year in Taiwan. . . . My five-year-old son and I had a wonderful time planning a Chinese New Year celebration for his nursery school. . . . We acted as host family for Asian students as well as other Asian visitors at Harvard and tried to make them feel as welcome in our part of the world as we felt in theirs. . . .

The Asian experience enriched my life by giving me new interests and knowledge, but it also affected my life on another level. The experience of living in a country where family ties are valued highly and where parenthood is a respected calling played a role in propelling my husband and me into parenthood. . . . The dominant trend in modern moral philosophy is to treat actions —not moral agents—as primary in moral theory. It is believed that people's moral qualities are derivative of their actions. Chinese philosophy reverses that relationship: the qualities of agents are primary. Impressive Chinese philosophical traditions had been built on the belief that moral norms grow out of human sentiments. In my recent work on the moral basis of family, I have had to entertain both these ideas.

• More than a decade has passed since Jeffrey Laurence was a Luce scholar working on the faculty of medicine at Osaka University in Japan. He interrupted his medical studies at the University of Chicago to accept the Luce appointment and turned down a Rhodes scholarship to do so. In Japan, Laurence did his work at a one-thousand-bed cancer research institute associated with Osaka University, and he found that "the connection between cancer and immunology fascinated me." The head of the institute, Dr. Yuchi Yamamura, was working with mechanisms that increase immunity to lung cancer, "using technology that was spectacular back then, doing things in research that I had only heard about in the states. Things that were routine in Japan in 1974 would have been experimental in the United States." After living in a two-room apartment attached to a little family temple in nearby Kyoto for a year ("life, mixed with medicine and flower-viewing, was a grace," he says), Laurence returned to Chicago, got his M.D. three months later, and became a resident at New York Hospital–Cornell Medical Center.

There, in 1984, he started the hospital's laboratory for AIDS research. He has a tiny staff but says, "We need to get more people who are interested in molecular biology and immunology. This is the most important medical problem in the past fifty years." In New York, Laurence has acted not only as doctor but as fund-raiser: he raised $350,000 to expand the laboratory and now is trying to raise $2.5 million to fund an institute for the study of AIDS. "There is no place like that in New York City, yet half of all AIDS patients are here." Laurence does not assert that he would not be where he is had he not gotten a Luce scholarship, but the profound effect of Japan on his career is clear. He has returned to Asia many times since he completed his year in Osaka, but his memory of his first exposure remains sharp. He uses words like "amazing" and "phenomenal" to sum up the experience and finds himself still in agreement with his earliest response to the Luce opportunity: "It sounded like a great idea."

• Luce scholars are generally an adventurous bunch, but few can claim adventures like the one that Edward McNally had in his tour as a Luce scholar in 1985–86. McNally, then newly graduated from Notre Dame Law School and a special assistant to the attorney general's chief of staff in the U.S. Justice Department, was the first Luce scholar to work and study on the mainland of China. From the law school of Peking University, McNally made two extensive tours through China, traveling on both occasions in a Chinese-made motorcycle with a sidecar—"classic World War II style," he says. The first took him 3,000 miles across the Yangtze and the Yellow rivers from Beijing to Shanghai without ever having to present his credentials. In Shanghai, his motorcycle needed repairs, which were obligingly supplied by the Public Security Bureau. On the second trip, which came at the end of his year in China, McNally traveled in the company of John Burns, a correspondent for the *New York Times*, from Taiyuan, 250 miles southwest of Beijing, 1,000 miles to the border of Sichuan province.

Heading on, McNally and Burns arrived in the tiny town of Zhenba at 4:30 A.M., where, trying to arouse an innkeeper, they made enough noise to attract the local police. Formally placed under house arrest, they were comfortably accommodated for the night and interviewed by local television the next day: the news broadcast made no reference to the arrest. Two days later they were sent back to Beijing by train ("We could not have been treated more politely") and had a farewell lunch with Winston Lord, the American ambassador. A few days later in Hong Kong, McNally learned that John Burns had been arrested as he tried to leave China for a three-week vacation. Since he had been Burns's companion, McNally was briefly of interest to the press: among those interviewing him in Hong Kong was Margaret Scott, another Luce scholar, who was on the *Far Eastern Economic Review* and a stringer for the *Washington Post*. McNally, now an assistant U.S. attorney in New York, says, "I hope very much to go back to China. I would love to help each side to understand the difficult legal traditions and vocabularies of the other."

No better evidence of the high quality of those who apply for Luce scholarships, and of the difficulty of choosing between them, can be adduced than the history of one who was passed over. Jamienne Studley, a graduate of Barnard with a law degree from Harvard, applied for a Luce scholarship, intrigued by the idea, as she says, of looking at the field of health care, then her main interest, "from an entirely different perspective." She recalls: "At the time, I was twenty-five, and I'm sure I thought myself exceptionally grown up, enormously mature and insightful." When she came up for selection, Studley was interviewed by, among others, Peter Krogh, dean of the School of Foreign Service at Georgetown University. She found that her interviews' "expectation of vision, maturity, sense of self, ability to stand up for yourself and what you believe in—all that was miles beyond what people had demanded of me before. After all the gentility—we stayed at a gracious hotel and had a lovely breakfast on silver service—it was like a kick in the stomach. It had all of us reeling."

The kick, however, turned out to be one from which Jamienne Studley recovered very nicely. Soon after, she joined the staff of Yale Law School. Now thirty-eight and dean of the Graduate Program at Yale Law School, the one who was called but not chosen as a Luce scholar is thoroughly reconciled to the one setback of her career.

Since the Luce Scholars Program began in 1974, the Luce Foundation has spent about $4 million to send 185 Americans to East and Southeast Asia. The basic stipend for each scholar is $14,000 for the year, with an increase of $3,000 if a married scholar brings a spouse along. The foundation pays travel expenses—economy class—for all travel required by the program. A differential, provided according to a formula that assures parity among the scholars insofar as possible, may be paid where costs of living differ. The foundation also pays for medical insurance; the scholar must meet all other expenses from the basic stipend. As we have seen, many scholars work in professional positions in Asian institutions or agencies as part of their assignment, but they receive no compensation for that work. Some scholars dislike the provision that they get no academic credit for their time abroad, but the foundation continues to regard that provision as an assurance that the program will continue to stress experience with Asian life and not become academic in nature.

Criteria of success are elusive in the foundation world, and nowhere more than here. In achieving one of its objectives, as the narratives from the scholars demonstrate, the Luce Scholars Program has been a remarkable success. It seems certain that the horizons of the participants—and by association the horizons of many of their colleagues as well—have been broadened by their introduction to an area of the world certain to be of increasing importance to the United States for decades to come. This objective, remarked the foundation's staff in a report to the board, "has been almost universally applauded by Asians and Americans, by specialists and laymen alike."

Another key measure, however, will be the degree to which the elaborate selection process did indeed succeed in choosing people who become leaders, and that will be the hardest test of all. Remarks Robert Armstrong: "The payoff is long-term. The real benefits could be twenty-five years from now. But we are seeing signs of the results we'd hoped we would have." One sign, according to Armstrong, is the elevation of one Luce scholar through the ranks of CBS News. Missie Taylor went with President Reagan to China and Japan and is regarded, Armstrong remarks, "not as an Asian expert but as someone with Asian experience who knows what questions to ask." Of the first group of fifteen Luce scholars, four are teachers, three are lawyers, and three are doctors. The more prominent leader—the secretary of state, for example—has yet to emerge.

The Luce Scholars Program has some similarity both to Rhodes and Fulbright scholarships. All choose promising people and give them a chance for interesting experiences and broadened education. Like Luce scholars, Rhodes scholars are selected because they are judged "physically, intellectually and morally capable of leadership." And the Fulbright program, too, wants people of "potential, with ability and willingness to share ideas with people of diverse cultures." But the Luce Scholars Program is distinct from both of these. Rhodes scholars, for example, go to England and spend two to three years at Oxford University, not in the environment called "the world of work." About seventy Rhodes scholars—Americans and others—are chosen; the annual number has grown since the program was founded in 1903. The Fulbright program is administered by and paid for by the U.S. government, giving it a very different character from the other two undertakings. Also, it makes grants to citizens of other countries as well as to Americans; in the forty-two years between the time the Fulbright program began and 1986, some 155,000 people—54,000 Americans and 101,000 from abroad—have been named Fulbright scholars.

The 185 Luce scholars have been people of remarkable heterogeneity: as of 1986, they consisted of 123 males and 62 females; at the time of appointment 55 were married men, 26 married women; 44 have gone to Japan, 31 to the Philippines, 14 to Taiwan; 184 have advanced degrees, awarded by 97 different colleges, with Harvard leading: Luce scholars have earned 38 degrees from that institution. To choose the scholar with the most unexpected qualifications is not easy. But one candidate for that honor would be a 1981 scholar: Stephen C. Haus was a graduate of the Rhode Island School of Design who became a landscape architect specializing in zoo design.

With its concentration on Asia, its high degree of selectivity, its means of funding, and its uniqueness in placement, the Luce Scholars Program has found a niche of its own. Perhaps an early brochure about the program, written by Robert Armstrong—with a handsome cover drawing, *Bamboos, Rocks and Lonely Orchids* by the fourteenth-century artist Chao Meng-fu—best sums up the program, which he described as "the culmination of several years' activity by the foundation in support of projects designed to extend the parameters of American contact with Asia. With each new effort in this direction has come a confirmation of the need to do still more. Certainly the troubled history of Asian-American relations over the past several decades stands as tragic evidence of our failure to develop in this country a broad base of understanding of Asian realities. . . .

All can benefit immeasurably from an initiation into an equally important area of the world that will certainly affect—more directly than they may realize—the course of their careers and lives. Even a relatively small number of future leaders with such broadened insights could have a significant impact on the course of our future relations with Asia and on our own cultural, intellectual, and political development."

THE LUCE FUND FOR ASIAN STUDIES

An axiom of philanthropy holds that one successful program demonstrates the need for another. As the foundation's experience with the Luce scholars ran along in the 1970s, its familiarity with the academic community for East Asian studies in the United States, and indeed with the entire East Asian scene, also grew. Henry Luce III, Martha Wallace, Robert Armstrong, and others at the foundation became aware that, as Armstrong said in his Luce scholars summation, there was "need to do still more." That general belief was slowly refined as the thinking of Armstrong and the others swung around to a recognition that American academic institutions concentrating on East Asia were beginning to weaken their Asian programs—or, as the staff of the foundation put it to Henry Luce III and to the board in November 1975, "that the American academic community finds itself in a growing financial pinch with respect to Asian studies."

A merger of several elements explained the pinch. The American experience in Vietnam had so depressed and wearied the nation that support for any American effort in Southeast Asia was eroding. Military retreat had brought with it intellectual retreat as well. Looking to reduce costs, the federal government cut back its financial help for area studies and training. At the same time, however, President Nixon's opening to China in 1972 fueled renewed interest in Chinese studies. Access to China for the first time in nearly twenty-five years followed for groups of American scholars. Growing awareness of

Japan's economic prosperity was another stimulus for Asian studies in the United States. Still, the Ford Foundation, which had for many years encouraged research, training, and general education in Asian studies at American universities, changed its emphasis, devoting fewer of its resources to this field. "As a result," the staff wrote, "even the most prestigious centers of Asian studies find themselves hard pressed to maintain standards and to respond to new situations and demands."

Yet the lesson of Vietnam seemed to call for much more, rather than less, study of Asian history, character, and culture. So did the new developments in China and Japan. Henry Luce III, Wallace, Armstrong, and the others held discussions among themselves and with the leading figures in Asian studies to work out ways to bolster the Asian academic community in America. An early foundation decision barred any across-the-board effort to give some small degree of help to every university offering courses on Asian topics. Such action promised to make only a small degree of difference, and it would also have been enormously difficult for the small foundation staff to administer. Further, across-the-board strategies generally imply a paucity of ideas that has not usually afflicted the foundation. Instead, the foundation singled out twelve Asian programs which it determined stood at the head of the Asian field and decided to give help in concentrated doses only to those. As it turned out, that policy of selection was to bring benefits to many lesser institutions as well.

Once it was decided where to bring the help, the question became how to do it. The first idea was to offer support in a prefixed amount for similar projects at each center. But though trying to help everyone would have been too difficult, the idea of helping a few in the same way—administratively the model of simplicity—turned out to be too easy. Since each of the twelve selected programs had its own distinctive strengths and priorities, tailored projects showing an understanding of each center's individual character would clearly be the most promising, and that was the approach the foundation ultimately settled on. To increase "the understanding of U.S.-Asian relationships at

Ken Haas

Gerald L. Curtis, professor of political science with the East Asian Institute at Columbia University, calls at Japan House in New York City. Research projects at Columbia supported by the foundation include the institute's "Pacific Basin Studies Program" and its project, "Asia in the Undergraduate Core Curriculum."

every level: historic, economic, cultural and political" was the way the foundation finally articulated its broad and ambitious intention for extensive financing of these chosen universities.

The notably original emphasis in that broad definition was contained in the innocent-appearing phrase about "relationships." For the spading by the foundation's staff had turned up the truth that Far Eastern specialists in the United States had become very specialized indeed—working on specialty within specialty, concentrating, for example, on Japanese industrial development or Thai village organization or ethnic groups in Indonesia. They were becoming "more intranational than international in outlook" in the view of Henry Luce III. "Few have been inclined—or encouraged—to relate their specialized knowledge to the question of Asian-American relations" was the way Armstrong and the staff put it. And experts in American history, in turn, were adding to the trend toward specialization by concentrating exclusively on America: its diplomacy, its economy, its culture. Neither Asians nor Americans were sufficiently concerned with the constant flow—the flux and reflux—that took place between the two hemispheres.

From all this analysis, there was finally born an important undertaking of the foundation called the Luce Fund for Asian Studies, to which the foundation committed a total of $3 million over a seven-year period. And for the first time, the foundation made use of an unusual financial technique called a "set-aside." That amounts to a pledge by the foundation to the Internal Revenue Service (IRS) that the foundation will spend a given sum over a designated period of years. Once the arrangement is approved by the IRS, the foundation has the flexibility to make payments that vary from year to year but still conform to the IRS spending guidelines as long as the total given sum is paid out by the end of the time that is specified to the IRS at the beginning. It is a way to get credit for the payout at the outset, before the money is actually spent. To get a Luce Fund for Asian Studies grant, each university had to submit its projects for Luce Foundation approval. No single project, except for those that engaged more than one institution, was to get in excess of $75,000 of Luce Foundation money. No payment of a specific amount each year was guaranteed to any participant; the foundation made its separate judgments according to the nature of the requests and individual requirements.

Although all that sounds as though only the selected twelve institutions would be beneficiaries of foundation grants, matters in fact turned out quite differently. The initial twelve were, of course, the principal beneficiaries. But the foundation requested each of the twelve whenever possible to include other centers to do work on topics related to the one the foundation had funded—or, in the foundation's more formal language, each of the twelve was urged "to give serious consideration to proposals that encourage inter-institutional cooperation not only among the centers themselves, but also with respect to neighboring institutions or faculties with particular strengths in related topics."

Rewarding ripple effects followed that exhortation. For one thing, it brought within the foundation's purview two of the leading American scholars active today on Chinese-American relations. Warren Cohen is a diplomatic historian working in Chinese affairs and director of the Asian Studies Center at Michigan State University. Cohen is described by one enthusiastic associate as "the doyen in the curious field of Chinese-American relations—without him, lots of material might fall between the cracks." One of the most prolific scholars in the field of Asian-American relations is Akira Iriye, professor at the University of Chicago, also a beneficiary of the Luce Foundation's activities. Cohen says that as a result of the foundation's importuning the preferred universities on the subject of interinstitutional cooperation, he found himself included in work supported by foundation funds at Columbia, the University of Chicago, the University of Michigan, and elsewhere. Even though Michigan State was not on the foundation's preferred list, Cohen says, "I was enjoying the benefits of Luce Foundation money, attending conferences, getting what was in effect Luce money laundered through the University of Chicago or Columbia to finance my research. I think for six or seven years I attended conferences at the University of Chicago three times a year, with scholars from all over the country—all of this coming out of a grant that the Luce Foundation had given Chicago."

Although he does not overstate the case, Cohen emphasizes the importance of the foundation's timely entry in force into his scholarly field. With the shift in focus of the Ford Foundation, Cohen says, "money from the Luce Foundation became critical in the late 1970s and the early 1980s." As the foundation had concluded earlier, some decline in scholarly work had been taking place; following the Luce Foundation's substantial financing, though, Cohen says, "if you look at the literature, you find a tremendous boom of high-quality work being done." Partly as a result of the enormous amount of help that the major centers got from the Luce Foundation, Cohen says, "a whole stream of books has come out—some of the most important work of the past decade—that were either directly funded by Luce money, or people involved in the books somewhere along the line had Luce Foundation support that made their work possible." Some of the books are described below.

In 1978, the Luce Fund for Asian Studies largely funded what Cohen calls "one of the finest conferences I've ever attended," organized by the East Asian Institute of Columbia University. Under study was one of the periods so disrupting to Chinese-American understanding: the years of civil war in China between the Communist and Nationalist forces, which preceded the Korean War. During that time the Chinese Communists successfully completed their drive to power. The United States continued its support of the Chinese Nationalists and later made the fateful decision to push across the border of North Korea—north of what had hitherto been the zone of combat— toward the Chinese border, despite the warning from the Chinese government that in such an event China would intervene. Thus deepened the enmity long emerging between the United States and China. Some thirty American scholars attended the conference and presented papers. Each received some modest amount of Luce financing for travel and research.

Cohen and other authorities adjudge the resultant book, *Uncertain Years: Chinese-American Relations, 1947–1950*, edited by Dorothy Borg, a research associate at Columbia's East Asian Institute, a senior figure in the field, and one of Cohen's mentors (she was joined by Professor Waldo Heinrichs of Temple University) as one of the most important examinations of a crucial period of Chinese-American history. The book lays poignant stress on these as the turning-point years, the period when, with a different evaluation here, less political pressure there, fewer flamboyant decisions elsewhere, the disastrous sequels to 1947–50 might have been avoided. In his essay "Acheson and China," Cohen sounds the same dramatic theme: "Acheson's performance was not perfect, but it was perfectly creditable—until the decision to cross the 38th parallel [the U.S. invasion of North Korea from the south]. In the heat of battle, and bearing a burden of guilt as Americans died at Chinese hands, Acheson blamed the Chinese . . . then Acheson and the Truman Administration squared off against the plague of McCarthyism . . . and the Administration spent its last year staggering under McCarthy's attack."

Soon retiring from his job as a professor at Cornell, which has been called the premier campus for Southeast Asian studies in the United States, George Kahin is one of the most eminent of Asian scholars. To his works, which include an authoritative work on Indonesia, *Intervention: How America Became Involved in Vietnam* was added in 1986. The reviewer of *Intervention* in the *New York Times* first characterized Kahin by saying that "throughout the [Vietnam] war his was a voice of calm, well-informed reason and courageous dissent." The reviewer continued: "Kahin's account summarizes and interprets an enormous amount of research and writing on Indochina, in addition to providing new and extended interviews with central figures in the U.S. and Vietnam . . . the great value of this book is the calm, well-buttressed coherence with which Kahin presents a remarkable record of folly, stretching back to the 1940s." The buttressing included many hitherto secret documents that Kahin elicited from the Defense and State departments by judicious use of the Freedom of Information Act and that now form part of the public record on Vietnam. Kahin's book took ten years to write, with the Luce Foundation one of his financial supporters.

Tang Tsou is a professor of political science and Far Eastern languages at the University of Chicago, one of the premier institutions in the United States for Chinese studies. He lectures in formal style, with precision and a dry attention to detail about modern-day Chinese political parties and their forebears. His book *The Cultural Revolu-*

tion and Post-Mao Reforms: A Historical Perspective bears marks of the same scholarly care and makes no effort to popularize: his Introduction begins with the bold-faced phrase "Methodological Notes." The work, though, can tremendously inform the serious reader about the Chinese Communist political community and the interplay in that community between ideology and political development, which Tsou with typical frugality calls simply "ideas." Countering the view that the Chinese Communists were and are only tough pragmatists, Tsou patiently explains: "Particularly important for Western observers is the fact that for millennia the Chinese have given great weight to ideas, and they continue to do so in the twentieth century."

If these books can be called the children of the Luce Fund for Asian Studies, then it is interesting to note that the children also have had children. Nancy Tucker, then an adjunct assistant professor of Asian history at New York University, contributed an essay called "Nationalist China's Decline and Its Impact on Sino-American Relations, 1949–50" to *Uncertain Years*. Related to that essay was Tucker's book, which was also her dissertation, called *Patterns in the Dust*—a meticulous account of why the United States did not recognize Communist China in 1949–50. In that way, Luce dollars sometimes can set in motion generations of research.

Warren Cohen describes the chain of events: "Lots of ideas came out of that 1978 conference. When you have a conference like that, each of us is affected by the discussion that takes place. We may write something two years later, or we may decide to study something two years later—you can't attribute it directly to the conference. But it's the pyramid effect or the spiral effect or whatever you want to call it. We had that tremendous burst of activity in the field of American–East Asian relations, and I would say that 90 percent of it is directly funded or indirectly sparked by Luce Foundation grants."

Cohen also finds the Luce Foundation's approach—pragmatic, flexible, and oriented toward the merits of new ideas rather than toward the conventional paths of philanthropy—consistently effective.

Foundations as a rule get interested in a subject and they lay out lots of money to get university groups started on it. The term they're so fond of is "seed money." But once they get it started, someone else is supposed to take it over, maybe the university itself. Sometimes that happens, but my experience is that it usually doesn't happen, and what you get is decline afterwards. Maybe there will be a permanent residual effect, but I think there is generally a drop in activity. In a couple of years the money is gone, and they failed to come up with a way to provide it internally, and they are running around looking for foundations. One of the things that happens at universities, unfortunately, is that research direction, program direction, is determined by what foundations are willing to fund, rather than by intellectual or academic decision. There's a lot of resentment about that, but it seems to be an inescapable part of the picture.

The Luce Foundation for Asian Studies closed its books in 1982. (For a list of the books that resulted from this program, see Appendix I.) Of the $3 million expended, the largest part went to Chinese studies ($828,000). Then came Japan ($529,500) and then studies covering East Asia generally ($459,500). They were followed by Southeast Asia ($346,000), all-Asia studies ($334,000), Korea ($320,000), Philippine studies ($140,000), and Taiwan ($64,000). The twelve designated institutions were the recipients; among them, Columbia finished first, with grants totaling $435,000. Next came Harvard, with $423,000, followed by the University of Michigan ($363,000), the University of Chicago ($334,000), and Cornell ($321,000). Other recipients included Stanford ($266,500) and Princeton ($236,500).

Although the Luce Fund for Asian Studies was exhausted by 1982, the foundation has continued to support the work of Warren Cohen and other scholars. In recent years, Cohen has been at work on what he calls his "big project"—"Unfortunately, I'm distracted by twenty-two smaller ones"—to which the Luce Foundation gave $50,000 over a period of six months, starting in September 1983. The "big project," which addresses the American response to East Asian art, testifies to Cohen's virtuosity, as well as to the diversity of the foundation's interests. Cohen's work is part of what he describes as "a shift in the historical profession over the past twenty years, away from political and diplomatic history, and toward social and cultural history." When Cohen was a graduate student, he says, diplomatic history was the "hot field"; now, in some places, "if you're not doing social history, you're not a historian."

The part of social history that Cohen is working on concerns art broadly defined—"What we hang on our walls is part of our culture, like what we wear and what we eat"—in America and China: the connections between the two and how the perceptions of one influence the other. The history is a long one: "In colonial America, lots of the crockery that people had was exported from China. That was the cheapest you could get, you couldn't make anything of that quality in the colonies or in Europe." Adds Cohen: "We recently excavated a late seventeenth- or early eighteenth-century fort in upper Michigan and found pottery from Sichuan. Later people all over the East Coast were papering their walls with wallpaper that had been brought back from China. At one point some things from China were curiosities, some were necessities; at another point, suddenly all this is taken seriously as art." In doing his research on Chinese art, Cohen uncovered Henry R. Luce's role in working with a high-ranking Chinese diplomat in the late 1950s and early 1960s to bring a major exhibition of Chinese works to the United States for extensive travel around this country; the story is part of Cohen's narrative.

In this "big project" Cohen is dealing with some other subtleties as well: how America's perception of China and Japan has been affected by the collections of art from those countries that have been exhibited here and how curators came to collect that art in the first place. The ambitious work, Cohen sums up, "is designed to expand the horizons of American cultural history. Students of American history have long accepted the idea that the United States is a product of Western civilization. But the impact of East Asia on American culture has not received adequate attention"—a point with which the Luce Foundation emphatically concurs and a deficiency that the Luce Fund for Asian Studies was designed to help correct.

THE CHINESE SCHOLARS

The engine of many Luce Foundation programs concerning China is driven by the desire to promote better Asian-American understanding. The Luce Fund for Asian Studies and the Luce Scholars Program have been principal contributors to that purpose, but in accordance with that familiar axiom of philanthropy, "new efforts show new needs," as Armstrong puts it. In 1981 the foundation once again addressed itself to the "need to do still more" by creating another program, the Luce Fund for Chinese Scholars. The fund began in 1981 with a commitment of $1 million; a couple of years later, Henry Luce III and the other directors were sufficiently pleased with what that first million had done to lay out another $1 million. The total of $2 million funded the program for its five-year life.

Like the Fund for Asian Studies and the Luce Scholars Program, the Fund for Chinese Scholars grew out of the discovery of an overlooked need. Whereas the two earlier Asian programs in a sense began in America with the changing environment of American academic institutions and the changing attitudes of American young people, the Fund for Chinese Scholars had China as its starting point. In 1979, the United States and China established diplomatic relations after thirty years of acrimony and mutual isolation. In 1972, with the visit by President Nixon to China, the ice began to thaw; with Deng Xiaoping's trip to the United States in 1979, the relationship turned into a love feast. By 1981, the number of Chinese students and scholars coming to the United States was increasing rapidly from year to year. The Chinese government, however, was primarily motivated by its striving for economic development so that the vast majority of the Chinese coming here represented the scientific and technical communities; Chinese academics in the humanities and social sciences did not have a chance for comparable exposure to the United States. The principal centers of American scholarship on China benefited remarkably little from the flow, being largely unable to get what they wanted most: long-term visits to their campuses by senior Chinese academics.

Among the first to recognize this imbalance, the Luce Foundation was also early in seeking to redress it. The instrument it chose was a program to bring Chinese humanists and social scientists to universities in this country that had important commitments to Chinese studies. The purpose was to create new opportunities on both sides: the Chinese coming here could pursue their scholarship in first-rate American institutions, thus furthering the development of their disciplines in China; and Americans expert in the China field could have the benefit of a dialogue with Chinese scholars and could make associations that would be valuable later as they carried on, often in China, their study of Chinese culture, society, politics, and history.

Participation in the program on the American side was limited to seventeen universities prominent in the field of China studies; the foundation assured each of these institutions that it would pay the cost of the stay of one scholar each year for the five-year life of the program (which in fact lasted for six years for many of the seventeen). Nominations for Chinese scholars were made by a special committee, representing the several disciplines in the humanities and social sciences, which were established on each participating campus to coordinate an annual nomination to the foundation. There was no competition among Chinese scholars for any post: any request from the universities that met the requirements of the program was automatically funded. But no scholar could come more than once in the life of the fund, and no stay shorter than six months was permitted; one academic year was preferred. "We are eager," the staff told the Luce board, "to prevent the development of an intimate 'club' of scholars whose names appear year after year on proposals from the field." The annual amount for each scholar, which varied according to the circumstances of his or her stay, included a direct payment to the scholar (made by the host institution and not directly by the

Ken Haas

*Dr. Jiang Zejun (right) of the Foreign Affairs Institute in Beijing dis-
cusses an illustrated manuscript with a scholar at the Library of
Congress in Washington, D.C. As a participant in the Luce Chinese
Scholars Program, Dr. Jiang pursued his interest in diplomacy at the
Fletcher School of Law and Diplomacy, Tufts University.*

foundation), funds for housing and maintenance, some research support, and some money for travel within the United States. The foundation originally hoped that Chinese institutions would pay for international travel, but in most cases they have not done so. The average cost for each scholar came to around $22,000. By the end of the project in the summer of 1988, ninety-one Chinese scholars had visited America under foundation auspices.

Some of the visits by older scholars, long barred from the United States, were marked with poignancy. One of them, Zhang Mengbai, spent much of his time at Cornell catching up on the past thirty years of American history, which he teaches at Suzhou, where Henry W. Luce once preached. According to Cornell's account of Zhang's stay, he had "an almost overwhelming task here to digest decades of scholarship previously inaccessible to him." When he was seventy-one he was elected president of the Suzhou Historical Society and gave a series of lectures on the United States. Zhang's host on the Cornell faculty believes that he will supply an "authoritative and well-informed voice on the U.S." as he continues his teaching in China.

Cai Shaoqing, another professor of history, took a year off from Nanjing University to teach and study at the University of Washington in Seattle. His teaching there centered around his forthcoming book on secret societies in modern Chinese history, including such exotica as "vegetarian sects and Taiping-triad relations" and "origins of the triads and Elder Brother Society." Using a Shanghai municipal police file obtained by the University of Washington from the National Archives of the United States—the file is not available to scholars in China—Cai began a study of the infamous Shanghai Green Gang and continued his work on banditry during the period of the Chinese Republic. According to the University of Washington's report, Cai also established close contacts with American graduate students, who perhaps will benefit from that relationship later in their careers.

One Chinese scholar has to his credit the establishment of a link between two institutions that are half a world apart: the Metropolitan Museum in New York and the Palace Museum in Beijing. For his year in the United States, Yang Xin, a specialist in Chinese painting from the Palace Museum, was placed with the Department of the History of Art at the University of California in Berkeley. He spent much of his time traveling extensively to observe conservation, administration, educational programs, and libraries in American museums, giving special attention to the Metropolitan Museum in New York, where he gave lectures on Chinese painting. He reported his observations fully to his superiors in the Palace Museum after he returned there in January 1985. To the pleasure of those who looked after him at Berkeley, soon after his return to China he was promoted from his job as a researcher in painting to become manager of exhibitions at the Palace Museum. "My hope," wrote Professor James Cahill, director of the Department of the History of Art in a letter to Ira M. Heyman, chancellor of the university, "is that Yang Xin will pick up some of the ideas and methods of the more interesting trends in our art history and take them back to China, where art history is still a very conservative pursuit." Adds Cahill: "Yang's talks of Chinese methods of connoisseurship were quite valuable to my students. And on top of everything else, Yang turned out to be lots of fun."

Not every stay in the United States went so smoothly. The Chinese government refused to give permission to one academic to have his wife join him in the United States. "This lack of trust hurt him," commented one of his hosts on a university faculty. Another spoke not a word of English and had never before left China. "His experience began with a month of somewhat bewildering adjustment to an entirely new environment" commented an American associate. And as with all such exchange programs, there remain difficult questions such as what some of the visitors were really thinking about the American spectacle, in contrast to what they were telling their hosts, and whether upon returning to their home country they can really have much influence on the course of events there or whether they simply disappear into the larger scene.

Although the favorable judgment about the program from its sponsors in universities was predictable, some of the evaluations were convincing because they candidly admitted the sponsors' self-interest.

One of them, Professor Stanley Rosen, of the Department of Political Science at the University of Southern California, summed up his verdict: "It seems to me that the Luce Fund for the Chinese Scholars has performed at least two very valuable services. First, it has helped to train Chinese academics, or at least to introduce Western concepts to them. Even very senior people, having been cut off from the West for decades, benefited from this. At a minimum, they bring back to China new ideas (and books) to share with colleagues and students. Second, the Luce Fund has given American academics a chance to gain a much deeper understanding of the Chinese academic and intellectual environment. . . . We have learned about the possibilities for collaborative research, and the institutions receptive to such research. From a selfish perspective, I think the second service is the more valuable one."

Along the same lines, Michel Oksenberg, professor of political science at the University of Michigan, adds: "The Luce Fund has enabled the establishment of personal ties between leading Chinese scholars in the humanities and social sciences—bonds which were strong before 1949 but had atrophied in the subsequent thirty years. It enlivened and enriched the dialogue at major China centers. Our scholarly community is better as a result: more proficient in Chinese language, more precise and tactful in discussing China, and more informed." And James Cahill believes Berkeley gained because its Chinese visitors were "people of relatively broad humanistic learning, with some combination of language, literature, history, and philosophy. And their contributions to our programs were correspondingly broad and rich." Cahill expects to visit Yang Xin's exhibits in Beijing, already improved by the application of the methods of display and labeling that Yang Xin acquired here.

That American scholars are greatly enriched by the process is surely the judgment of William Parish, director of the Center for Far Eastern Studies at the University of Chicago. Parish recalls the visit to the University of Chicago of a Chinese scholar who was a lawyer, and for whom a law professor at Chicago arranged visits to state and federal prisons in five different states, including Texas, where state prisons partly pay for themselves by inmate labor. Later a young American lawyer from the University of Chicago doing research on Chinese law visited his Chinese lawyer friend in Beijing and since has spent a third of every year doing legal research in China—"so you build contacts that last far beyond a single meeting."

Another Luce scholar at Chicago was Jing Qicheng, deputy director of the Institute of Psychology in China. Jing, who speaks excellent English, toured the United States under the auspices of the University of Chicago. At the University of Illinois at Urbana, Jing started his own little exchange program: thanks to his efforts, the University of Illinois agreed to admit ten or twelve graduate students from China from the Institute of Psychology to pursue their Ph.D. studies at Urbana. Parish also reports that "Jing has also invited me to work on projects through the Institute of Psychology. These are enduring connections."

THE CHINA INSTITUTE

The Luce family and the Luce Foundation have had a long and intimate association with the China Institute in America. That organization, which one close observer calls "the granddaddy of all China exchange and educational institutions," was founded in 1926. A quarter of a century before, the Boxers, an antiforeign Chinese secret society, had attacked foreigners and Chinese Christians, especially in North China (the attacks drove Henry W. Luce and his family, including young Henry, from their mission in Shantung to safe haven in Korea, but the indomitable Luces returned to China six months later). After the Boxers were put down, the United States and other powers exacted indemnities from the Chinese government. Then the United States, often afflicted with guilt on matters concerning Chinese, returned the U.S. share of the indemnity to China on the condition that the funds be used for educational purposes. Endowed with part of those funds, the China Institute in America started up, first by providing information about China to Americans and about the United States to Chinese—mostly students in both cases.

Over the years, the China Institute expanded its role to become a cultural center with a presence in both countries, and it had many contacts with the Luce family in ways that spanned the generations. Mrs. Henry Winters Luce helped and befriended, both in China and in the United States, Mrs. Chih Meng, whose husband was one of the early directors of the China Institute. At various times Henry R. Luce, Henry Luce III, and Henry Luce III's late wife Claire McGill Luce all served as trustees of the institute. Henry Luce III was chairman of the board of the institute from 1976 to 1979. Elisabeth Luce Moore has been a trustee of the institute since 1943.

In 1943 the China Institute was looking desperately for a place in New York to carry on its work. At the time, the Nationalist government of China was carrying on two wars—one against the Japanese and the other against the Chinese Communists. Chih Meng, whose American first name of Paul was conferred upon him by Henry Winters Luce, impressed on Henry R. Luce his government's need for help to continue its cultural mission. Paul Meng persuaded Luce in a lengthy conversation in Luce's office that the China Institute was "doing good work on a shoestring" but could not continue without an office in New York City. "The urgent thing was a headquarters," recalls Elisabeth Luce Moore. "Soon Harry had us looking all over New York for one."

Frequently in those days, as we have seen, concerns of Henry R. Luce quickly became those of the foundation as well. In January 1944, for the now unbelievably small sum of $49,641, the foundation bought China House, a lovely townhouse on 65th Street in New York, for the China Institute. (A provision in the transaction, inserted with characteristic foresight by Charles Stillman, stated that if the Institute were to leave the building, it could under certain circumstances revert to the foundation. China House would probably bring $4 to $5 million in the present market.) Relative to the assets of the foundation, though, the "unbelievably small sum" was fairly sub-

Ken Haas

*Foundation program officer Terrill E. Lautz at the offices of the
China Institute in America. With him are institute vice president Lily
Chang and its president, Dr. Douglas Murray.*

stantial: at the time total assets stood at around $260,000. The $49,641 grant to the China Institute was by far the largest the foundation had made in its seven-year life. From 1946 onward, scarcely a year went by in which the Luce Foundation did not give money to the China Institute for one purpose or another, usually for general operating expenses: $25,000 in 1947 and 1948, for example, and between $10,000 and $25,000 a year from 1950 to 1965. From 1944 to 1966, the foundation's contributions to the China Institute totaled $588,782, including the gift of China House. Later years show $150,000 in 1970, $141,400 in 1974.

All that help, however, does not mean that relations between the institute and the foundation were always smooth. In the 1950s the institute was perceived as symbolizing support for Chiang Kai-shek and the Kuomintang, by then driven off the mainland to Taiwan, and the perception damaged the institute. Evidently, however, the dissatisfaction of the foundation with the institute was not linked to that point. "In fact," remarks Henry Luce III, "the China Institute was a cultural agency, and had no political dimension." He says that the unhappiness of the foundation with the institute came instead from the institute's weak administration and its inability to organize efficiently and operate effectively. The board of the foundation, for example, made a $150,000 grant to the institute in 1974 to cover a three-year period, during which the institute was to phase in broader support from other sources. The $150,000 was a challenge grant to help the China Institute raise a $2 million endowment, the fear being that the institute was becoming too dependent on Luce Foundation help. But the institute was not to gain that broader support. There was also concern that the institute was putting too much emphasis on programs for Chinese in New York: instead of centering its attention on cultural relations between the United States and China, it featured vocational training and bilingual education for local Chinese. "At that time the Institute was not doing what it does best," remarks a person close to the situation. "It was becoming a dinosaur"—and was no longer representing the mainstream of U.S.-Chinese relations.

Then a new president, Wan-go Weng, appointed in 1982, gave the institute new vigor and viability. A skilled proponent of the institute's purpose to resume its prominence in cultural affairs and educational exchange, Weng succeeded in eliciting support from the Starr Foundation and other sources. He also renewed the institute's emphasis on Chinese art, culture, and history and strengthened its school for instruction in the Chinese language. The institute's small art gallery now averages two popular shows a year that one admirer describes as "perfect gems." Wan-go Weng resigned in 1986 after four successful years as director. The new president, Douglas P. Murray, formerly vice-president of the East-West Center in Hawaii, says, "Education has been our big role, and it will be that again." That role, Murray says, will take different forms but will include a renewed emphasis on services to Chinese students and scholars from China, Taiwan, and Hong Kong. In 1984, encouraged by the momentum that Wan-go Weng had generated, the Luce Foundation made that $300,000 commitment to the China Institute for program support over a period of three years.

CHRISTIANITY IN CHINA

The exchange of scholars (Luce scholars to Asia, Chinese scholars to the United States) and the support for academic work on East and Southeast Asia (Luce Fund for Asian Studies) testify to the foundation's commitment to the proposition that East and West must understand each other better. Better understanding means a better knowledge by each country of the history of the other, especially of the early experiences that both have shared. The history of Christianity in China stands as a long and important episode shared by the two nations—an early stage, one might say, of the lengthy and complex love affair between them. Both Henry W. Luce and Henry R. Luce partook of that history—Henry W. as one of the players and Henry R. as one who by birth, by inheritance, and by intellectual commitment took a lifelong interest in it. Scholarship in the field, therefore, has a natural, almost irresistible, appeal for the Luce Foundation.

Photograph by Wei Hsein Station   Courtesy of Henry R. Luce Estate

The colleagues and family of Henry Winters Luce gathered for a photo taken at a railroad station in China, probably in 1915. Dr. Luce is in the second row from the top, third from left; his wife, Elizabeth Root Luce, is in the third row, third from left. Their daughter Elisabeth is seated in the front, at left, and their son Henry is in the front at right.

In the early nineteenth century, in a phase of the love affair when both sides were just getting to know each other, Protestant missionaries from the United States were major communicators about the progress of the courtship—major sources of information for both countries. They were hardly the first foreign divines to arrive in China: among their predecessors were the Jesuits, many of them Italian, who had a conspicuous presence in the court of the Ming emperors. But the Americans were the first churchmen to become cultural brokers between China and the New World, linking village China with small-town America. To the Chinese they were a font of information about the distant country of the United States. The images of

Christianity and to a degree of the entire Western world formed by Chinese were transmitted to them principally by the voluminous writings and religious tracts of the missionaries. Just as important, the missionaries were directing rivers of information the other way: in a characteristic display of their indomitable spirit, they were forever trying in the screeds they sent back to America to describe China to their kinfolk, for example, to the people of Middlebury, Indiana. The reports of the missionaries form today a large body of knowledge of key importance to Chinese-American history, key, that is, to a better grasp of one facet of the love affair.

The literature of the missionaries is an ocean of information that has not been fully explored. One batch of manuscripts, for example, that was slowly collected over the years by the American Board of Commissioners for Foreign Missions remained for decades beyond the easy reach of many students and scholars. Ultimately this archive found its way to Harvard, where it remained secure but still remote in the Houghton Rare Book Library and the Harvard–Yenching Library.

In those formidable redoubts the trove stayed, out of sight and out of mind, until in 1976 the Luce Foundation's directors approved a grant of $70,000 over three years to enable American scholars of China to examine and analyze the Harvard–Yenching Library documents. In 1985 the work of these scholars was published by Harvard in a book called *Christianity in China: Early Protestant Missionary Writings*, edited by John King Fairbank, long the dean of China scholars, and Suzanne Wilson Barnett. Contributors to the book— some eminent Sinologists, some more junior—in their essays reveal and explicate the strength of the early missionary beliefs and the missionary vigor in proselytizing. But they also reveal the colorful and courageous nature of those who delivered the message. Notable among them, for example, was Justus Doolittle, who in 1850 left his family of poor farmers behind in Middlebury, Indiana, in full expectation of enduring "hardship, suffering, and peril" in Foochow. A benevolent man who embraced God and love, believed in their powers of redemption, and kept his faith in the face of temptation, Doolittle found Chinese society "heathen, sensual, vicious and sinful," and his writing passionately deplored the web of traditional superstition and idolatrous ritual that he believed entrapped the Chinese.

Christianity in China also shows that other forces were impelling missionary thought in a very different direction. Some missionaries came to understand that the Chinese, heirs to a culture that long antedated the civilization of Greece, much less that of America, resented being thought of as heathens; they looked on missionaries, whose presence they perceived as sustained chiefly by gunboats, as invading barbarians. In response, as disappointment in the sparse results of proselytizing grew and understanding of Chinese hostility improved, the nature of missionary activities and the tone of their literature changed. Chinese society—trapped according to Doolittle in "idolatrous ritual"—was less and less held up by the missionaries as exemplary of the devil's work. More sensitive to the cultural chasm that separated East and West, some missionaries shifted the direction of their efforts, proselytizing less and working more to spread secular learning and Western medical training among the Chinese; medical missionaries became an important part of the secular missionary movement. Many missionaries turned away from religious tracts and began instead to produce educational material—explanatory writing on history and geography rendered in a manner familiar to the Chinese rather than in the forms of the West. The missionary began to put aside his devotional robes to assume the garb of a learned man— a highly respected figure in Chinese tradition. As a group the missionaries did not relinquish their beliefs, but some of them did go through a crisis of faith. In the case of Walter Henry Medhurst, a leading figure among nineteenth-century missionaries, the shift toward schools and toward educational literature led to a poignant reappraisal of missionary tenets and purposes.

The book *Christianity in China*, like the Luce grant, is of modest dimension. But it puts new perspective on an important formative period in the love affair, in the long and entwined history of the United States and China down to the present day. The expectations of the Luce Foundation's board were surely fulfilled by the outcome of the grant.

But *Christianity in China* was also a forerunner of a major commitment of the foundation. Initial thoughts in this new direction came from the foundation's examination of the findings of a conference in 1983 held under the auspices of the United Board for Christian Higher Education in China, with which the foundation and the Luce family have had long and close relations. The chairman of the conference was Nathan Pusey, the former president of Harvard. Academic and religious leaders attending that conference concluded that "we should encourage a systematic, comprehensive, multi-dimensional review of the history of Christian missions and of Christianity in China." They agreed that first-rate scholarship on the missionaries in China had been coming to the fore in recent years—presumably including some of the work then going forward for *Christianity in China*—and they urged that scholars press ahead with their research "to assess, combine and supplement the Chinese and the Western approaches" to the history of the mission movement.

Impressed with those findings, the foundation considered the ways it might pursue the field. Then, in 1985, the Luce board agreed in principle to fund a major and multisided study of the China mission movement and of the history of the Christian church in China. Given the foundation's traditional interests in higher education, in Christianity, in China, and in U.S.-Chinese relations, it would be hard to imagine a topic closer to the foundation's core beliefs. The agreement in principle was followed by two specific and important grants authorized by the board. The first pays for a number of research projects at the highest level of scholarship; in their totality, these projects will shed new light on the Christian experience in China, particularly from the Chinese perspective. The second has the ambitious and technically challenging objective of cataloging the huge number of missionary documents scattered around the United States. When completed, the 750-page volume will make it far easier for students and scholars to locate the materials for their scholarly work.

The larger of the foundation's two grants in the field is a $650,000 grant for a six-year study being directed by Daniel H. Bays, a highly respected scholar of Chinese history and a professor at the University of Kansas. The ambitious undertaking is intended to advance comprehension of the effects of Christianity in China by exploring the ways Chinese culture and society have responded to and been altered by their interaction with Christianity. The topic is vast, with many facets, but Bays is giving special attention to what he calls "the Chinese part of the experience with Christianity." Bays's method in managing the grant has been to solicit from scholars in the field proposals for examining various segments of the long and complex interplay between China and Christianity. Bays then weighs the proposals, and after consultation with an advisory board and the foundation, he parcels out money—up to $25,000 for one-year fellowships—to enable applicants to carry out the research they have proposed.

One exciting new proposal, Bays says, came from Emily Honig, at the time a thirty-four-year-old assistant professor of Chinese history at Lafayette College in Easton, Pennsylvania. Following her application, Honig received a $25,000 grant to undertake a biography of a remarkable Chinese woman, now in her late eighties, named Cora Deng (Chinese name: Deng Yuzhi). Born in Hunan Province, brought up by her Christian grandmother, Cora Deng attended a missionary-run school, broke away from an arranged marriage, went to college, and then went to work for the YWCA. At that organization, to which three women in the Luce family—Elizabeth Root Luce, Emmavail Luce Severinghaus and Elisabeth Luce Moore—devoted so much of their energy, Cora Deng held a variety of jobs for sixty years, throughout and in the aftermath of the Cultural Revolution; she still worked there in 1987. In the YWCA's Industrial Bureau, Cora Deng studied and wrote about the conditions of women workers in Shanghai; she also conducted a literacy program for them. She established night schools for women workers, where they were taught skills to make them more active in the labor movement; one favorite was public speaking. Honig's biography will tell the story of the accomplishments and trials of this extraordinary Chinese woman. Honig's analysis of the ways Cora Deng's work and social consciousness were formed and informed by her Christian faith, to which she was devoted from the time of her girlhood, relates directly to the purposes of Bays and the Luce Foundation.

Honig's discovery of Cora Deng was one of those lucky strokes that come from diligent research. Honig's earlier book, *Sisters and Strangers: Women in the Shanghai Cotton Mills, 1919–1949*, led to her discovery of Cora Deng's M.A. thesis on the economic status of women in Chinese industry. Honig then sought out Cora Deng in Shanghai. After a long talk, says Honig, "I realized that the story of her life was not only intrinsically interesting, but acquired more interest still because it offered a perspective on Chinese history radically different from, yet in some ways complementary to, the accounts of women's lives that are already available . . . in part because Cora Deng was first and foremost a Christian."

Examples to match that fascinating finding are not easy to come by, but Bays has a list of topics that sound as good and that are being submitted by imaginative scholars of Chinese history and Christianity. The author of one of those ideas is Norma Diamond, an anthropologist at the University of Michigan, who now has a Luce grant to do research on the Hua Miao, a linguistic and ethnically distinct minority group in southwest China. Two principal missionary groups working among the Hua Miao at the turn of the century were the United Methodist church and the China Inland Mission. In that unlikely setting, the two missions were outstandingly successful in planting Christianity among the Hua Miao, where the native as well as the foreign faithful put down roots in native soil. There Christianity thrived beyond the expectations even of its most optimistic believers: so widely accepted did it become in the Hua Miao region that the central government of China, which does not casually make such decisions, recently recognized Christianity as a "native religion" of the Hua Miao people. Diamond's research will show the part Christianity played in strengthening both the ethnic boundaries and the stubborn resistance to assimilation of the three hundred thousand Hua Miao people, touching along the way on such subordinate themes as how church affiliation affected education, literacy, family organization, and village self-government. Diamond will also have a look "at some breakaway Christian sects among the Hua Miao, highly millennial in tone, proclaiming the End Days and the Second Coming."

In its second grant, which in a way supplements Bays's project, the foundation in 1985 recognized how important to the subject of Christianity in China were the widely scattered missionary writings. The task of this undertaking is to locate the writings and to catalog them. The scholar in charge of this $225,000 grant is Archie Crouch, a seventy-eight-year old bibliographer who was a missionary in China from 1936 to 1946. The rich accounts, such as those that form the background for *Christianity in China*, which the missionaries gave of their early encounters in China are spread in many unlikely spots throughout the United States. Major depositories also contain large collections of these writings. And many religious denominations in the United States, such as the Presbyterian Historical Society in Philadelphia, have established their own archival centers. Besides all the material in central locations, thousands of other documents are believed to be dispersed around this country in rural libraries, churches, attics, and basements. (Extensive stores probably exist in China as well, but no local records of American missionaries there have yet been made accessible for scholarly purposes.) Anyone in the past who wanted to dig into the mine of information in the United States would have had great and sometimes insurmountable difficulty just trying to find out what is located where.

In pursuit of all these hidden bits and pieces, and some major collections as well, Archie Crouch has been working in the Speer Library at the Princeton Theological Seminary with a staff of two bibliographers and two research assistants, one of whom speaks Chinese. Crouch and his team are producing a work called *Christianity in China: The Scholar's Guide to China Mission Resources,* which Henry Luce III believes "will bring much improved access and scholarly attention" to the missionaries' correspondence, diaries, manuscripts, magazines, pamphlets, journals, and tracts and which offer a great deal in the way of running commentary on the history of Christianity in China.

The Scholar's Guide has turned out to be a monumental undertaking. Crouch and his people have queried thousands of libraries and repositories about their material, ranging from extensive collections at Yale and at Union Theological Seminary in New York to such minor fragments as the twenty letters held by the Lottie Moon Room in the First Baptist Church on Cherokee Avenue in Cartersville, Georgia. Having had close relations with missionaries and educational missions in China for decades, the Yale Divinity School has a large original collection of its own, largely the archives of the former Christian colleges in China. Yale has also added to its holdings by gathering missionary-related documents from other sources. Yale compiles its own register of the materials in its possession, but the register is not published; interested scholars have to go to New Haven to conduct their search. *The Scholar's Guide* will provide a description of the contents of Yale's collection, as well as of the contents of other sizable collections.

Yale, though, is an exceptional case. Many of the depositories that Crouch has queried have never given careful attention to their China materials, especially if the collection is small relative to the library's other resources. The Houston Public Library in Houston, Texas, for example, is a major library in an urban area, but its librarians have never had the time to itemize the few China-related items it holds. Among the documents from Houston that *The Scholar's Guide* will list are fifty pages written by John Milsaps, a major in the Salvation Army, who traveled extensively in China in the 1890s. Milsaps wrote pamphlets and kept a diary, which he turned over to the Houston library many years ago. His diaries tell an intriguing account of travel around China in 1899. The pamphlets he donated to the Houston library include a series entitled "The Mission Crisis in China," giving Milsaps's observations during the Boxer Rebellion and during a south China famine, as well as an unusual account of an unexpected subject: the use of Chinese music in evangelization. Milsaps's Chinese-language materials, also in the Houston library, include a Baptist hymn book of 1875, a Chinese translation of Bunyan's *Pilgrim's Progress* (1870), and the Gospel of St. Matthew in Mandarin (1899), which was set in numeric characters designed by another missionary, W. H. Murray.

The Kentucky Library of Western Kentucky University in Bowling Green has a letter from Mamie Sallee Bryan, who lived in the Baptist compound in Shanghai, to the Women's Missionary Society of the Hartford Baptist Church in Hartford, Kentucky. Written in 1929, the letter thanks the local society for its support, without which Bryan says she could never have gone to Shanghai. Enclosed with the letter were two sheets of Sunday school lessons in Chinese, one for primary schools and the other for "junior schoolers."

At Cartersville, Georgia, the First Baptist Church's Lottie Moon Room, Crouch's research led to the discovery by Margie Black, an Atlanta historian, of twenty letters that Lottie Moon, a well-known missionary who was in China from 1873 to 1912, sent to the Women's Missionary Society in Cartersville. Lottie Moon was born in Albermarle County, Virginia, not far from Monticello; she attended what was later to become Hollins College, where she won a reputation for having intellectual interests unusual for a female of that era. After the Civil War, the Foreign Mission Board of the Baptist church persuaded Lottie Moon that a single woman could spread the gospel among Chinese women more effectively than men could. She paid her own way to Shantung, where she served around the time that Henry W. Luce and his wife were there. (The Luces arrived in 1897.) A tiny woman just over four feet tall, Lottie Moon stayed in China for thirty-nine years, teaching and evangelizing. Despite her size, she could be a formidable figure, once facing down a Chinese father who wanted his daughter to bind her feet ("He backed down completely," Lottie Moon said in one of her letters home). Like other missionaries, she served not just as teacher but as nurse. A biographer comments, "Lottie worked with a tenderness to human need. When she visited a woman whose treasured son had died, she offered sympathy first, then the message of heaven." Lottie Moon stayed in Tengchow during the bombardment by the Japanese in 1895, ignoring danger and traveling unceasingly through the province, "radiating strength and stamina," says her biographer.

During all those work-crowded years, Lottie Moon found time to write continual accounts of what she saw, following her own advice: "Write. Write at least a half hour each day," she urged a colleague. "Write constantly to America of the need of these dear people for Christ." Her letters, written in a strong, legible hand, cover almost half a century and touch on nearly every aspect of Chinese and missionary life. Included, for example, are discourses about the Chinese government's pronouncements concerning missionary activities, even the most hostile of which did not daunt her: "In the army of the Lord, it is no mere idle boast to say that foreign missionaries constitute the van," she wrote. "Theirs is the post of honor; the post of danger."

Her accounts of the persecution of Chinese Christians ends with the call for reinforcements: "Virginia has only one representative in all China, and that one a woman," she told church authorities back home. "I do not complain of the burden laid upon me by teaching heathen men in addition to my legitimate work among the women and girls. I merely come to you and state the facts. . . . What are you going to do, *yourselves in person?*" On another occasion she wrote, "Truly the harvest is great, and the laborers are few. May I ask you, dear sisters, to make it your constant prayer that the Lord of the harvest will send laborers. . . . Oh, that many, many women would give their lives to this blessed work of elevating their degraded heathen sisters!" And Lottie Moon practiced what she preached, "bearing the gospel directly to the women and girls in their own homes. . . . Now I am on the threshing floor, sitting on the newly gathered wheat, teaching a few pages of the catechism. Under the light of the stars, I am hearing girls sing such hymns as 'Jesus Loves Me.' " The letters of Lottie Moon, a testament to the vigor and fearlessness of the missionaries, will be cataloged in *A Scholar's Guide.*

Debbi Soled, an editor and researcher who works for Crouch, visited Wellesley College, an especially important repository, in search of missionary materials. Wellesley sent a number of missionaries and wives of missionaries to China in the late nineteenth and early twentieth centuries and also had an institutional connection with Yenching University, one of the foremost colleges in China founded by Christian missionaries (Henry Winters Luce, as we have seen, was one of its organizers). In turn, many young women from missionary families, including Elisabeth Luce Moore and Emmavail Luce Severinghaus, attended Wellesley, further strengthening the connection between Wellesley and China. *A Scholar's Guide* will contain biographical files on some forty Wellesley alumnae, faculty, and staff who went to China and will also include two collections that bear directly on the Wellesley-Yenching connection. Correspondence in those collections includes letters between several of Wellesley's presidents and the Wellesley people in China as well as a letter that Elisabeth Luce Moore wrote to Margaret Clapp, then Wellesley's president, in 1964, long after the bamboo curtain had dropped. The letter gives a concise account of the earlier relations between Wellesley and Yenching.

The Sisters Adorers of the Precious Blood, a cloistered and contemplative order, were about to build a monastery in Tientsin when, with other Western missionaries, they were banished from China in 1949. Many of the sisters who were expelled from China, along with some Chinese women who had joined the order, returned to their motherhouse in St. Hyacinthe, Canada. But the bulk of their records on their mission in China ended up in the sisters' monastery houses in Manchester, New Hampshire. Tucked away in those buildings are manuscripts, diaries, letters, and photographs that detail the history of the sisters' mission in Tientsin from the time of its foundation to the moment of its compulsory closing. Recounted are particulars about the hardships and imprisonment of some of the sisters in 1948. Also related are the adventures, many of them sad, of the native-born Chinese sisters, the Chinese Jesuits, and other Chinese missionaries who evaded expulsion in 1949 but were driven from mainland China to Taiwan and Japan in the early 1950s. These documents, which otherwise might have been lost to historians, are among those being listed in *A Scholar's Guide*.

5

Art: An Enhancement of Scholarship

A watershed year in many ways, 1981 saw the birth of one of the foundation's major undertakings. The jump in the value of its assets to $100 million that year, caused principally by the increase in the price of the 2,723,076 shares of Time Inc., stock that the foundation then held, brought new and ambitious programs within its reach. With enlarged means in hand and more still in prospect, the staff began discussing new directions for foundation programs. Led by executive director Martha R. Wallace and program director and vice-president Robert E. Armstrong (who was soon to be Wallace's successor) these discussions soon swung around to the field of art. Henry Luce III, a collector, expressed interest and gave encouragement to a thrust in that direction. The search for an appropriate locus for foundation support began.

That the foundation should take up a significant position somewhere in the field of the arts constituted a revival of an old interest rather than the invention of a new one—another demonstration of the foundation's regard for its roots, so often repeated in its history. Aside from his appreciation of Chinese calligraphy, Henry Winters Luce, judging from the historical records, had no very strong devotion to the arts. His son, Henry R. Luce, was not a sophisticated critic, but he was a tireless and enthusiastic visitor to museums and art galleries, and a collector as well. As a trustee of the Metropolitan Museum of Art his membership on the Purchasing Committee was his favorite eleemosynary assignment—the only role of his life in which he was able, he said, "to spend somebody else's money."

Luce had a special engagement with the art world. He accepted the truth that art is a central expression of a civilized society, and he regarded art as an ultimate measure of a society's worth. On one occasion he expressed the wish that art might become "the dominant or unifying purpose in American life." Like Nathaniel Alden in George Santayana's *The Last Puritan*, Luce thought it "a public duty . . . for those who could afford it to encourage art in a new country," and, also like Alden, Luce accepted art unquestioningly as a prima facie good cause: one needed neither finely tuned sensibilities nor a mastery of precious prose to admire its beauties.

Both Henry and his wife, Clare Boothe Luce, were collectors of art. Henry Luce acquired Oriental ceramics—T'ang horses and camels were his favorites—mostly in 1946 during a swing around China (on the trip, typically, he met General George C. Marshall, General Douglas MacArthur, and Emperor Hirohito, the principal players in the Asian drama). Painting and sculpture had an important place in the many Luce homes. And art was given some prominence in the offices of Time Inc., including the company's headquarters, the Time and Life Building in New York, which was constructed under the management of Henry Luce III. Art of note in other offices includes Henry Moore's *Reclining Woman* and wall relief at the London Time and Life Building. When Luce died in 1967, he left the Metropolitan Museum $80,000, which was used to purchase a painting by John Haberle, an American artist whose photographically detailed trompe l'oeil and precise work was described by one critic as "a celebration of the ordinary." Luce had previously given the Metropolitan a painting by Monet, and he also gave a Monet to the Yale University Art Gallery.

As it was to do with the other interests of its founder, the Luce Foundation during the 1950s and 1960s responded appropriately to Luce's ideas in the field of the arts. It made several grants that nurtured one or another artistic activity. For example, in a grant that foreshadowed its important present engagement with the arts, the foundation mingled art and education by giving $20,000 to the University of Michigan so that it could obtain a copy of an important photographic archive of Asian art belonging to the National Palace Museum, Taipei.

From that modest beginning grew the foundation's present innovative and successful program, which is major in terms of money, unique in approach, and very broad in scope. The initiative that began with those early talks about art among Henry Luce III, Martha Wallace, and Robert Armstrong gathered momentum as Wallace and Armstrong began soliciting from distinguished figures in the art world suggestions for ways the foundation might best apply its resources there. Ideas poured in from such people as Nancy Hanks, former chairman of the National Endowment for the Arts; Tom Lippmann Freudenheim, director of museum programs for the National Endowment; Philippe de Montebello, director of the Metropolitan Museum in New York; the late Joshua Taylor, then director of the Smithsonian's National Collection of Fine Arts, now the National Museum of American Art; Thomas Armstrong, director of the Whitney Museum of American Art in New York; and other authorities. Then Robert Armstrong and members of the staff began to analyze and evaluate the flood of suggestions, on a quest to identify an important need in the arts that the foundation could fill. The small size of the foundation's staff, which Henry Luce III and Armstrong remain reluctant to enlarge, imposed a limitation on what was possible.

Diligent search led to surprising discovery. The burst of artistic creativity in America had long before given this country preeminence in the arts and a delayed but finally secure popular recognition of its artistic primacy. Still, the consensus of the most knowledgeable was that no work of a quality that matched the originality of American artists was being done by American critics and scholars. One of those consulted, Thomas Armstrong of the Whitney, remarked that as far as curatorship and scholarship on American art were concerned, it was "as if nothing had happened" in the realm of creative art. Paul Cummings, a curator at the Whitney and author of the *Dictionary of Contemporary American Artists*, called American art history "an empty field." Only fourteen universities in the entire country offered continuing studies in American art, and good Ph.D. programs were even more rare.

Opinions such as those led Wallace and Armstrong to conclude, as they told the board in November 1980, that "the basic intellectual foundation without which the institutions working to preserve and interpret American art for future generations cannot be effective" was being neglected. "The vast majority of institutions that train this country's curators, critics and art historians have seemed loath to consider American art on any regular basis. European art or other more exotic specialties continue to be their major concern. Our few outstanding scholars of American art have been courageous pioneers who have made their own way in the face of academic indifference and, occasionally, disdain."

With the weakness identified, the search swung around to the means of correcting it. Choices quickly narrowed down to two. One was to give money to traditional academic institutions such as universities, graduate schools, and schools for professional training. The other was to assist museums, which were carrying the burden of putting art on public display but scratching for the resources that would enable them to go forward with serious scholarship. Tom Freudenheim of the National Endowment for the Arts described to Armstrong the pressure on museum directors to mount blockbuster exhibits—the exhibition of Egyptian artifacts from the tomb of King Tutankhamen was a case in point—as "approaching hysteria." John Walsh, a curator of paintings at the Boston Museum of Fine Arts, expressed the view that the "exhibitions have changed our lives greatly. For all the benefits we gain from temporary shows, we pay a high price: there is ever less time and money for the care and study of our collections and for the intellectual growth of the professional staffs." Another authority agreed that museum curators live with tight schedules, never take sabbaticals, and rarely have time to devote themselves to research and writing about their own extensive collections of Americana, the topic of absorbing interest to them.

In traditional academic halls, American art was said to be relegated to a secondary position. European and other art were given priority. It would be an exaggeration to say that everyone in academe was studying the Italian Renaissance, but great numbers of people—perhaps too many—surely were. And the differences between that sometimes aloof academic world and the solid museum world were too vast to be bridged. One prominent museum director told Armstrong that some professors of art history at universities stubbornly assume that all the best students will spend their lives in academe and that only the second-raters will go into museum work. Such misunderstandings and suspicions made cooperative projects hard to start and very chancy in outcome. With all that in mind, and with substantial help from the foundation's several advisers and from Armstrong of the Whitney, Luce and Wallace settled on the final recommendations that they would take to the foundation's directors.

Thus museums emerged as the more promising place for the foundation to apply its leverage. "Just as they have led the way in the collection and exhibition of American art of every era, the professionals in the museums have the potential to lead the way in scholarship as well," Wallace and Armstrong told the board in November 1980. "But American museums, which have led the public to an increasing understanding of American art, have not been able to fill the gap in scholarship. The pressure on curators and directors in recent years to mount blockbuster exhibitions designed to build attendance and attract financial support has made sustained scholarship a virtual impossibility. Museum professionals are eager to see a new emphasis on introspection and research, but scholarship is not as easily financed as showmanship."

No group of experts has ever agreed entirely about anything. The conclusion that museums constitute the proper point of entry for foundation grants to encourage scholarship in American art—to develop that "basic intellectual foundation"—was immediately challenged. Barbara Novak, a brilliant scholar and professor of art history at Columbia University, who in Robert Armstrong's opinion has "as broad an overview of aesthetic education as anyone in the country," thought that "most museums are content to limit their activities to docent programs and the usual student tours" and have no desire to pursue the more serious purposes of education. From Novak also came heartfelt opposition to a commitment to grant to museums alone the opportunity to pursue scholarship in American art. With deep feeling Novak spoke of "the beleaguered scholarly community in the universities," which she described as "struggling valiantly to maintain our programs in American art, while funds go to students in Renaissance or Baroque or anything *not* American." She added the personal note that "I have been trying desperately against tremendous odds to train scholars to make genuine and important contributions to the American field." This sensitive plea was heard and heeded: in 1986 the foundation made a series of grants for dissertation support in American art precisely because of the validity of Novak's position.

Such moving arguments, however valid, at the time came from a minority. Beyond question the consensus favored the position taken by Joshua Taylor of the Smithsonian, who in a long conversation with Wallace and Armstrong deplored "the enormous gulf that now divides museums from other centers of intellectual activity." Taylor urged the foundation to "encourage museums to reach out into the intellectual community in the area of American art and culture." That path, Wallace and Armstrong agreed in the elegant proposal that Armstrong drafted for the board,

> would constitute another effort by the Foundation to encourage maximum use of an important American resource. It would foster serious intellectual inquiry in an area—American art—where such activity has been woefully inadequate. It would stimulate the return to scholarship by an academic resource—the American art museum—that has been distracted in recent years from one of its major functions. And in the process, it might encourage the sort of intellectual "bridging" between disparate elements of the intellectual community [academia and museums] that has come to typify the work of the Foundation in other fields.

In its meeting in December 1980, with Luce in the chair and leading the discussion, the board approved an allocation of $4 million for the establishment of the Luce Fund for Scholarship in American Art. Under the provisions of a set-aside plan, the $4 million was made available for commitment over a period of five years. Three years later, in an expression of satisfaction with what the fund was accomplishing, the board assigned another $3 million in an additional set-aside. The foundation initially decided to limit access to the fund to thirty-six museums with important collections of American art. Included were such major institutions as the Metropolitan Museum in New York and the Museum of Fine Arts in Boston, excellent museums such as the Walker Art Center in Minneapolis, and a few smaller, specialized institutions such as the Amon Carter Museum of Western Art in Fort Worth. Later, when the new set-aside of $3 million was added, the foundation put seven more museums on the list. The lists were worked out in consultation with experts in the museum field, including not only Tom Armstrong, Freudenheim, and Joshua Taylor but also such authorities as Charles Child Eldredge III, an art historian who succeeded to Taylor's post after Taylor died, and William Innes Homer, author, scholar, and chairman of the Art History Department at the University of Delaware. Together, the group of museums that were selected held the most prominent collections in the world of all periods of American art and offered the most promising potential for scholarly achievement through the talent and interest of staff members.

When it came to specific projects, the foundation decided to await and pass judgment on suggestions from the museums themselves. Generally, the foundation determined that its grants were to be spent not for exhibitions of American art at the selected museums (such support would have to come from the National Endowment for the Arts, from corporations, or from the other sources that traditionally fund them) but for research projects and the production of books and catalogs that would break new ground in American scholarship. From the chosen museums, the foundation solicited proposals that it hoped would cover a wide range—all the way from the study of the life and work of a single painter culminating in a book or monograph to a survey of the evolution of realism in American art. Such a survey, suggested Martin Friedman, director of the Walker Art Center in Minneapolis, might start with the once-neglected but now increasingly celebrated Hudson River School and come down to the present day. "Other possibilities," Wallace and Armstrong told the board, "would be limited only by the imagination of the participating institutions."

As it turned out, those imaginations have brought to the foundation proposals of remarkable scope. Their concrete realizations over the past few years have traversed both time and space. They have included catalogs that accompany exhibits and studies that add knowledge and insight to artists and genres already comfortably positioned in the history of American art. And they have included fanciful undertakings that stretch the conventional frontiers of art and stretch at least as much the minds contemplating the newly staked-out areas, some of which, not without a note of defiance, go so far as to include the emotions of the artist in art's purview.

Such startling and challenging ideas about what constitutes art and how to display it come from Marcia Tucker, the founder and guiding spirit of the New Museum of Contemporary Art in New York. Superbly educated in the arts, dedicated to their prosperity, and intellectually formidable, Tucker has spent her life as student, organizer, and critic of modern art. She worked as curator of painting and sculpture at New York's Whitney Museum for about eight years. Then perturbation and ambition led her to found the New Museum, which is now entering its eleventh year.

It stretches the lay mind to understand the governing concepts of the New Museum, much less to phrase them coherently. What seems clear is that the New Museum is devoted to expanding the frontiers of art far beyond the most familiar forms of a canvas stretched on wood or a figure mounted on a pedestal. What is not so clear is where, by Marcia Tucker's cartography, the frontiers lie; she probably intends to stimulate just such uncertainty. In any case, the frontiers define territory formerly reserved for the realm of ideas: that is, Tucker and the New Museum believe that ideas and emotions can also be art and can be put on public display.

The museum's expansive philosophy is best explicated by Tucker herself. She starts with her disapproval of present currents in the world of art:

From around the mid-1970s on, attitudes about the arts, their public presentation, and the responsibilities of museums changed completely. Art began to be considered a business. Works of art became increasingly commodified. As a result, museum directors now find they can do only exhibitions that are corporately funded. Shows that are controversial are just not fundable, so they just aren't done. Art as a method of inquiry, as a scholarly and intellectual pursuit, has been very seriously neglected. I started to hear things like "Museums are businesses and should be run as such." But museums are not businesses, and if they were, people like myself and many others would not be here. We are in museums for other reasons.

Foremost among those reasons is Tucker's dominant conviction that art is not simply beauty—not simply what elegant artists like those of the nineteenth-century Boston School thought it was (see page 146). Art is "an expression of the totality of our culture," asserts Tucker. Indeed, art may not be beauty in the traditional sense at all. She continues:

Post-modernism postulates art as a kind of production in society, just as other things are produced, and urges an analysis of the work of art apart from its creator. Our view is far different from looking at art as painting or sculpture done by a single gifted person with certain kinds of skills. The New Museum sees art as a repository for valuable and relevant ideas, though history might say "This artist was less important and this work wasn't so important." The museum is an attempt to respond to the interests of living artists, to the interests of the art community, and not to commercial interests. We may be the only museum in this country that does shows even when they are not funded— and that really is an amazing thing.

The foundation's interest in the New Museum dates from early in the museum's history, following a visit there by Henry Luce III. At

Ken Haas

*Barbara Haskell, curator at the Whitney Museum of American Art,
holds a photograph of Jasper Johns's 1958 painting,* Three Flags.
*Among the Whitney's projects supported by the foundation is a
study of contemporary American art in European collections.*

that time, Tucker put on a show of the work of Alfred Jensen, an
American artist of geometric style, who painted a mural for the Time
and Life Building in Paris. "I wanted to do the show when I was at
the Whitney," remarks Tucker. "But the Whitney thought it was nuts
to do that. After I got here, the Whitney changed its mind and offered
a show to Jensen. But he said he was a young artist and wanted to do

a show at a young museum—which shows he wasn't so young after all." Henry Luce III was a collector and a patron of Jensen, and, says Tucker, "wanted to see the museum that Alfred had chosen over the Whitney. He came to an exhibition here called 'Bad Painting.' He introduced himself and said that he disliked just about everything in the show. I said, 'You can't say something like that and not let me take you to lunch, and we'll fight it out.'" Tucker's later judgment about Luce coincides with a judgment often rendered about his father: "He is a great believer in the power and the validity of ideas, and they don't necessarily have to be his ideas." Presently, the museum board elected him its first president.

Once the New Museum made the list of invited institutions for the Luce Fund for Scholarship in American Art, the museum proposed three projects, all of which were granted. In all, grants to the New Museum totaled $1.72 million over a period of several years. Of that amount, $1.5 million was given for capital improvements and for long-term planning and development. That sum came from the foundation's regular program funds, not from the special Luce Fund for Scholarship in American Art. Most of the money has gone to complete the construction of the museum's new home in lower Manhattan, including more gallery space, offices, a library, and an auditorium. The initial stimulus for so large a grant came from Henry Luce III. Luce was sufficiently intrigued even by exhibits such as "Bad Painting" to stir up the interest of his staff and then, with the encouragement of his aunt, Beth Moore, herself ever the enthusiast for the shock of the new, to get the project before the board, which approved it.

The balance of $220,000 carried forward the foundation's encouragement of scholarship in American art by supporting a series of three books to be done at the New Museum. The first was a collection of critical essays (*Art after Modernism*) and the second a series of monographs by young artists (*Blasted Allegories: An Anthology of Writings by Contemporary Artists*). The third elucidates the social thought of the artists themselves, expressed in their own words (*Discourses: Conversations on Post-Modern Culture*). The three volumes, taken as a whole, have as a theme Tucker's fundamental idea that "art arises from discussion and dialogue—and it is precisely this sense of dispute and dialectic which is too often lost and cannot be reconstructed." *Art after Modernism,* Tucker says, is "dangerous stuff—extremely controversial. There are pirated dog-eared copies going from hand to hand in Europe right now. With this kind of scholarship, we are putting something into the world. We're not saying 'This is right, this is the way you must think about contemporary art.' We are opening up another kind of thinking."

Tucker would hardly deny that there is room for argument about many of her judgments. Many of the political and social views of the artists seem scarcely worth recording, much less preserving, on their own merits. Tucker would probably say in response that while that may or may not be true, the ideas of the artists tell us something important about their art. The point is not always entirely convincing. For example, arguments made in *Art after Modernism* by a photographer named Martha Rosler ascribe validity to the contention that "the doctrine of art's uselessness was the result of the fear of the upper classes after the French Revolution that they would lose control of art. The lie of official culture is that society-invested art is sullied. . . . To rescue ourselves from this damaging fiction surely requires a new emancipation from market relations. The leveling effect of money [is that] all photographs are equal regardless of what they depict."

And a recent show at the New Museum included comments by Hans Haacke, a politically oriented artist, which decry the evils of American multinational corporations and of the American political system with a palpable lack of balance and understanding. One work by Haacke shows a portrait of Ronald Reagan at one end of a red carpet and at the other an antinuclear demonstration, implying that the complex matter of nuclear weaponry and U.S.-USSR relations can be reduced to the personality of the president. Haacke also speaks of art as "a tool and a bargaining chip, a way of legitimizing amoral practices of business and politics." But even those opinions, which seem highly dismissable to this writer, do not negate the worth of the three-volume work by the New Museum or suggest that the foundation's support was misplaced. For all their internal deficiencies and illogicalities, the works stand as a badly needed challenge to widely accepted but just as widely unexamined assumptions about what art is and for whom.

The originality of exhibits at the New Museum is just as great a challenge as the books to the conventional idea of what is suitable for museum display. In a recent exhibit, for example, the New Museum featured a woman making little electronic signs that go on and off; another exhibit offered a woman who appeared once a month and answered questions for an hour or so; yet another put on display a vacuum cleaner encapsulated in a Plexiglas case (artist: Jeff Coombs). A show called "Damaged Goods," presenting "the role of the object in a variety of contexts," featured photographs that were accompanied by short texts, as much a part of the art as the photographs, which were written by the photographers. One photograph called *Perfect Vehicles* showed randomly grouped vases with a few cans of paint scattered among them. As a photograph, it appears to the un-skilled eye to be successful—it makes an interesting array of shapes and shadings. But to the same eye, the photograph hardly seems jammed with social significance. The photographer's comments, how-ever, contend that "a common vase becomes an art object upon the suspension of its utility; that is, it is filled with meaning and value only after it is emptied of its substance. With my newest work, I feel I have solved the tiresome problem of having to remember not to fill the vase." Make of that what you can.

Rising in defense of such spectacles, Tucker quickly broadens the argument. She remarks with considerable penetration: "The medium is not the issue. The issues are what should a museum be for? Should it only address an intellectual elite and speak with the voice of au-thority to those who are not in the know? Or is it to act as a populist mirror, to serve the community—and what is the community? Fur-thermore—what is an exhibition, and why is it an exhibition?" One could hardly ask for—or hope to be able to cope with—more pene-trating questions.

The principle that disturbing questions should be asked and widely accepted conventions should be disputed, sometimes for the simple pleasure of argument, has historically been attractive to various members of the Luce family and, indeed, was part of the charter that Henry R. Luce wrote for *Time* magazine. A good deal of the Luce Foundation's interest in and support for the New Museum originates in that belief and seems to ensure that the museum and Tucker will continue to disturb the conventional, dispute the obvious, and display the subtle.

At the Met

The Metropolitan Museum is rich enough, and its artistic domain wide enough, that even Hercule Poirot might find it challenging to determine where to help and how much. The Luce Foundation's well-delineated aim concerning scholarship in American art, however, provided a clear angle of entry. Two very different foundation projects are now being carried out at the Metropolitan, each distinctly advancing the foundation's special purposes. One of them, a capital grant, complements the capital grant made to the New Museum.

The Metropolitan has the finest and largest collection of American sculpture in the world. But the most recent catalog of its sculpture was done more than twenty-five years ago. Since then scholarly and popular interest in the distinguished collection has grown, and so has the number of pieces that make it up. "We know the interest is keen," Philippe de Montebello told Henry Luce III. "We see it every day in the response of visitors." The inadequately cataloged collection now includes some 250 pieces by 100 sculptors, featuring great works by neoclassical sculptors (e.g., Horatio Greenough and William Wetmore Story), by naturalists (John Quincy Adams Ward) and by practitioners of the Beaux-Arts style such as Augustus Saint-Gaudens. For the catalog now in progress, the foundation in 1983 made a grant of $180,000.

The work will be a compendious guide to the collection and an analysis of its importance. The catalog starts with an introductory essay on the history of American sculpture. Then the text provides biographies of each sculptor whose work is represented in the collection and critical essays for each piece included there. The director of the research is Lewis Sharp, curator of American paintings and sculpture at the Metropolitan, who did his doctoral dissertation on John Quincy Adams Ward. Says Sharp: "It's going to be an important building block in the total scope of our understanding of American sculpture." And according to John Howat, chairman of the Departments of American Art at the Metropolitan, "this publication will fill an undeniable gap in American art studies. Our format will set a new standard and serve as a model for other catalogues in this field."

A little-understood and long-neglected aspect of the sculptor's art will be emphatically brought to public attention by the catalog. After Saint-Gaudens died in 1907, the Metropolitan asked his widow to select works of his that she would like to see included in the Met's collection. Mrs. Saint-Gaudens chose several pieces, which then were specially cast for the museum. Recently, though, the Met has been inspecting those pieces and has found that they do not have the same high quality as the sculptures cast during Saint-Gaudens's lifetime. Notably, the newer pieces lack the fineness and delicacy of detail on which Saint-Gaudens insisted. "In terms of appreciating sculpture, that is very significant," says Sharp. "It shows that the hand of Saint-Gaudens was very important in the final piece. You put two pieces alongside each other, look at the patination, and it's the difference between night and day." Thus, Sharp continues, the discovery highlights the crucially important and subtle point that "the history of sculpture has been the history of a relationship between artist and artisan."

Catalogs such as that one on the Met's collection serve as maps to buried treasures. But often artifacts in museums may remain hidden for decades, affording some credence to those who hold the popular view that although curators give adequate care to what they superintend, some also take unholy pleasure in keeping the treasures buried—sometimes literally underground in museum basements but in any case always safe from the public gaze. (Frederic Vergne, curator

Art: An Enhancement of Scholarship

Ken Haas

John K. Howat, chairman of the Departments of American Art at the Metropolitan Museum of Art, visits one of the museum's vast store rooms. The foundation is providing the museum with funds for the establishment of the Henry R. Luce Center for the Study of American Art.

of the Condé Museum just north of Paris, did not help to dispel my notion when he made an ill-advised comment to a reporter: "My overriding duty is to preserve the [fifteenth-century] manuscript. No one will be allowed to see it again . . . I suppose some visiting head of state might be shown it if he asked, but the public and scholars no longer have direct access.") Howat and de Montebello of the Metropolitan Museum assert that the primary purpose of museums is to put collections on public display for public education—to open a great segment of intellectual life to a substantial part of the population. "Museums should not serve just as resorts of delight," de Montebello told Luce.

But especially over the last twenty-five years, museum collections have grown so rapidly that even the managers at the Metropolitan have had to relegate increasingly large numbers of their art objects to storage areas. There, in a jungle where the objects are safe but visitors travel at their peril, many artistic pieces of unexceptionable beauty now sit or hang in the dark. Those who want to see them have to make appointments; then they must be escorted through the jungle by a staff member. Because the objects are fragile, the Met staff small, and the potential audience large, the Met has had severely to restrict access; many applicants are turned down. "Much of what we have," says de Montebello, "remains inaccessible and of small benefit to scholars and the public." He adds: "Any suitable solution requires space and funds."

The suitable solution that the Metropolitan—doubtless encouraged in part by the role that the Luce family has played at the museum—proposed to the Luce Foundation will clear away a large part of the jungle. The museum has a huge American Wing, which includes great stretches of space on the mezzanine floor. Now being installed on the mezzanine, which can be reached readily by stairway from the main floor of the American Wing, is what will be called the Henry R. Luce Center for the Study of American Art—"by far the most complicated and also our most revolutionary installation," says Lewis Sharp. There just about the entire reserve collection of Americana at the Met—the decorative arts, the long-hidden sculpture, and the paintings, which, Howat says, "in any other museum would be the primary collection"—will go on permanent display. Every one of some eight thousand objects lodged there will be numbered. Visitors and scholars will be able to take that access number back to computer screens, where they will probably find everything they want to know, and maybe more, about the numbered item.

Of utmost importance to the center will be the way the artifacts are displayed. Members of the curatorial staff traveled throughout Europe studying the options, especially cases and lighting systems. The experts finally selected stainless steel and glass cases manufactured by Glasbau Hahn in West Germany, which makes what Howat calls "the Rolls-Royce of the industry." Glasbau Hahn's glass cases are three-eighths of an inch thick, designed for temperature-controlled rooms, and ingeniously designed so that they can easily be opened by curators but are almost impossibly difficult for the more mean-spirited. Into them will go cups, saucers, and pewter mugs; paintings done over a long span of years; and furniture, silver, and pottery. Thus will be included, in effect, all the art entwined with the life of former times. That once "buried treasure" will be visible at last.

Glasbau Hahn has not lost touch with the marketplace when it comes to pricing its immobile glass Rolls-Royces. For curators' salaries, installation costs, and the cases themselves, the foundation is bestowing on the Metropolitan Museum a total of $3.5 million. The grant to the Metropolitan and the one to the New Museum are complementary, each augmenting the physical plant for the display of art in a great city. The returns on that $5 million given to the two museums may not be in for decades—until the quality of latter-day artistic scholarship can be assessed, or until other museums follow the Met's lead in getting their reserve collections out of basements and on display.

The Henry Luce Foundation

Beauty in Boston

Art reflects the values of its age, which was probably the feature that made it most attractive to Henry R. Luce. The homily is never more clearly affirmed than in the work of the artists of the Boston region in the late nineteenth and the first three decades of the twentieth centuries. Earlier the nation's acknowledged and envied leader in every aspect of American culture—social, artistic, literary, educational— the city of Boston in that later era was in slow and elegant decline, much like the fabled old ladies who still dictated the city's social code. But Boston's art was in glorious renaissance: art schools, notably the one started a couple of decades earlier by the Boston Museum, were flourishing; the country's most prosperous art dealers were located in Boston; and the most celebrated names in American painting were linked to Boston and its environs. John Singer Sargent, described by one critic as the "spiritual leader" of the Boston School, was in the full bloom of his international fame in the 1890s. In the 1890s Winslow Homer, born in Boston in 1836, was turning out the powerful and dramatic watercolors that ensured his place in art history. Childe Hassam, like Homer Boston-born, was not only displaying his mastery of the dazzling impressionistic technique he acquired in Paris but was also, in a manner very non-Bostonian, moving to the forefront of the emerging post-Impressionistic school.

Striking as the talents of the individual members of the Boston School were, however, a greater importance lay in its collective impact. Independent of the better-known and foreign-influenced movements in New York, the Boston School was coherent, strong, and especially in its portraiture reflective of Boston's conservative traditions, its gentility, and its idealism. Yet according to Jan Fontein, director of the Boston Museum of Fine Arts, the splendors of the Boston School had been overlooked for too long. What little scholarship was devoted to American art, says Fontein, made "the old mistake in searching for a single mainstream and identity for American art, overlooking the genuine accomplishments of America's regional (that is, non–New York) schools." Since such accomplishments were nowhere better exemplified than in the Boston School, it best offered the prospect of a foundation grant that would work to correct the "old mistake" of scholarship that Fontein deplored. The grant would also help to kindle public interest in perhaps the most significant and best-defined of all the regional schools of American art.

That dual opportunity came with a proposal from Boston's Museum of Fine Arts, which has a long history of distinguished scholarship. One of the first formal schools of art instruction in America began as an adjunct to the Boston Museum, and it continues there today. The museum has also sponsored important exhibits, established a prominent position in its community, and elicited financial support from many of the corporations in the Boston area. The proposal from the museum that came to the foundation in 1982 was two-edged—and just what the foundation was hoping for. The museum suggested a major exhibition of the works of the artists of the Boston School, including Sargent, Homer, and Hassam, as well as William Morris Hunt, Maurice Prendergast, and many others, funded by the Shawmut Corporation, and in addition a sorely needed volume about the Boston School. Both book and exhibit were to attract new attention to that group of artists—the exhibit by drawing crowds to the American Wing of the museum and the book by becoming the definitive scholarly work on the subject. "We aim for a book," commented Fontein, at the time, "which will make a large and lasting scholarly contribution to the American field."

To this end, the foundation made a grant that stands as prototypical of the help it gives in this area. The grant to the Boston Museum, made in December 1982, came to $150,000. The largest single chunk of that amount went to pay the salaries of members of the Boston Museum's curatorial staff to do the research and write the book. Forty-six of the total of 112 paintings and drawings in the exhibition came from the Boston Museum's own collection; the others were gathered from museums and private owners around the country, but principally in the East. In an interesting side effect prompted by the occasion of the exhibition, several owners contributed their treasures first to the show and then permanently to the museum. For example, five sisters gave the museum an enchanting portrait of their family—including the five sisters themselves—seated in the comfortable living room of their cheerful home in Manchester, Massachusetts. The painting, with its aura of grace and ease, was done by their father, Charles Hopkinson, and called *The Hopkinson Family*. And an inviting, softly lighted painting by Ernest Major—mysteriously titled *Portrait of Miss F.* and possessing some of the provocative qualities of John Singer Sargent's *Madame X*—was donated to the museum by its owners, Harold and Esther Heins. That painting stood in the anteroom of the exhibit as a frontispiece to lure in the crowds. The exhibit and the book were both given the resounding title *The Bostonians: Painters of an Elegant Age, 1870–1930*—intentionally evocative of Henry James's novel *The Bostonians*. ("I shall be much abused for the title," James predicted in a letter to his brother when his novel appeared, and he was right.) Several genres were represented at the exhibit and discussed in the museum's book. But both were dominated by splendid portraiture, including portraits of individuals, delightful familial scenes, and charming depictions of meetings between lovely young women, set in spacious rooms full of sunlight and grace. "There's none of the psychological interest you get from a French impressionistic interior," says Trevor Fairbrother, the assistant curator, who for two years was paid out of the Luce Foundation funds. "You never wonder—is that person happy or not? What are they thinking about? The Boston pictures are very cheerful, optimistic—everything exists to delight you and to say that art is about beauty."

For a glimpse of that bright and bygone age, some 157,000 people flocked to the museum to see *The Bostonians* over a hot Boston summer. The number set no record: it was far exceeded by some huge attractions such as the great Renoir show in 1985, which made its only U.S. stop at Boston's Museum of Fine Arts. But by the more modest criteria usually applied, *The Bostonians* did very well indeed. And the local press was full of praise for the exhibit of native talent in a history-minded region.

The book about the Boston School, which also served as a catalog for the show, delivers on Fontein's promise. Trevor Fairbrother is the principal author. Theodore Stebbins, Jr., a Harvard-trained expert in American art, and William Vance, professor of English at Boston University, contributed essays. Vance's monograph examined the intertwining of Boston's social and intellectual history with the history of its art; its originality and erudition led Fairbrother to comment in his acknowledgments, "I take pride in the fact that such a fine piece of writing results from this exhibition." And art expert Erica Hirshler, like Fairbrother paid out of the Luce grant, wrote the ninety-eight brief biographies of the artists at the book's conclusion, which help to assure that the book will become a source for future scholars. Further, as a benign fallout from the foundation's grant, Fairbrother has joined the museum's permanent staff as assistant curator for American paintings, now that the foundation's grant has run out. The show traveled from Boston to Denver and Chicago.

Arts and Crafts in Boston

At the Museum of Fine Arts, the locale of *The Bostonians*, in the spring of 1987 an exhibition was held and a catalog published that were original in nature and connected in substance to other Luce Foundation–sponsored projects. Catalog and exhibition reinforce the theme of that museum's earlier show of paintings and display an interdisciplinary character that furthers some of the purposes of another very different foundation undertaking, the Henry R. Luce Professorship Program already discussed. At the same time, the museum stakes out new ground in this extensive effort. Both the gratifying interconnections and the originality began a couple of years ago with a proposal from the Boston Museum to the National Endowment for the Humanities for a grant to finance an exhibition of American arts and crafts from 1875 to 1920, roughly the period covered by *The Bostonians*. The National Endowment's grant of $50,000, however, fell far short of the museum's needs. That led Museum Director Jan Fontein and Jonathan Fairbanks, curator for decorative arts, assisted by an enthusiastic and erudite associate curator, Wendy Kaplan, to turn to the Luce Foundation for assistance with a scholarly book on the subject of the exhibit.

Thoughts by the layman that "arts and crafts" are a narrow interest must be quickly dispelled. Arts and crafts includes an important movement in this country's intellectual history, an account of a significant exchange of political ideas between the United States and England, and the display of artifacts of unchallenged beauty. The main character in the movement in England after the great critic John Ruskin was William Morris, noted nineteenth-century English reformer, who had a thousand interests. Morris's philosophy centered around his troubling observation, in the words of Jonathan Fairbanks, that "the common man, who shaped things out of the natural environment, found himself competing with manufactured goods that took away the spiritual values of craftsmanship." In the society evolving during the industrial revolution, Morris feared—rightly, history now tells us—that the spiritual value of making things by hand would be lost. The machine was not exactly Morris's enemy—he thought that it could be used to do routine, repetitive, uncreative tasks—but he also thought that when it was used, as Kaplan says, "to ape hand work, it was a disfigurement to human kind." The Society of Arts and Crafts, based on Morris's principles, aimed at putting up organized resistance to the machine as disfigurement and to restore the decorative arts to their rightful place beside painting and sculpture.

In Boston, fertile soil for his ideas, Morris started another Society of Arts and Crafts, the first in America. Morris also put together a company to assemble painters, sculptors, architects, engineers, and decorative arts people in a cooperative workshop, whose message—a foreshadowing of Marcia Tucker—was that all the sister arts were equally important. Morris's workshop also advanced the idea put forward by the Victorian John Ruskin that we should not have "one man always thinking and another always working." So "unity of art" and restoration of "joy in labor" became the battle cries. The objects created by the artisans in his company, Morris thought, should be put on international display in recognition of a new art form. Exhibitions were staged around the United States, and, says Jonathan Fairbanks, "a whole culture grew up around this rejuvenation of handcrafts-manship." Morris's socialist politics had little appeal in America, but his messages about arts and crafts were very popular.

In its exhibit—"The Art That Is Life"—the Boston Museum re-vived both the ideas and the objects of the period. To assemble examples of the arts and crafts of that age in America, the museum's curators and their assistants traveled first to professional collectors and then to private homes, from whose closets objects of surprising beauty emerged. Experts lent their talents: helping with the collection of the silver of the period, for example, was one expert who has spent his professional life working with precious metals. Selection of the furniture of the movement, made of solid native woods in simple rectilinear forms, was conducted by yet another specialist. Splendors from pencils to pianos—not quite but almost—numbering 225 items in all, make up the exhibition. Its breadth and inclusiveness resulted in a huge display.

More enduring than the exhibit, the accompanying catalog is ex-pected to become the standard reference work on the Arts and Crafts Movement in America. The book covers the period when the move-ment, led by disciples of Ruskin and Morris, profoundly reshaped American art and culture, when, according to Jan Fontein, the move-ment "changed not only how objects looked, but how people looked at objects." Since interdisciplinary skills are required to examine the breadth and complexity of the Arts and Crafts Movement, Fontein says, contributors to the work include a professor of archaeology at Princeton, a professor of library science at Columbia, a professor of art at the Corcoran Gallery, and a curator of cultural history at the New Jersey State Museum. The work is called *The Art That Is Life: The Arts and Crafts Movement in America, 1875–1920*, by Wendy Kaplan, with contributions by many others. That seems like a bar-gain for the foundation at only $120,000.

Art at Berkeley

An exhibit that the *Chronicle of Higher Education* described as "one of the year's most exhilarating and introspective experiences" began in the spring of 1987 at the University of California at Berkeley, helped by an $80,000 grant from the Luce Foundation (whose role the *Chronicle* overlooked). Called "Made in U.S.A.: An Americanization in Modern Art, the '50s & '60s," the exhibition put its emphasis on "the context in which the art was produced," in this case the period from the end of the Korean War to the height of U.S. involvement in Vietnam. "Made in U.S.A." was comprehensive: its 112 items included works by Robert Rauschenberg, Andy Warhol, Claes Oldenburg, Jasper Johns, and many less familiar names. Paintings, sculptures, and half-painted–half-carved items (such as a portrait painting of Bob Hope from which projects a replica of Hope's nose done in wood) were all on display.

According to Sidra Stich, senior curator at the university's museum and the show's organizer, the show was intended in part to counter "the prevalent critical voice that looked at significant art as being abstraction." Critics fascinated with abstract expressionism have undervalued later work done in a variety of styles that has focused on American mass culture, Stich believes. So the exhibit she put together features works itemized by the *Chronicle* and inspired by the commonplace in American life: an old heel nailed to the upper left corner of a piece of weathered wood—Oldenburg, 1960; a dollar bill on which George Washington's head is being transformed into a brick wall—Phillip Hefferton, 1963; an oil painting in which the towers of the Golden Gate and Bay Bridges are replaced by dollar-and-cent signs—Peter Saul, 1967; a comic-strip painting in which Elvis Presley is weeping tears of blood—Ray Johnson, 1955; and a painting in which a fat white figure is surrounded by the empty uniforms of a butcher in bloody apron, a policeman, a soldier, and an executioner—May Stevens, 1968.

After it closed at Berkeley, the exhibit traveled to the Nelson-Atkins Museum of Art in Kansas City, Missouri, and then to the

Virginia Museum of Fine Arts in Richmond. Among the sponsors were Best Products Foundation, AT&T Foundation, and California First Bank.

The scholarly work the foundation wants to see flourish, and for which it made its grant, is an important accompaniment, and in one sense the basis, of the show. Along with the exhibit, a symposium was held at the university conducted by scholars from different disciplines—sociology, political science, film studies, journalism. The seminar touched on "all the topics of the time, such as patriotism, consumerism, media communication, and modern man's anonymity in the technological age"—surely an impressive listing, even from a place as broad-gauged as Berkeley. Stich treats with the ideas brought together in the show in a book, supported in part by the foundation and published by the University of California Press. The book serves as the catalog for the show and bears the same title. One local account calls it "the first major work to examine thoroughly the breadth, historical significance, and conceptual richness of the Americanization that took place in art during the 1950s and 1960s." Comments Stich: "This art doesn't provide answers. It just sits there on the edge of saying 'America—isn't it great?' and 'America—my God, what's happening?'" That's saying a lot for a total of only $80,000.

Archives in New York

To some like me, whose archaic artistic tastes are not especially stimulated by pieces of wood representing Bob Hope's nose, and whose knowledge is not so sweeping as that of the modernists at Berkeley, some small grants in small places seem more attractive. More than one hundred years have passed since Frederick Law Olmsted and Calvert Vaux drew their spacious plans and did their exquisitely detailed drawings for Central Park. These drawings, related work of Vaux and Olmsted, and other similar items in a collection now in New York's Municipal Archives are a landmark in themselves—a broad and once badly neglected collection of more than

Ken Haas

Program officer Mary Jane Crook (left) at the Museum of Modern Art with Riva Castleman, director of its Department of Prints and Illustrated Books.

two thousand watercolors and engineering drawings and plans. Included are the celebrated Olmsted/Vaux Greensward Plan of Central Park, along with original drawings by others of the New York Public Library, the Metropolitan Museum of Art, and the Museum of Natural History; maps and plans not only for Central Park but for smaller parks in boroughs other than Manhattan; and surveys and architects' designs for bridges, roads, and monuments within the parks of New York, many of which were never built.

The entire collection has lived the dangerous life of a transient practically since it left the architects' drawing boards. For many years, the collection was stored in the Parks Department's Arsenal Building in Central Park, where it languished until Robert Moses became parks commissioner. In the 1930s, Moses moved the collection to an outbuilding in Sara Delano Roosevelt Park, in the lower East Side of Manhattan. There, cold, heat, and humidity ate away at the collection for decades; thieves broke into the outbuilding and plundered some of the prizes. Then in 1973 the Parks Department, which had been the collection's rightful owner but neglectful guardian, stored it for latter-day safekeeping in the Avery Art and Architectural Library at Columbia University. Better protected than in its old shack but still ignored—and just as far out of reach of scholars and as far out of the public eye as it had ever been—the collection spent another ten years. Finally, in 1983, Columbia transferred the collection to the New York City Municipal Archives, where it should have gone years before and where it probably would have gone in 1973 had not the city, in the grip of its famed financial crunch, judged it impossible to make the necessary expenditure for proper care and storage.

Then the city came into money, and laid out a chunk for a fine new archival facility, complete with storage rooms that have humidity and temperature controls, safeguards from fire, and the other accessories appropriate to the worth of what is stored there—and staffed the facility with a small group of competent professionals. Now in the basement of New York's grandiose municipal building, the drawings are being unrolled, given superhumidified flat storage, treated with fumes of dissolved thymol to retard mold, and dry-cleaned. Still missing, however, was an item-by-item catalog of the drawings, which the city could not finance. In stepped Catha Rambusch, executive director of the New York Archival Society, a privately supported organization. Rambusch approached the Luce Foundation, which approved a grant for the catalog, to be added to another similar grant supplied by the Mellon Foundation. Thus the original renditions of the ornate scrolls, pediments, and pedestals that decorate some of New York's architecture are being properly recorded and cataloged at last and some day will be available to scholars and students of the period. It is hard to see how $28,000 of Luce money could do more. That modest amount, not a great deal larger than some of the grants made in the foundation's early years, came not from the Luce Fund for American Art but from the public affairs category, described further in Chapter 7.

By the end of 1986, the total of $7 million—$4 million in 1981 and $3 million in 1983—that the foundation had set aside for the Luce Fund for Scholarship in American Art was entirely committed. But no new program offered more promise than a continuation of the old, marked by an impressive number of successful books, catalogs, and scholarly projects. The Luce board therefore decided that the foundation should go on with its support of serious scholarship in American fine and decorative arts, the field the foundation had properly identified as undervalued by art historians in 1980. In December 1986 the board committed another $3 million to be appropriated over three years for that purpose. The new $3 million will come from general program funds allocated to the arts, not, like the original $7 million, from a special set-aside. The governing policies for the program may shift a bit: more encouragement may be given to larger grants to museums for more ambitious research—the largest single grant under the Luce Fund was $180,000—and support may also go to exhibitions that are judged essential components of the research endeavor. But the overall direction of the program will not change. The $3 million brings the amount that the Luce Foundation has allocated to scholarly work in American art to $10 million. To that should be added capital grants, such as the $1.5 million to the New Museum and $3.5 million to the Metropolitan Museum. The total of more than $15 million gives the foundation a clear position of leadership in the encouragement of American artistic endeavor.

6

Theology: High Education for High Purposes

About thirty years ago in Rome, Harry Luce and I had lunch with a learned monsignor from the Vatican. As I usually did to prepare for such occasions, I boned up on Roman history. At the lunch, though, it immediately became obvious that my preparation was unnecessary. For one thing, Harry was especially eager to talk that day, and if I had had anything intelligent to say I would have had a hard time breaking in. Beyond that, though, Harry and the monsignor rapidly took the conversation way over my head. As it went on and on, I got bored and spent my time watching Harry. I could practically see him flipping through that three-by-five card file in his head, producing names, dates, and issues in a stream; he was a match for the monsignor from the beginning. And, of course, the Vatican was not Harry's theological home; he knew a lot more about his own church and would hold forth about it whenever he got a chance. As John Jessup remarked in *The Ideas of Henry Luce*, Harry "could preach a strict Calvinist theology when he felt like it."

Still, for all his high education in the field of theology, Luce preferred in his talk and writing to hitch up his religious faith to the immediate world, and particularly to American society. As Jessup says, "Among his favorite themes was the question of whether, and in what sense, America is a Christian nation. . . . Luce believed firmly in the religious base of American democracy and in its Providential purpose." Luce's speeches are full of comments that confirm that judgment of Jessup: more than forty years ago, in a remark that might have been made yesterday by Leon Kass of the University of Chicago, Luce said that the world needs the church "because man's technology has outrun man's morality." In other addresses that he made around the same time, Luce continually associated American society and world affairs with religion: "There is only one wholly legitimate and self-justifying end in politics, and that is human freedom ... and there is only one permissible source of authority: God. The essential America expresses the goal of freedom under the guidance of God."

The Luce Foundation is one of the very few national foundations that maintains an active interest in the field of theology. Like Henry R. Luce himself, the foundation has always been attracted by proposals that promise to explore the meaning of religion in contemporary American life. Studies evaluating that complex issue have constituted a major category of the foundation's theological grants: a current grant in that category, for example, supports a study of possible improvements in the way this country accommodates immigrants of the Christian faith. Another grant takes a giant stride even further into the contemporary world and ends up behind prison walls. With the foundation's help, members of the New York Theological Seminary are now teaching courses to prisoners in Sing Sing who are studying to be ministers and who someday will carry the word to other prisoners in that forbidding fortress, and perhaps outside it too. Another important category for foundation support links theology to the foundation's enduring interest in higher education. The foundation has funded a number of programs intended to lift the level of excellence of religious education in seminaries and divinity schools; it is guided by the principle that the strength of theology will always be dependent on the intellectual vitality of theological educators. These grants will also have social consequences as better-equipped religious educators in turn educate those who will alter society by what they teach and preach.

Christian beliefs and social flux are the twin phenomena that underlie the flood of immigrants from the Republic of Korea into the United States over the past two decades. About 750,000 immigrants have come here in that time, and their ranks are increasing by some 30,000 a year. Around 70 percent of those immigrants are Christians, coming from a land that has a large Christian population. Thomas Gillespie, president of the Princeton Theological Seminary, notes that "today there are probably more Presbyterians in Korea than there are in the U.S." The largest Presbyterian congregation in the world, the Yung No Presbyterian Church in Seoul, has 60,000 members. "We used to say that the Presbyterian Church in Prairie Village, Kansas, had 6,000 members, and we were very impressed with that," remarks Gillespie. According to Sang Lee, a professor at the Princeton Theological Seminary, who was born in Korea, about 2,000 Korean immigrant churches are now active in the United States, heavily concentrated around Los Angeles, New York, Washington, D.C., and Chicago. The number of churches is growing at a pace commensurate with the increase in the number of immigrants. Many of the churches conduct their services entirely in Korean. Most are Presbyterian; many are Episcopalian; some are Methodist and Baptist ("the Baptists being less rigorous and strict than either Presbyterians or Methodists," Lee drily remarks) and Catholic; many are independent of any sect. To support a center that would develop a ministry to care for the problems that arise from this influx, as well as to help those who are caught up in it, the Luce Foundation in December 1983 made a grant of $95,000 over three years to the Princeton Theological Seminary, later supplemented by a $400,000 challenge grant in 1986.

To describe the circumstances and attitudes of the growing numbers of his compatriots now in America, Sang Lee turns to his Bible. "We are a pilgrim people," he says. "Like Abraham we have been called by God to live in a wilderness as in a foreign land as strangers and exiles, not wholly at home where we are, nor comfortable any more about returning to where we or our parents came from." Lee contends that "we Asian immigrants are aliens, tolerated yet unwelcome guests. After 20 years in this country, I am still asked when I am returning to Korea. Almost every glance and gesture of many white Americans says to me 'What are you doing here?'" He calls himself and the 750,000 other Koreans "marginal people—in between two cultures or societies without wholly belonging to either one, poised in psychological uncertainties, reflecting the discords and harmonies, repulsions and attractions of these worlds."

Although the problems that these Koreans face have obvious social and psychological components, Lee stresses most the religious aspect. "This is so at least to those of us who embrace the assumption that human beings are essentially religious, and cannot but ask questions of an ultimate nature"—like Henry R. Luce, he might have added. "The problem of how to live an honest, authentic life in the face of marginality," continues Lee, "is in the final analysis a religious issue." Furthermore, it has American as well as Korean roots. "It's an interesting twist," comments Gillespie. "The church for many years sent people like Henry Luce III's grandfather out as missionaries. The Presbyterian mission in Korea was enormously successful. Now the people of Korea are flocking to the land that sent the message out to them in the first place." The Korean immigrant church—with its problems and its pains—Sang Lee says "is the fruit of the missionary movement of the late nineteenth century."

The pastors of the immigrant churches, Lee says, have been having a hard time coping with the conflicts and tensions within their flock. The divisions exist not just between the two cultures—Korean and American—but also between the Korean generations, with "a vast distance" separating older Korean immigrants from their teenage, native American children. Church leaders tend to be first generation; they have had a lot of trouble understanding and communicating with American-born, ethnic Korean high school kids. In anger and frustration, many of these young people have declared their intention to withdraw from the church. Unless Korean parents and pastors act, Sang Lee says, "they may lose the second generation." The pastors themselves confront "a debilitating confusion" about the directions of their church, life, and work. They share with their communities "the deep and urgent yearning among Asian immigrant Christians for ideas and strategies that would guide them toward a discovery of their true human and religious vocation."

Acknowledging the troublesome circumstances of the immigrant church, a committee of Korean ministers belonging to the United Presbyterian church in 1981 proposed the establishment of a center for Asian-American theology, to be located at a seminary related to that church. The committee expressed a preference for the Princeton Theological Seminary because it had a long association with Presbyterian churches in Asia and because it is located close to cities with large Korean and other Asian immigrant populations. Besides tending the immigrant church, the center would do theological research and train second-generation church leaders, but it would always be centered on Asian immigrants. A month after the Luce Foundation's first grant for the purpose, the Princeton Theological Seminary named Sang Lee director of its Program for Asian-American Theology and Ministry.

Just the existence of the program at Princeton Theological Seminary has made a difference in the character of the place. The number of Asian-Americans applying to the seminary for admission as candidates for the degrees of Master of Divinity and of Master of Arts in Christian Education doubled in 1985, and the number of Koreans among those applicants nearly tripled. Of the ninety Korean-Americans who applied, seventeen were admitted to the seminary—by far the highest number ever. At the same time, Sang Lee says, first-generation pastors have shown their growing understanding of the church's needs by expressing ever-increasing interest in having bilingual second-generation pastors and educators join them. It looks, therefore, as though there will be a market for the new product now being educated at the seminary. To determine just what the newly educated will have to cope with, the Asian-American program has sponsored a study of the attitudes of second-generation Korean youth who belong to immigrant churches.

Further, Lee himself has been preaching the gospel. One of his courses at Princeton is called Marginality and Pilgrimage, which is especially designed to instruct Asian-American students on the meaning of Christian pilgrimages, including the ones their parents undertook. He has also marched his Asian-American students to the firing line by sending them out to local congregations, where they learn what the pastor in combat has to face. Then they all assemble once a month to discuss and evaluate their experiences. And Lee has sponsored a series of seminars related to his favorite topic—or perhaps his second favorite topic, his first being the theological thought of Jonathan Edwards, the early American determinist theologian and preacher who became president of Princeton (then called the College of New Jersey) in 1757. Among the seminars are a conference for Chinese-American pastors working in New York; a seminar on evangelism for Korean-American pastors; a teacher training conference for Asian-American Christian educators; and retreats held in pleasant settings for English-speaking young people from the immigrant churches. Comments Lee: "Many of these young people felt that someone had communicated with them for the very first time about the Christian faith and their immigrant life."

Encouraged by the accomplishments and the drive of Sang Lee, the foundation made its additional grant to support his work and to ensure that the center would continue. This $400,000 took the form of a one-for-two challenge grant: for every two dollars that the seminary raised, the foundation gave one dollar.

The Madison Avenue Presbyterian Church has played a role in the life of the Luce family since Henry R. Luce joined the church on April 19, 1924, one year after he brought out the first issue of *Time* magazine. Henry Luce III says that his father "was always alert to the quality of sermons" and at the time was attracted to the Madison Avenue church by Henry Sloan Coffin. Coffin was a Yale man (Class of 1897), who attended the Union Theological Seminary and went back there as the seminary's president after twenty-one years at the Madison Avenue church. Coffin left the Madison Avenue church in 1926, but Henry R. Luce stayed on to hear deeply resonant sermons, which filled the church with tones of Doomsday foreboding, delivered by Coffin's successor, George Buttrick, a pacifist. Pacifism was a long way from Luce's beliefs, and the two men engaged in endless arguments, friendly and unyielding on both sides. The high level of sermonizing set by Coffin and Buttrick is carried on today by David H. C. Read, a great figure in the field, who was named one of the best preachers in America by *Time* in 1979. Luce often commended Read on his Sunday sermons; according to one of his biographers, Luce heard of a sermon of Read's about the serpent on the rock and eagerly telephoned Read to ask for a copy. Today Read runs a ministry effective in the local community. Of the avenue churches, Madison Avenue Presbyterian is known as perhaps the most demographically representative. Read has served on the Selection Committee of the Luce Scholars Program since its inception. Over the years, the foundation has supported several of the activities of the Madison Avenue church. In 1974 the foundation gave the church $225,000, most of which went into endowment and for remodeling.

Concern with contemporary life and a commitment to the importance of theological education mingle at the New York Theological Seminary, one of the country's most unusual religious educational institutions. Wilbert Webster White, a Ph.D. in Biblical Studies from Yale, founded the seminary in 1900 to fill a basic lack: White believed that theological education at the time took an inadequate approach to the Scriptures. He set out to supply that crucial nourishment at his seminary, which had the further distinctions of being interdenominational (although by its nature it attracted those of an evangelical bent); of admitting women (the Divinity School at Harvard first admitted women more than fifty years later, in 1955); and of offering in a dingy neighborhood sliced by the Third Avenue "El" a gymnasium and other facilities for neighborhood youth (a forerunner of the seminary's present social work).

Depressions and financial crises, however, could not be overcome by scriptural readings, and by the time George W. Webber took over as president of the New York Theological Seminary in 1969, its very existence was threatened. Webber and the board of trustees kept asking, "Is there something important that this place can do, or should we bury it?" The board, half of which came from the laity, hit on an unusual answer, the Storefront Pastors Program; and the seminary offered programs leading to accredited degrees to black and Hispanic clergy who had never been to college. (For more on the foundation's support for the Storefront Pastors Program, see Chapter 7.) These people could pay part of their own tuitions, so that the financial drain on the seminary was lessened. Webber remarks: "After that, the place took off." Webber retired as president in 1983 and was succeeded by Keith A. Russell, the present president. But Webber, a man of boundless energy, continues in a whirlwind of seminary activities, notably those that the foundation supports.

Pulpits and prisons rarely meet, but the two come together behind the gray walls of Sing Sing prison—the Ossining Correctional Facility is the name that prison administrators prefer—in one of the foundation's most unusual grants. Webber engineered the merger, and he explains how it came about:

A young man out of Harlem who had worked as a church volunteer came to see me. His point was that there were over 450 men in prison who had gotten an accredited B.A. degree while they were there. A lot of these men had a faith commitment and wanted to do graduate studies. He asked whether there was any way the New York Theological Seminary could arrange for graduate theological studies for prisoners. It sounded like a fantastic idea, but I figured there was no way the prison system would allow something like that to happen. There were no graduate programs in prisons. The ethos is to punish, not to correct. Give a prisoner a chance to go to college, that's pretty bad. But graduate school was beyond the pale.

But there happened to be a black man responsible for family and ministerial services in the prison at that time. Just three years before he had gotten a Doctorate of Ministry from our seminary. His doctoral project concerned how to humanize ministerial and family services work in prisons. Here was a guy who knew us, and who had the leverage. So I drew up a prospectus: transfer men with accredited degrees to Sing Sing. They go to class every morning, five days a week for eleven months. They carry a full load, and commit themselves to a whole year of study—they won't take early release. As long as they are in the prison system, they must be involved in some creative work helping prisoners. In the end, they'll get a Master's Degree in Professional Studies, an accredited discipline. My board said "Webber, if you can find money, you can do it."

Helped by the Luce Foundation, which granted $90,000 over four years, Webber did find the money, and in 1982 he began running the only postgraduate program for prisoners in the United States. He teaches at Sing Sing once a week; so do four other members of the seminary, one of them a black woman who teaches the New Testament. Says Webber, "It's an incredible experience for all my colleagues—so physically tiring and emotionally draining that it wipes them all out. All the fall-out, all the problems you hear about. . . . There's a Jewish medical doctor who was in one of our classes, doing twenty-five years to life for murdering his wife. He's sixty-three years old, and he works for the prison rabbi. A hospital in Zambia was desperate for doctors, he wanted to go, but the State Department said no. Now we're trying to get approval for him to go to Liberia. He's always there waiting, wondering if I've got any word for him."

Five classes with a total of sixty-five prisoners have now graduated from the seminary's classes with master's degrees. Webber describes many of them as "wonderful people, remarkable human beings." He remembers one or two who were "loners, tough, hard-nosed types," but they made it, too. One year, four or five dropped out: "They didn't belong, they hadn't really taken the covenant seriously." One, a Muslim, is now a chaplain in the state prison system—"incredible that a guy who had been a prisoner would be appointed chaplain, absolutely a wonderful guy," says Webber. Being a Muslim does not change the nature of the religious education, explains Webber: "The Old Testament and the New Testament are part of Islam's religious heritage. The Koran is a further revelation of the story. The oldest Muslim here, the elder statesman who had done the best academic work, was the Imam at Sing Sing. He had to give that up to take this program."

Those who will soon be teaching the word of God to people who need to hear it as badly as anyone in the world sit attentively in a room with thick brick walls and tiny barred windows a foot or so below the low ceiling. Music from a nearby room where the prison band is practicing comes through too loud and too clear: hard rock drowns out the message of God. ("That noise next door tells me that the prison authorities are saying 'We don't care about you,' " says one prisoner.) The lesson for the day (Ephesians 4:11–4:16—the meaning of discipleship) is not only nearly smothered in rock; it is also punctuated by the sound of rifle fire from a nearby range, where the prison guards are sharpening their skills.

The reading from Ephesians is followed by an intense discussion among those present—murderers, felons, scarcely one who is not in jail for a stretch of at least fifteen years, scarcely one who has not been already imprisoned for almost a decade. They comment:

> Paul calls himself an apostle. He was not a disciple. [Someone replies:] That doesn't make Paul right, because he calls himself an apostle. I mean if I call myself Jesus does that make me right?

> There's a difference between an apostle and a prophet, so to speak, like you got these guys like Moses and Abraham. These guys are clearly prophets. So I'm asking, are the apostles more important than these prophets?

> If you say I've been given these gifts, I've been given these gifts. I'm a saint, I'm an apostle, I've been given a gift—what we start thinking about is hierarchy. But if you have been given as a gift to the saints or to apostles, it brings back the idea of servanthood—the idea of being a prisoner for the Lord. The hierarchy concept comes from someone who is obsessed with power, a capitalist ideology. To be used to serve the Lord, yes, but not as part of the hierarchy.

> I want to make another point. . . . [groans] All right, I won't.

> [Comment from one prisoner to another:] I think you could do better if you don't get so fixed, so stubborn. You just say "No, that's not it."

Prisoners in the class tell their own story:

Prisoner #1: I'm here to get my last two units of theological seminary program . . . this is my calling, to get into ministry. After this I will be able to go back to Auburn and work with the clergy there in family ministerial services under the pastor or the chaplain, counseling other inmates. Those married men need some form of special ventilating, someone to talk to of their own association, their own peer group, rather than the embarrassing question of talking to the chaplain.

Prisoner #2: My main interest is in pastoral care and counseling. I've been in the New York State prison system since 1980, and I've seen many things in the system that are not being addressed. I want to take the knowledge that I've gained in the system, and to apply what I get out of this program in a moral sense, in a spiritual sense, by helping other inmates . . . a little counseling occasionally, just someone to talk to occasionally.

Prisoner #3: I came down from Attica. An inmate here may have a few privileges that wouldn't be considered privileges in another facility, like here you can go by yourself to the school or the yard. At Attica you definitely would need an escort, and possibly two, just to go to the yard recreational area and back to your cell. I earned a bachelor's degree in prison because it was important to me not just to be in prison and let the time go. . . . When I first came to prison I had a need to find some sense of security and some sense of forgiveness and atonement. Basically, I think I just had a deep need for spiritual values.

Prisoner #4: My colleague and myself have a convenant in which we spend the next two years together working on pastoral counseling for inmates. He comes from a background of Islamic faith and I come from a background of Christian religious faith. We have agreed to take the best of both worlds and work with the teachings of Christ and Mohammed and not necessarily the personas. There are inmates who go through incarceration without any help, without anyone who cares. Hopefully, we can supply some care.

Prisoner #5: I'm thirty years old and I have about seventeen more years to go. I've been waiting for eight years in prison for a chance to do something constructive. I'm a Muslim and I felt that here is an opportunity to learn skills and help my Muslim brothers. I run into individuals thirty years old, thirty-three years old, who can't read. My parents were religious people, they were good providers, they did the best they could.

Many of the men expressed disappointment with the religious services behind the walls at Sing Sing.

I was concerned that the imagery of God that was being preached to the guys was somewhat authoritarian. God was being depicted as just another corrections officer, the Big Warden. You expect to hear from the pulpit something about human concerns ... all we heard was sin, sin, sin. If you don't believe, you're going to hell. If you're a Muslim, you're going to hell. If you're a Christian, you're going to hell. The theme got ragged, after a while you stopped listening. And it's a sickening thing to see a man tell you one thing on Sunday, and another on Monday. Yesterday he was talking about brotherhood and all that kind of stuff, today he'll meet you in the corridor and don't speak.

None of the men denies the crime, but all question the punishment. Says one: "I had six years of military service, three in combat in Vietnam. The readjustment was not all that easy. I got into heavy drinking. I resorted to crime, specifically extortion, theft, and robberies, and so forth." Another: "I come from Harlem, 109th Street between Lexington and Third. I've been around drugs all my life. I shot every drug you could think of. Prostitution, pushing females just to get drugs—I have been reduced to subhuman levels. I went out and killed and robbed to take care of my mother. I got on my knees in my cell and prayed to God that He would enlighten me." Another: "What brought me here was killing a man who did not deserve to die. I thought it was his fault that I killed him. The biggest part of being in prison has been accepting responsibility for my acts."

All declare that their purpose is to help other inmates: "You meet a lot of people here that won't admit they had problems before their incarceration. They are not much interested in your sincerity and your positiveness, that's all pie in the sky to them. I've killed, I've hurt people, now I start turning things around and helping people. This program will give me the skills to do just that." The oldest in the group, a big quiet black Muslim about fifty years old, states the common objective:

Inmates come to us for advice. How shall I plan before I get out? You can be a teacher and use the word of God without mentioning the word of God. We are considered eggheads out there—the best of the worst. You have to be humble: if they get hostile you can't help, there's jealousy and hostility out there. You have to work in your religion very carefully, you're walking on eggs. Sometimes you get a chance to say "There's a place in the Scriptures." They know we have been where they are now, sometimes you can get a dialogue going. "If you look at me, you see yourself." Giving people some kind of hope is our ministry.

Some less dramatic programs that the foundation supports also take religious beliefs into social realms. The Luce Foundation's help to the Presbyterian Progress Foundation, for example, began in 1956, when the Luce Foundation gave the Progress Foundation $75,000 for general support. In 1964 the Progress Foundation came back with a request for renewal. Commenting on it, Henry R. Luce scribbled in his heavy rapid hand at the bottom of a memo: "Not exciting, but fair enough, I guess." From 1956 to the mid 1970s, the Luce Foundation gave $200,000 to the Progress Foundation. That amount included support for the Mount Washington Presbyterian Church's program for day care in the Bronx. Much of the money went to renovate an obsolete facility. In 1975, when the foundation made its final payment, about fifty black and Hispanic children were being cared for there, with church members making up half of the day care center's board of directors.

In the field of theological education, where a large number of its grants have been made, the Luce Foundation has concentrated chiefly on the divinity schools at Yale and Harvard and on the Princeton Theological Seminary. At Princeton, the foundation's assistance began in December 1964, in response to a confluence of a couple of the interests of Henry R. Luce. At that time, the foundation made a grant to the seminary to fund the Henry Winters Luce Chair of Ecumenics and Mission. Henry Winters Luce, as we have seen, was a missionary; he was a member of the Princeton Seminary's class of 1896 and did some teaching there in later years. Henry R. Luce, said John Jessup, "inherited from his father an interest in the Protestant ecumenical movement, the great effort to end 'the scandal of disunity' among the churches." In a talk he gave forty years ago, Luce spoke of "we Christians—Christians of all sorts, good, bad and many of our friends —we number 600 million." Since he had thus begun to grapple with ecumenism, and since his father had been so closely associated with the Princeton Theological Seminary, the chair seemed a logical choice for foundation help and, continuing an established pattern, a further memorial to Henry Winters Luce.

The early choice made by James I. McCord, then the president of the seminary, of a man to fill the chair was undeniably a happy one, since the same man still teaches the same course very successfully. Samuel Moffett had been a student of Henry Winters Luce at Princeton in 1940. Moffett recalls today that Henry W. Luce "deluged us with material—much more than we could ever read—Confucianism, Taoism, Buddhism. He knew these religions not just from books but from personal contact. Then he would just sit down and talk about some of the things that he had been through."

One of Moffett's recent lectures put forward for examination the proposition that John Calvin—the protesting Protestant who rejected

James I. McCord

the views of the Church of Rome, of the Lutherans, of the Anabaptists, and of a number of other divine groups and gave the world Calvinism—was really a believer in an ecumenical church. After opening with a word of prayer ("There are a good many empty chairs today because the seniors are taking their ordination exams and we should have a word of prayer for them as well"), Moffett declared,

> You cannot leave Calvin out of any proper discussion of ecumenicity during the Reformation. All his life as a reformer Calvin worked for the union of French and Swiss Presbyterians. All his life he worked for cooperation in the gospel with the Lutherans.
>
> Calvin called the divisions of the church the mutilation of the body of Christ. This spirit of ecumenicity chimes through all of Calvin's writings. He dreamed of a great ecumenical Reformation council that was never held. "Even if a church otherwise swarms with many faults," Calvin said, "as long as it keeps to the essentials, the lesser faults are not sufficient reason for leaving it. What were the three essential doctrines? One was the unity of the Godhead. The second was the deity of Christ. And the last was that salvation is by God's grace and not by our works."

To laughter, Moffett made a final point: "Then Calvin added the phrase 'and the like.' That's the lawyer speaking."

After Henry Luce III became a trustee of the Princeton Theological Seminary, its board was asked to drop the requirements for proficiency in biblical languages. To offset this deemphasis in basic scholarship, Luce and the board in 1973 approved an amendment to the effect that English-language Bible courses should be augmented. McCord agreed; he was especially troubled by the prospect of neglect of biblical studies because "it is through investigations of the biblical texts themselves that formative new insights for the life of the church have arisen." In recommending McCord's request to the Luce board for a foundation grant, Martha Wallace and Robert Armstrong expanded on the point: "Since Biblical studies should logically provide one of the key focuses of any theological curriculum, it is ironic that this vital area has suffered severe neglect in most seminaries and divinity schools over the past several years. Even more ironic is the fact that this unfortunate development is the unintended result of well-founded efforts to streamline the study of theology." McCord's appeal, they continued, "represents both an effort to redress a serious imbalance that now exists in theological education and a reinforcement of more traditional values and concerns."

In response, the Luce board awarded the seminary three annual grants of $25,000 each, which were followed by a grant of $90,000. Thus blessed, McCord added two faculty members to the Department of Biblical Studies at the seminary, chosen after a search committee went through the dossiers of some two hundred applicants. One of the two, Thomas W. Mann, who holds a Ph.D. from Yale, taught at the seminary for six years. The buttressing of biblical studies at the seminary, McCord believes, not only sent young seminarians out to their work better equipped but also stimulated interest in biblical study at the seminary on the part of applicants. "An upsurge of interest in Greek and Hebrew," McCord thinks, can be attributed to the improved course of study. In a note he sent to his father on October 13, 1965, Henry Luce III reported that "McCord would still like to name the chair in ecumenics for Grandfather"—which, of course, was done. In all, the foundation gave $1 million to the Fifty Million Fund, the foundation's first grant of a round $1 million.

In November 1965 the foundation made yet another grant to the Princeton Theological Seminary. It committed a total of $500,000 to the seminary, earmarking its contribution to the Fifty Million Fund then being raised for the capital needs of the United Presbyterian church in the U.S.A. Henry R. Luce, then sixty-seven and only fifteen months from his death, was chairman of national gifts for the $50 Million Fund. (Luce had good company: Dwight D. Eisenhower was honorary chairman.) Of the $500,000 of Luce funds that went to the Princeton Theological Seminary, $300,000 was used to build a power plant for the seminary, which at the time had an inadequate coal-burning boiler that spewed smoke from an unsightly stack. The remaining $200,000 went to the purchase of the only contiguous piece of property around the seminary that ever seemed likely to come on the market and whose price today would surely be in the millions of dollars.

During the years of the foundation's relationship with the Princeton Theological Seminary, McCord argued that basic research was galloping ahead in many different fields—in science and in industry, he noted that "the quest for knowledge is proceeding at a logarithmic rate"—but while such "radical relocations in man's relationships to time, space, and activity" were going on, research within the church was being neglected. "New patterns touch the very heart of religion," McCord said, but religious research remained a secondary interest in theological schools, narrow in its inquiries, and "primarily directed toward immediate problems of the church's day-to-day existence."

All this led to a Center of Theological Inquiry, "where selected scholars may be free of ordinary teaching and administrative responsibilities to concentrate on research and creative study." McCord saw the thrust of the research taking three directions: the state of religious and quasi-religious consciousness in the modern world; the relationship between theological and nontheological disciplines; and the relationship between diverse religious traditions. McCord drew a parallel between the center he wanted and the Institute for Advanced Study in Princeton, where research is primarily devoted to mathematics and the natural sciences.

Discussions between prospective recipients of grants and foundation people often sharpen thoughts and alter the shape of proposals. In this case Henry Luce III was already deeply involved as a trustee of the Princeton Theological Seminary. In correspondence with McCord he urged that the relationship between theological and nontheological disciplines, the second of McCord's three-sided schemes for research, be emphasized. Luce found both the first and third concepts overlapping somewhat with two other theological institutes, one at the holy city of Jerusalem, the other at Notre Dame in South Bend, Indiana. Luce and McCord exchanged views for several years while the research institute was hatching. The relationship continued after the center finally came into being, fifteen years after the concept began percolating.

During the first five years of its existence, the Center of Theological Inquiry had no building. Then the Luce Foundation made a loan of $1.5 million to the center for a building close to Princeton Theological Seminary. The building was named Henry Robinson Luce Hall; it was dedicated by Henry Luce III. (For his address at the time, see Appendix B.) McCord, now president emeritus of the Princeton Theological Seminary, moved his office a few hundred yards to become chancellor of the new center. Henry Luce III serves on the center's board of trustees. Under the terms of the $1.5 million loan, one dollar of the loan was to be forgiven for every two dollars of endowment raised from other sources. The full amount of that challenge was reached in 1987. In this case the foundation got adequate acknowledgment of its generosity: "Henry Robinson Luce Hall was made possible by a generous gift of The Henry Luce Foundation Inc., to which both the Center and the world owe a debt of gratitude," says a center brochure. Reads the commemorative plaque at the center: "Luce Hall, 1984: Given in memory of Henry Robinson Luce (1898–1967), founder of TIME, The Weekly Newsmagazine. 'Meaning was built into life, in the beginning, by the Creator.' "

The foundation's long and close association with the two theological institutions in Princeton has not been matched elsewhere. But other divinity schools have also been beneficiaries of important foundation grants. Notable among them is the Yale Divinity School, which has been awarded sizable foundation grants in the field of education. One of the largest was a grant made by the Luce board in June 1986 of $300,000 to be spent over a period of three years to enlarge the pool of prospective faculty for theological schools. The scarcity of good faculty members at religious graduate schools is a nationwide phenomenon.

This scarcity has complex origins, with which Leander E. Keck, the dean of the Yale Divinity School, has had considerable experience. "In the 1930s and 1940s," says Keck, "divinity schools got their faculty from graduate schools of theology, from college departments of religion—a kind of farm club for the seminaries—and from the pastorate, where some able and articulate people, not all of whom held advanced degrees in theology, wanted to teach." Among those "able and articulate" pastors, Keck notes, was Reinhold Niebuhr, one of the most famous theologians of the century—and a participant in occasional lively debates with Henry R. Luce.

But, Keck continues, after World War II the situation changed. Pastors became more and more involved in all kinds of activities— social affairs, community affairs—and "it became difficult to find learned pastors who could hold their own on a faculty. That supply dried up. At the same time, there were fewer and fewer Ph.D. programs training people to teach in 'practical' areas, like Christian education. Finally, a Supreme Court decision allowed public universities to create religious studies departments, on the theory that they taught *about* religion in the same way that you taught *about* East Asian culture. With this came a whole upsurge of research and publication in the colleges and universities. It was no longer college teachers' ambition to go to a seminary in order to become published scholars—they could do that where they were."

Furthermore, explains Keck, college faculties began splintering into specialized disciplines—that familiar pattern—and biblical teaching, for example, broke down into highly concentrated specializations like legal texts, Wisdom literature, or the Gospel of John or pursued sophisticated forms of literary analysis. Many people in those specialized areas, says Keck, have no interest or desire to teach future ministers. And all the separations of specialties led to a greater separation—the separation of the teaching of religion from religion itself. "Say you have four Ph.D.'s in biblical studies. Two want to go back to college to teach as they were taught, by interesting, scholarly people—that's their sense of vocation. And the other two might not be competent to teach ministers. They know their Hebrew, but ask them a theological question and they might not know what you are talking about."

But while the supply was diminishing, demand continued. To find candidates who wanted to enroll in the Divinity School at Yale has never been a problem; the problem is to find people to teach them—to teach what Keck calls "the art of ministry. . . . In some places you can find people who teach speech and can tell you how to hold your diaphragm, but they don't know much about psalms." And, as if all these difficulties didn't suffice, Keck also fears that current scarcity may lead to yet another division—between seminaries so deeply committed to preparing persons for the ministry that their faculties become content to retail the research done in religious studies departments in colleges and universities. Such a schism would be disastrous, because "you must expose future ministers the finest minds engaged in basic research."

When Keck's case came before the Luce board, it got sympathetic attention. The proposal that the board reviewed was enthusiastically endorsed by A. Bartlett Giamatti, then president of Yale. The proposal read in part: "We seek to create a postdoctoral program which will bring to the profession men and women who show promise of becoming outstanding theological school faculty members. Each year, three individuals would be offered a two-year appointment as Fellows in Theological Education . . . he or she would work closely with an experienced faculty mentor during each of the first three semesters; in the fourth that person would offer his or her own course. Over six years, the program would create a significant pool of young faculty members capable of assuming teaching positions at theological schools throughout the country." The program that the foundation funded started in the autumn of 1987.

Movement in those directions was not new to the Luce Foundation. Under the same rubric of assistance to theological education, the foundation years before had made a grant somewhat similar to the one given to Yale. That earlier grant went to Columbia University's Department of Religion, $75,000 to augment its faculty in the field of phenomenology of religion. In those years, also, the foundation sought by various grants to encourage studies and research aimed at examining the value systems in theology. The foundation's substantial support for the College of Wooster, discussed later in this chapter, has such study as its partial objective.

However grave the scarcity of theological educators in the nation's leading divinity schools, it could hardly have been more serious than the sadly inadequate supply of black clergy in the United Presbyterian church's Synod of the South, the group of Presbyterian churches in the southern states. In 1978, the United Presbyterian church told the Luce Foundation, only forty-nine black clergy were working in pastoral ministries in the Synod of the South. Of them, about twenty-five were then over fifty years of age; only seven were under forty. Only seven black candidates from presbyteries within the geographical limits of the synod were enrolled in seminaries so that the already sparse current ranks of black ministers faced ever more severe reductions over the next decade. At the same time, as supply was shrinking, demand was growing. Churches attended largely by blacks were undergoing unexpected expansion in their congregations as the population of blacks in the region grew, in part from the then current phenomenon of reverse migration.

As a result, the United Presbyterian church embarked on a campaign to fund a black clergy recruitment and training program. It was part of a huge nationwide effort to raise $60 million for 15 synods and 151 presbyteries in the United States. The Luce Foundation contributed $100,000 over three years, beginning in 1978, toward the United Presbyterian church's recruitment of black candidates for the gospel ministry and toward the cost of placement of the new ministers by the church. The shortage has not disappeared, but in the six years during which the church's recruitment, training, and placement programs have been running, twenty-four black ministers were added to the synod—in relative terms, a very significant increase.

Although for the sake of convenience the foundation's programs are categorized, in fact many of them bridge the foundation's principal interests. One of the most unusual of those hybrid grants is now in operation at the Yale Divinity School. John W. Cook, professor of religion and the arts at the school, had a kind of divine inspiration when he took note of the foundation's support for religious education and its continuing concern with the arts. He saw a chance for a very attractive merger. He put before the foundation a suggestion for a program at the school that would train future theologians, especially those who will be ministers, in the traditions of the role of arts in religion. Impressed, the directors gave Yale $315,000 to support Cook's courses. Cook has been teaching a course titled Christianity and the Arts for nine years and is now also director of Yale's Institute of Sacred Music and the Arts.

Cook's experiences with the foundation as he put together his proposal are as unusual as the content of his courses. He first came in contact with the foundation at a time when Yale University officials were trying hard to win more grants from the foundation, having made a series of unsuccessful proposals. After he reviewed a history of ruffled feelings, Cook talked at length with Robert Armstrong, then program director at the foundation, where Martha Wallace was still executive director. Cook asked Armstrong to "give us some guidelines so we'll know how to come through the front door."

Flattery is all too pervasive a commodity in the foundation world. But Cook's sincerity in his evaluation of Armstrong's responses and of the reception he got later from Henry Luce III is beyond doubt—and not just because he is a man of the cloth. "I've dealt with a lot of foundation people, but I've never found anyone with the kind of clarity, the up-front treatment that Bob has. If it's no go, it's no go—nobody is disappointed, no false hopes." And of Luce, Cook says: "He understands the issues involved, and what is at stake in these courses becoming a curricular possibility in theological education. . . . He was very keen." Of the perspective that Armstrong and Luce brought to his concept, Cook says:

With some foundations, you feel like they were on an agenda that made promises about changing and rewriting history. Armstrong and Luce had none of these pretenses. They are very realistic—you take one step at a time. They asked for an annual report that wanted us to concentrate on strengths and weaknesses. As we went along it was possible to talk about what was working and what was not working in terms of curricular aspects. It was a learning process for us. Nobody came and said,

"Now you really ought to do A rather than B." They'd say "You said you'd do A and B, now go do it, but let us know how it is working." They didn't sit on our shoulders and rewrite or redirect. They asked for clarity where there was some vagueness. It was an investment in our vision without trying to change it, and that's a good relationship. . . . It wasn't just money to pay our bills.

Cook's survey courses are called Christianity and the Arts and are given over two semesters. The first covers the period from medieval times to the mid-eighteenth century, as Cook says, "the way that the history of Christianity has appropriated the arts for its own purposes." The second runs from the mid-eighteenth century to the present day and studies, in Cook's words, "the shift from the institution to the individual." In a fascinating analysis, Cook notes, "As art has moved toward radical individualization, the church has really separated itself formally from the world of the arts. The way that the world of art expresses that separation is to put the religious aspect back into the consciousness of the artist. From Van Gogh to Mark Rothko, there's a line of artists who are expressing something specifically religious in what they do." The subject of religion rarely appears inside the frames of the paintings of such artists, Cook says, but there is a subtle religious consciousness "that has to do with intuition, self-conscious relationships to a spirit, subconscious responses to reality." And, he adds, "When the artist claims that this is a divine spark of inspiration for some divine principle, or is a cry of outrage against an inhuman society, you have to take that seriously as the religious consciousness of the artist expressing something specifically religious."

That subtle concept of Cook's has far-reaching importance for religious education as well as for art. Marcia Tucker, the director of the New Museum, has lectured at the Yale Divinity School. "The recognition of a whole religious constituency of the art world is a contribution to us—otherwise we would never be in touch with that constituency," says Tucker. Nor does the reach of Cook's subject end there:

Some students who go into a Protestant ministry buy into a language of the arts about which they have no opinion, and which they have no critical facilities to evaluate. Then they are unable to use intelligently the set of tools that they inherit with their religious leadership. So the country misspends millions of dollars annually on faulty architecture, and on misinformed appropriations for furnishings and liturgical objects, because we are not training our ministers or rabbis or priests to pick up on the fact that they are going to be investing annually in the world of the arts. They are wasting the money, or they're misstating what it is they stand for religiously.

Foundation officers love the phrase "seed money"—funds that start enterprises growing. The Luce Foundation's investments in Cook's classes at the Divinity School seem likely to have just that effect. Religion in the arts as part of theological education has been the subject of a recent study by Professor Wilson Yates at the United Theological Seminaries in New Brighton, Minnesota, near St. Paul. The Yale Divinity School is identified in the study as having hit on a novel and rewarding approach to the subject, which is viewed as a model for other programs. As a result, Cook and a colleague have been participating in a range of activities at seminaries and other theological centers around the country. They lecture and explain what they are doing at Yale—preaching the gospel of God and man at Yale, one might say. They are also consulting at the Graduate Theological Union in Berkeley, California, and at the Candler School of Theology at Emory University in Atlanta, as well as the consortium of seminaries in Washington, D.C.

Yet another Luce grant supported an entry by the College of Wooster into the field of religion and social values. The college asked for foundation help in developing a series of undergraduate courses focusing on "contemporary problems of interest to social and natural sciences such as racism, poverty, war, social systems, economic systems and ethical problems in the life sciences and natural sciences." To help faculty development, faculty seminars were to be organized along similar lines and lectures of a more general nature made available to residents of Wooster and the surrounding area of east central Ohio. The effort to involve the local community more actively in the programs of the college was based on the traditionally strong tie that Wooster, an outstanding liberal arts college associated with the United Presbyterian church, has with the local Presbyterian congregation. The Luce board found the most compelling aspect of the proposal "the effort to strengthen the teaching of religious and ethical values at a church-related college, and to relate the strength not merely to the college itself but also to the broader civic community." The foundation made grants to the College of Wooster totaling $75,000 over 1973–75 for that purpose.

7

Public Affairs: Civil Rights and Civic Duties

No foundation of the size and with the public sensitivity of the Luce Foundation, whatever its original orientation, could ignore the urban riots that ripped at the country in the 1960s. "We felt obliged, and rightly, to respond to the civil rights disturbances in a major way," recalls Henry Luce III. Besides believing that the foundation had such an obligation, Luce also thought that it had a well-rooted tradition for its entry into this difficult field: in a comment already cited, but especially relevant in this context, he stressed that any "pressing social issue" would be "a subject of great interest" to his grandfather and added that "even more explicitly can this concern be ascribed to my father."

To the foundation's social conscience and to its historical ties to pressing social issues must be added yet another factor that facilitated action by the foundation during the years of the civil rights crisis. The foundation organizes its areas of interest by topic. But it has reserved one rubric called "public affairs" as a catch-all for engagements that cannot easily be classified but that merit foundation attention and are consonant with its history. Of all the foundation's areas of interest, public affairs is the most general, deliberately designed without a fixed program or a precise definition, so that the foundation can respond quickly to the changing needs of American society and to compelling new ideas as they emerge. Under that category, the directors can make commitments in a wide variety of fields whenever a tempting opportunity comes along. "The Public Affairs Program of the Henry Luce Foundation," Henry Luce III declared, "is a continuing reflection of the social awareness and concern with the condition of mankind which were so important to Mr. Henry R. Luce and his father." Thus "public affairs" became the journal, in a sense, under which entries were made of foundation grants in the field of minority opportunity.

In his comments at the time, Henry Luce III made clear the foundation's reasons for immediate social action. "The directors felt," Luce wrote in 1969, "that the emerging struggle for equality by the American black minority and the national crisis involving racial unrest and urban blight had become priority matters. They decided that this was a timely opportunity to employ the Foundation's flexibility to direct resources quickly toward an urgent need. And yet they upheld the standards maintained by most foundations of seeking lasting values rather than engaging in emergency relief, the value of which can easily dissipate." Therefore, Luce continued, "programs were developed to promote cultural identification, to assist black education at various levels from secondary through graduate (including theological) training, and to provide extra thrust to major agencies in the field." All these foundation efforts, over the course of about four years, came to around $3 million.

Among the "major agencies in the field" were the Urban Coalition, the National Urban League, and the National Association for the Advancement of Colored People (NAACP). In 1968 and 1969, the foundation's board committed a total of $400,000 for the New York Urban Coalition, enabling it to provide risk capital for minority businessmen, with an emphasis on "those businesses which will provide the local communities with sound investment possibilities, and open up additional employment possibilities for members of minority groups." And it gave the same amount to help establish the National Urban Coalition, which was intended to catalyze "the combined efforts of local government, business, labor, minority groups and religious organizations . . . and function as a center for the exchange of information on methods of dealing with urgent urban issues." The third major agency to benefit was the Special Contribution Fund of the NAACP's Youth Employment Program (YEP), to which the foundation made a total grant of $180,000. YEP was intended to assist unemployed and underemployed ghetto youths in finding better jobs;

it was designed especially for young blacks who then were thought to be "apprehensive about existing training opportunities—or totally unaware of them." Another celebrated program aimed at young blacks was Broad Jump, Inc., a summer remedial program for disadvantaged New York City boys ages nine to fourteen; the foundation funded a $50,000 study of the program to evaluate its effectiveness and to provide for some follow-up in winter months.

The foundation also contributed in those years to programs more specifically designed to develop the potential for leadership among disadvantaged young people. The effort was intended to give support to programs "that identify academic needs, reinforce motivation, develop remedial techniques, and strengthen cultural identity."

The Consortium for Graduate Study in Business for Negroes received $150,000 to help underwrite the Summer Studies Program at Washington University in St. Louis, Missouri. Participating universities included the business schools of Indiana University, the University of Rochester, the University of Southern California, and the University of Wisconsin. The purpose was "to prepare Negroes for managerial positions in business through a Master's Degree in Business Administration." The Summer Studies Program was intended to give such students better preparation for graduate school by having them do advanced course work over the summer.

The Intensive Summer Studies Program was given $105,000 to support its visiting faculty program at Harvard, Yale, and Columbia. Fifty teachers from predominantly black schools did graduate course work or guided independent research at one of the three universities.

The National Association of Independent Schools (NAIS) was granted $105,000 to expand its activities in black affairs. NAIS serves as liaison between member schools and various agencies involved in recruitment and placement in schools of black teachers. Through an Afro-American Study Center at the Choate School, NAIS has encouraged exchange of information on curricula for black studies. It also has aided new independent schools in inner-city neighborhoods to profit by the experience of older established schools.

A grant of $43,000 went to two programs operated by the New

York Theological Seminary, an institution with which the foundation has long maintained a close relationship. The programs combined the foundation's interest in theological education and in the development of inner-city leadership. One of them, popularly known as the Storefront Pastors Program, was begun by the seminary in response to the specific plea of a group of Pentecostal ministers, who requested help "in understanding how a Biblical faith both requires and enables one to relate to such human problems as welfare and education"— an interesting question of bottomless depth. The foundation gave $30,000 to the seminary to serve this unique group of leaders in the black community. The second grant of $13,000 permitted thirty seminary or preseminary students to get a year's experience in dealing with inner-city problems by working in secular jobs and community projects.

Like other periods of brave actions and brave words, the 1960s, in the judgment of many, ended in disappointment. Those who are disappointed argue that rarely have such good intentions—and, one might say, so many good dollars—produced so little that one can point to in the way of secure and demonstrable accomplishment. Henry Luce III, who is not among the cynical, says that the foundation never tried to get, and probably never could have gotten, follow-up reports about the concrete results of the dollars thus spent. But he believes that in the field of minority leadership, the foundation had specific goals in mind and made a "meaningful difference in the needs we targeted." He believes that by "responding to that major crisis in a major way," the foundation acted as it should have acted—indeed, as it must have acted in view of its provenance—at the time. "It was a national emergency, and I would have felt insensitive if we had not responded, and helped out at a critical period of need. Then we tapered off."

Despite the tapering off, though, the foundation has never withdrawn from social programs that favor minorities. It continues to fund a number of them from its public affairs category. Almost all the later grants have maintained the foundation's early focus on leadership via enhanced minority education. In 1973 the foundation made a grant of $110,000 to the National Urban League for a professional management training program for executives from the league's 102 affiliates. The foundation also granted over the years $90,000 to St. John's College in Santa Fe, New Mexico, to enable minority students to participate in the college's Graduate Institute in Liberal Education; the last payment of that total was awarded to St. John's in 1980. In 1974, $102,000 went to Harvard University to support graduate students belonging to minority groups who were doing graduate work there. And much more recently, in 1985, the foundation gave $50,000 to its old friend in the field, Broad Jump, Inc., to give talented minority students a chance to attend private New York preparatory schools. In that same year, the foundation also made a two-year $66,000 grant to the National Association of Independent Schools to enhance minority student representation in the member schools of the association.

Whether with reference to minorities or not, the idea of leadership is likely to continue to be the guiding criterion for grants in the public affairs field. Indeed, the general concept of leadership—its nature, its practice, ways to enhance its quality—threads through many of the Luce Foundation's principal activities, concentrated as they are in academia, East Asia, theology, and American art.

In this same category of public affairs, the Luce Foundation has played a role in the education of new members of the U.S. Congress. The first Luce grant of $100,000 for that purpose was made in 1982 to three organizations: the American Enterprise Institute, the Brookings Institution, and the Congressional Research Service, an arm of the Library of Congress. Another grant of about the same amount was made to the same institutions in 1986. Supported by the grants, the three organizations held "policy seminars," in 1983 and 1987, to brief newly elected members of the new Congress on national issues.

In January 1987 two freshmen senators—Kit Bond of Missouri and Terry Sanford of North Carolina—attended the three-day "new member seminar" at Williamsburg, Virginia. Also present were twenty-three new members of the House of Representatives—twelve Republicans and eleven Democrats. Scholars from the three institutions made introductory talks on a wide variety of issues, which were followed by panel discussions. Topics included the economy and federal policy, new directions in federal policy and welfare, health issues facing the one-hundredth Congress, and national defense. Outside speakers invited to address the group included James Schlesinger, former Secretary of Defense; Paul Volcker, then Chairman of the Federal Reserve Board; Caspar Weinberger, then Secretary of Defense; Clayton Yeutter, U.S. trade representative; and Barber Conable, now head of the World Bank. The basic goal, in the words of the organizers, was "to create a situation removed from the press of actual legislative business where new members of Congress could exchange ideas on what might be done to resolve current national problems." The judgment of the sponsors and the attending congressmen is that the seminars served a useful purpose by fostering a grasp of the complexity of current issues which could be discussed in a forum where it was unnecessary to strike political postures.

8

A Look Ahead

In 1987, as it embarks on its second half-century, the foundation is beginning two important new undertakings in the favored and familiar directions. Higher education in Asia, since the earliest years of the foundation a central interest, now gets fresh impetus from a newly designed foundation program. And American education at large will also presently receive both a lift and a nudge from a projected series of new foundation grants.

With respect to higher education in Asia, the pinch on scholarship, as already recounted, has hurt most in the study of Southeast Asia. The Luce Fund for Asian Studies, discussed in Chapter 4, was designed to ease the squeeze on the academic community that was concerned with Asia at large. Now the foundation is launching a sister program to the Fund for Asian Studies, which will address itself principally to the narrower but still vast region of Southeast Asia, an area that includes the mainland and insular Asia south of China and east of the Indian subcontinent. The region is a marvel of heterogeneity in every respect—linguistically, ethnically, and in religion, as well as in political organizations and economic systems. For decades, peacetime trade and wartime hostilities have made Southeast Asia a principal concern of American foreign policy. But the concern—occasionally to our sorrow, as our experience in the Philippines and in Vietnam testifies—has not been matched by academic studies of like intensity. Had they been going on, our foreign adventures might have had a different character and a more favorable outcome. In a way, American academia has been repelled by the complexity of the region, which makes impossible its treatment as a coherent unit; no central tradition or lingua franca gives the area a semblance of integrity. In the past ten years or so, after the U.S. disillusionment and defeat in Vietnam, Southeast Asian studies, never a strong interest of the American academy, have eroded even further, with the decline of federal support, a paucity of new teaching material, and a dwindling of the ranks of leading scholars all making negative contributions.

Yet the winds of change are beginning to stir. The fading of the bitter memories of Vietnam, the presence in this country of large numbers of Southeast Asian immigrants, and an ever more internationalized platoon of scholars—many of them of Southeast Asian origin—have all stimulated a modest revival of interest in Southeast Asia. A study done in 1984 at the Wilson Center, which was partly funded by the Luce Foundation, turned up further evidence of a renaissance: some five hundred scholars now in the United States actively study and write about the area. Ten American universities now have comprehensive Southeast Asian programs.

To build on those beginnings is the major purpose of the new Luce Fund for Southeast Asian Studies. The program is committing $8 million over five years in grants to support work at the universities already strong in area studies. Each of those universities has been invited to apply for grants from the fund. They have been asked to submit proposals for long-term projects—from two to four years in duration—that will enhance their own institutional development. In February 1988, the foundation announced grants totaling $4,048,500 to eight universities, including Cornell ($664,000), Yale ($600,000), Northern Illinois, and the University of Wisconsin, Madison ($572,000 each). These grants will make possible a total of fourteen faculty and language teaching positions. Cornell, for example, will develop new teaching material for Tagalog, a major language in the Philippines. As it has in so many other of its activities, the foundation is being assisted in the evaluation of the proposals by a panel of advisers. Among the categories to which the foundation is most receptive are further undertakings that will support faculty development as well as strengthen libraries of Southeast Asian materials, award student fellowships, and increase public understanding of Southeast Asian countries. According to Donald K. Emmerson, director of the Center for Southeast Asian Studies at the University of Wisconsin, the new Luce Fund "is going to help ensure the spreading around of quality and opportunity, by supporting fundamental, bread-and-butter higher education."

The new commitment makes the Luce Foundation a major U.S. provider of financial support for Asian academic work. The commitment, as Henry Luce III recently told the *Chronicle of Higher Education*, is an important new addition to one of the foundation's oldest and most highly respected interests, stemming from the engagement with Asia of his father and grandparents. "It doesn't require much explanation to indicate that my father's magazines had an enormous impact in raising the level of interest and knowledge of Asia and its people among readers in America," Luce said. Said Robert Armstrong to the same publication: "We're the principal player in this field, although not the only one. But we're not looking for exclusivity—we hope our actions will cause other foundations to look at the needs in this area. We're now doing more than we ever have, but we're still not doing as much as we know needs to be done." What has been done by the foundation, though, is substantial: about $18 million since 1976 to foster American-Asian understanding

The second major new program will assist American academia at large by speeding the progress of women through higher academic ranks. The proposal for the new program made by the foundation's staff to the Luce board declares that although recent professional advances achieved by women "are nothing less than spectacular, the academic community continues to be resistant to change and to the professional advancement of women." Cited support for that argument comes from the Russell Sage Foundation's Task Force on Women in Higher Education: "The apparently generous hiring of women assistant professors is at best an artifact of data collection . . . women who seek faculty positions are competing with men for a very scarce and highly valued resource, and are not welcome." Similar contentions come from the National Association of Women Deans, Administrators and Counselors, from Miriam Chamberlain, who is president of the National Council on Research for Women, and other sources. Continues the proposal: "It is against this background that we now propose a program that will identify a limited number of truly outstanding women academics from a wide range of disciplines, offer them significant support at an important point in their professional development, and bring them to the attention of those who are in positions to make the most senior academic appointments in coming years."

Responding affirmatively, the board of the foundation in 1987 approved the Clare Boothe Luce Visiting Professorship Program, named after the late wife of the foundation's founder. Mrs. Luce was described by Armstrong as "a national symbol of achievement among women." The program offers two-year visiting professorships for women at a selected group of major research universities. Nominations, now coming into the foundation, are restricted to one candidate per year per institution, with no overlapping appointments. Candidates can come from any discipline, but eligibility is limited to American citizens holding faculty positions at colleges or universities other than the nominating institution. The stipend will vary according to individual circumstances but will run in the neighborhood of $60,000 a year. The recipient will offer one course in her specialty each term and, beyond that sole requirement, will be free to pursue her own research and writing while in residence. The board expressed the hope that "a significant piece of scholarship might emerge from each award." For the first year of the program, which was academic 1987–88, only four awards were made.

The estate of Mrs. Luce, who died in 1987, was bequeathed in very large proportion to the Luce Foundation, of which she was one of the original directors. To the foundation, also, she left most of the marital trust established for her by Henry R. Luce, over which she had the power to dispose. Together, the bequests to the foundation constitute a gift of well over $60 million, an amount now designated The Clare Boothe Luce Fund.

Mrs. Luce's will names fourteen educational institutions, each of which is to get the income from $3 million of the fund. The income from the remainder is also to go to educational institutions. At least half of all the institutions must be Roman Catholic.

The Clare Boothe Luce Fund in its entirety will be dedicated exclu-

Ken Haas

Eight months before she died, Clare Boothe Luce met with Henry Luce III to announce the foundation's new university professorship program named in her honor.

sively to funding scholarships, fellowships, and professorships for women students and professors. The purpose will be "to encourage women to enter, study, graduate and teach" in the natural sciences, in engineering, in computer science, and in mathematics. In her will, Mrs. Luce says that she selected those fields "in recognition that women today have already entered the fields of medicine, law, business and the arts, and in order to encourage more women to enter the fields of science." The awards must be used for study and teaching in the United States, and not for travel or study abroad. A six-member grants committee will review proposals for all scholarships, fellowships, and professorships; three members of the committee are to be chosen by the Luce Foundation, and three by the Heritage Foundation of Washington, D.C. No less than two, nor more than three, members of the committee are to be women.

A FINAL WORD

Foundations are the children of the business world, but they lack the precision of their parent. The platitude—"there is no bottom line" by which foundations can be judged—is, like so many other platitudes, quite true. Still, judgments remain possible: this book, by recounting in detail what happened after the Luce Foundation made many of its grants, is intended to make such judgments better informed. Especially, the judgments should be made about the Luce Foundation's activities in academia (Luce professors), in East Asia (a plethora of programs), in art (an encouragement to museum scholarship), in theology (improvement of faculties in theological seminaries and divinity schools), and in public affairs (especially leadership among minority groups). With these accounts in hand, the reader is free to draw his own conclusions; those of the writer, I believe, are clear enough throughout. All programs in all areas have not been equally effective; even those that I judge to have been least successful, however, may have been warranted by the times in which they were begun.

A Look Ahead

In its direction and its policies, the Luce Foundation seems to me to have a special and distinguished place in the foundation world. The Luce Foundation has a clear sense of where it is going and what its capacities are; it has avoided entry into regions too vast, too populated, or foreign to its principal interests (such as medicine, agriculture, and the theater). This clear perspective I find to have been of great help to the foundation in deciding where to put its considerable but still limited resources; in that connection it is well to note that the foundation, sizable as it is, was ranked fifty-first among American foundations in 1986 in terms of total assets. Many of the Luce Foundation's grants build on earlier grants, and encourage others in the same or closely related areas, and that I believe adds considerably to the grants' impact. At the same time, the foundation is willing to take chances and experiment even in the most familiar areas and occasionally is sufficiently adventurous to reach out to new pastures (as it did in American art). As a brief visitor to the foundation, and one who is no longer associated with it, I find those qualities impressive. I hope the Henry Luce Foundation thrives for another fifty years.

Appendixes

APPENDIX A
The Board of Directors, Past and Present

PRESENT DIRECTORS OF THE FOUNDATION

The Luce Foundation now has nine members on its Board of Directors, two of them added since 1986. Over the years since the foundation began, the board has been remarkably stable: only fourteen people have served on it, and there have been only two presidents: Charles Stillman and Henry Luce III. In 1936, the foundation's first year, four people were appointed to the board: Clare Boothe Luce, Elisabeth Luce Moore, Charles L. Stillman, and Roy E. Larsen. Clare Boothe Luce later resigned from the board. Elisabeth Luce Moore still serves. Roy E. Larsen remained a board member until he died in 1979; Charles L. Stillman served on the board for fifty years—from 1936 until he died in 1986. The only director to resign other than Clare Luce was Martha R. Wallace, who was the program director and executive director of the foundation for five years before she joined the board in 1972; Wallace resigned both as executive director and as board member in 1983. Henry Luce III joined the foundation as a director in 1957 and became its president in 1958; he continues in that capacity today. Nancy Bryan Luce, the wife of Henry Luce III, had a sadly abbreviated tenure as board member: appointed in 1986, she died in 1987.

HENRY LUCE III has been president of the Henry Luce Foundation, Inc., since 1958. From 1951 to 1981, he was employed by Time Inc., was publisher of *Fortune* and of *Time*, and was vice-president for corporate planning during the last eight of those years. He continues as a member of Time Inc.'s Board of Directors, to which he was elected in 1967.

Beginning as a Washington correspondent for *Time* in 1951, Luce held various positions with Time Inc. prior to being elected a vice-president in 1964. He became director of research and development and in 1966 joined the Time-Life News Service as its London bureau chief. During that assignment, he was elected president of the Association of American Correspondents in London. He returned to New York in 1968 as publisher of *Fortune* and then became publisher of *Time* (1969–72). Before joining Time Inc., Luce served on the staff of the Commission on Organization of the Executive Branch of the Government (the first Hoover Commission) and as a reporter for the *Cleveland Press*.

Luce's educational commitments include being president of The New Museum of Contemporary Art and trustee of Princeton Theological Seminary, the College of Wooster, the United Board for Christian Higher Education in Asia, the Center

Appendixes

of Theological Inquiry, the Pan American Development Foundation, the Yale-China Association, and the Eisenhower Exchange Fellowships. He is former chairman of the board of the China Institute in America.

Connected to the foundation by family and long tenure, Luce's influence is pervasive. East Asia, theology, and higher education, all centers of focus for the foundation, are also Luce's continuing concerns. The field of American art has also been a preoccupation of his, and there, as elsewhere, his leadership has made the foundation a major force.

To judge how well any proposal put before the foundation will work out after the grant is made, Luce says, is always difficult. "There's no hard answer. If something seems to have worked out well, then you are encouraged to do something like it again. If something doesn't work out, you may avoid that kind of thing in the future. But you don't worry about that effort having been wasted—it's a good idea to take a certain amount of risk. There's a great tradition that private foundations are intended to innovate, to do imaginative things rather than just perpetuate the routine. If there's an occasional failure, you don't kick yourself—we expect that."

ROBERT E. ARMSTRONG is vice-president and executive director of the Henry Luce Foundation, Inc. Armstrong joined the staff of the foundation as program director in 1970, was elected vice-president in 1977, and succeeded to the position of executive director in 1983. Before joining the Luce Foundation, Armstrong served as associate and acting executive secretary of the Special Studies Project of the Rockefeller Brothers Fund.

Armstrong earned his baccalaureate degree from the University of Illinois, where he was elected to Phi Beta Kappa. Following graduate work at the Woodrow Wilson School of Princeton University, he served as an intelligence officer in the United States Army, both in this country and in Japan. Armstrong worked briefly with the Executive Office of the President in the Eisenhower administration before being sworn in as a United States Foreign Service officer in 1959. His diplomatic posts included Kathmandu (Nepal) and Moscow, where he was aide to former U.S. Ambassador Foy D. Kohler. Returning to this country, Armstrong joined the Rockefeller staff early in 1966.

Robert Armstrong was a founding member of the board of the Chelsea Theater Center in New York and of Opportunity Resources for the Arts. He is currently a director of the Center for Arts Information.

Armstrong remarks:

> Success is a difficult term in the foundation world. If we don't have an occasional program that doesn't work, then we aren't reaching far enough to new ideas. We could guarantee success by making sure that everything we

undertake is perfectly safe—we could do that. But we want to make some awards that are riskier. Because we make our academic chairs for a limited time period, universities are willing to bring us high-risk, more imaginative proposals. They know they won't be stuck with a named chair for all time. One chair we funded—an examination of the nature of the universe and man's place in it—wasn't successful because professors would come for only one semester at a time. The whole program became episodic. But it was a very exciting idea. I'm not sorry we made the award—we all learned from the process.

The strength of American philanthropy is its diversity. Specificity is something that marks our operations, for which I'm very grateful. It's quite clear to all of us what we do and what we don't do. We track the number of rejections that we make every year. The number has dropped markedly since the 1970s—our identity became clear to the outside world. There's a great sense of collegiality within the board and within the staff. We don't second-guess the board, but Hank and I go through an elaborate review process before board meetings, and we X-out things we know won't get board approval.

JOHN C. EVANS is advisory director and consultant to Morgan Stanley & Company, Incorporated. He has been associated with Morgan Stanley since 1967 and has served as general partner and managing director as well as vice-chairman and managing director of Morgan et Cie International S.A.

Before joining Morgan Stanley, Evans was associated with Prudential Insurance Company of America, International Finance Corporation, and Philip Hill Higginson Erlangers (later to be known as Hill Samuel), where he was executive director in London from 1960 to 1966.

An active participant in community and civic affairs, Evans is chairman of the board of the National Theatre of the Deaf, Inc., a director of the New York Policy Board, Cities-In-Schools, Inc., and a member and director of the Dia Art Foundation in New York. Evans joined the board of directors of the Henry Luce Foundation, Inc., in 1977. A member of the Bond Club of New York and of the Council on Foreign Relations, he also serves as a director of Benmarl Wine Company, Ltd., Fishers Island Development Corporation, Fishers Island Electric Company, and Fishers Island Telephone Company. Evans is, in addition, an elected member of the Board of Commissions of the Fishers Island Ferry District.

Evans's interest in the National Theatre of the Deaf led to a proposal for assistance to the theatre, which came to the Luce board from David Hayes, an officer of the theatre. The grant that the Luce board approved enabled the theatre to perform in China. Evans comments: "It was a proposal that the board would have approved if it had never heard of me. A board with no outside interests impoverishes a foundation, and deprives it of people with the cast of mind that can focus on what a foundation does. Sometimes board members are too timid, rather than speaking up to encourage foundations to get into things that the members care about."

JAMES I. MCCORD, who was president of Princeton Theological Seminary for twenty-four years, is now chancellor of the Center of Theological Inquiry in Princeton, the only research institution in the country devoted to the study of religious issues. Previously he had been, at age 26, a dean at Austin Presbyterian Theological Seminary. The recipient of numerous awards, including twenty-four honorary degrees, McCord was most recently recognized with the prestigious Templeton Prize for Progress in Religion, established to honor those who have pioneered ways of understanding God. A native of Texas and a Presbyterian minister, McCord also serves as chairman of the United Board for Christian Higher Education in Asia. He joined the Luce Board in 1986.

Says McCord:

The grants made by the Foundation to the Center were all to enhance academic excellence. One of the most recent grants could lead to a breakthrough on how the growing Asian community can be integrated into American society. The Asian community is intelligent, many are college graduates, and should be engaged at a level that will challenge them and use them for the betterment of American society.

ELISABETH LUCE MOORE (Mrs. Maurice T. Moore) was chairman of the board of trustees of the State University of New York for more than a decade. Appointed to that position by Governor Nelson A. Rockefeller in 1968, she was the first woman board chairman at this largest of all university systems in the United States. Her interests in education and in the Far East, where she was born of American missionary parents, are reflected in her work as trustee and long-time president of the United Board for Christian Higher Education in Asia, as trustee of the China Institute in America, the National YWCA, and the Asia Foundation, as past chairman of the Institute of International Education, and as a former trustee of Wellesley College.

For many years Moore has worked with the national and international YWCA with special responsibility for training leaders for volunteer service in seventy-six countries. An elder of the Brick Presbyterian Church in New York, she edits its bulletin *Church and Society*. She has served the United States government on various commissions, including the Advisory Committee to the Marshall Plan. A graduate of Wellesley College, Moore holds honorary degrees from several universities, among them Columbia, Duke, Princeton, and Wellesley College.

Elisabeth Luce Moore's enthusiasm for the work of the foundation is as much a tribute to her as to the foundation itself. She often comments about how much pleasure Henry R. Luce would take in the foundation today and how much he would approve of the direction that Henry Luce III has given it. She remarks: "The marvelous thing is that the foundation has such a balanced program. Funding the museum work gave us a new dimension—it was there from the beginning, and Harry's interest was there, but we never did anything much about it until Hank put it together. Harry would be absolutely delighted."

DAVID V. RAGONE retired as president of Case Western Reserve University in Cleveland, Ohio, in 1988 and held a concurrent appointment as professor of metallurgy and material science there. Ragone holds an S.B., an S.M., and an Sc.D. degree from the Massachusetts Institute of Technology. He has taught at both the University of Michigan and Carnegie-Mellon University and directed research at the General Atomic Division of General Dynamics. In 1970 Ragone was appointed dean of the Thayer College of Engineering at Dartmouth. Two years later he returned to the University of Michigan as dean of that institution's College of Engineering, a position he held for eight years. Ragone assumed the presidency of Case Western Reserve University in 1980. He is now a visiting professor at M.I.T.

Ragone serves on the boards of directors of a number of corporations, including Augat, Inc., the Cleveland-Cliffs Iron Company, National City Bank, the B. F. Goodrich Company, SIFCO Industries, Inc., and the Cabot Corporation. In addition, he is chairman of the Ohio Higher Education Facility Commission and a panel member of the White House Science Council's Study on the Health of the University. A trustee of the Mitre Corporation, he is also a member of the Council on Foreign Relations, the PaineWebber Venture Management Company Technical Advisory Board, and a consultant to the National Science Foundation. Ragone joined the board of directors of the Henry Luce Foundation, Inc., in 1981.

Says Ragone:

There's a very important role for foundations in this country. Government has a risk-averse strategy: they are afraid somebody will come back and say why did you study the sex life of the tsetse fly or the sea gull? At the foundation, we'll risk X dollars on some guy who thinks that he has a better way to do this or that—a better way to think about the combination between music and literature, for example. Hank and the foundation seem to have that kind of spirit. With the Luce professorships, the foundation's attitude was—come on, why don't we support something a little out of the ordinary?

One mustn't turn one's back on immediate social needs; there are problems in this world. But foundation money is so precious and so pivotal and so important, we shouldn't just throw it in the pot and say, look, that's for poverty, by God. Housing in Newark? Leave that to New Jersey. Don't throw money at the obvious. The special role of foundations is to identify future problems, the longer-range ones, that government agencies are just incapable of doing. Foundations ought to be thinking about those problems that will confront mankind and lay the intellectual basis for solving them. We're going to fall apart if we don't think in those far-reaching terms.

At the foundation it isn't whether the staff initiates ideas or the board initiates ideas. It's somewhere in between—it's through conversation. There's good valid conversation at the board meetings. We get into some of the biggest disagreements you have ever seen. After a vote on some of the proposals for Luce professorships, we sat around and decided we had done a disservice: "There are some people out there who are really good, and we didn't offer them anything." We decided to see whether we could do something for them—as we did in the case of Fordham and the music and literature grant.

I had to drop a board six years ago to accept this one. It's great fun—really worth it.

CHARLES C. TILLINGHAST, JR. is a fellow of Brown University, on the corporation of which he has served for more than thirty years, fourteen of them as chancellor. He began his professional life as a lawyer in New York City, served on the staff of District Attorney Thomas E. Dewey, and later was a partner in the firm of Hughes, Hubbard and Reed. In 1957 he left the law to become vice-president for international affairs and a director of Bendix Aviation Corporation. In 1961 he joined Trans World Airlines and served as its chief executive officer for sixteen years. Following his retirement, he became vice-chairman of White Weld & Company, which in 1978 merged with Merrill Lynch & Company, of which he was a vice-president until his retirement in 1983. Previously he had served on the boards of numerous businesses and charitable organizations. He has been a member of the board of the Henry Luce Foundation since 1974. He was the first director with no connection to the Luce family or to Time Inc.

Tillinghast says:

The foundation has gone through a process of evolution as it has moved away from the tightly knit family control. One place this shows is in the sale of Time Inc. stock. The question was whether the decision should be made for financial reasons or for reasons of the heart. Do we hold on to it forever? The point is not whether the assets would have grown more rapidly if no Time stock had ever been sold—the point is that the larger you get as a foundation, the more people are dependent on you, and the more important it is to minimize risks. Earlier, Hank was probably somewhat more reluctant than other members of the finance committee to lighten the foundation's holding of Time stock as a matter of policy. Since then, there has been general agreement on diversification—the function of the fiduciaries is to protect the assets of the trust.

I'm here because as an older man, I'm interested in good works. Different membership on the board has brought useful diversity of viewpoints to the foundation. Sometimes I'm concerned because many of our efforts seem to go toward upper-crust problems—the academic world, the artistic world, high policies of international relations. Yet those are the clearly delineated areas of the foundation. When that happens, a whole world of people with the same interests starts to come to a foundation and flood it with ideas. The impetus builds up, the direction is hard to change. I would like to see more efforts in the social area, but the foundation does very well at what it does now—any change would have to be slow and slight.

The job gets more and more difficult as the amount of money to be given away grows. Doing something useful gets harder, not easier. With the professorships, for example, how many times can you find new things to do in that area? The time may come when what has been done is enough. It's harder and harder to find enough compelling programs to satisfy one's conscience.

NEW DIRECTORS OF THE FOUNDATION

Late in 1987 and early 1988, the Luce Foundation added two new members to its Board of Directors.

Ken Haas

MARGARET BOLES FITZGERALD, a granddaughter of Emmavail Luce Severinghaus, is vice-president and director of community relations for Hill, Holliday, Connors, Cosmopulos, Inc., a Boston-based advertising agency. She is account manager for about sixty charitable organizations, and serves on the board or as a committee member of a dozen of them. On the occasion of her appointment, Henry Luce III said "her professional experience and her commitment to various causes in the public interest will add to the scope and outreach of the Foundation."

Corporate Photographers, Inc.

THOMAS L. PULLING is chairman and chief executive of Shearson Asset Management, Inc., a subsidiary of Shearson Lehman Hutton. He is a graduate of Princeton, and has spent his entire working career in the field of finance. Among other activities, he is a trustee or director of the Metropolitan Opera Association, the National Conference on Christians and Jews, and the Opera Orchestra of New York.

PAST DIRECTORS OF THE FOUNDATION

Alfred Eisenstaedt

ROY E. LARSEN was a director of the Luce Foundation from the time the foundation began in 1936 until he died in 1979. An early associate of Henry R. Luce, Larsen was president of Time Inc. for twenty-one years. He played a crucial role in the creation of the "March of Time" on the radio and on film, and was the innovator of many of Time Inc.'s ventures in the field of communications. He is judged to have been the most important figure in Time Inc.'s early history after its founders, Henry Luce and Briton Hadden. He was a graduate of Harvard and onetime president of its Board of Overseers; the building of the Graduate School of Education there is named Larsen Hall, a reflection of his long interest in public primary and secondary education.

Henry Luce III wrote in a foundation report: "I wish to express the sadness of all the directors and staff at the death in 1979 of Roy E. Larsen, who had been a director and vice president of the Foundation since its inception in 1936. During those forty-four years, Roy Larsen was an enthusiastic supporter of the Foundation's work, an innovative philanthropist on his own, and an understanding friend to all of his many admirers."

Appendixes

John Dominis

CLARE BOOTHE LUCE died in October 1987 at the age of eighty-four. Editor, playwright, war correspondent, congresswoman, and ambassador, she had enough careers, wrote the *New York Times*, to satisfy the ambitions of several women.

A native New Yorker, Clare Boothe Luce first gained renown as managing editor of Condé Nast's *Vanity Fair* magazine. Wider fame came when she wrote two successful plays, *The Women* and *Kiss the Boys Goodbye*, and for her reportage during World War II for *Life* magazine. Elected to Congress as a representative from Connecticut in 1943, she served two terms and then declined to run again. But she remained active in Republican party affairs. President Dwight Eisenhower named her U.S. ambassador to Italy in 1953. Although her departure from Rome in 1957 marked the end of her diplomatic career, she was not offstage for long. She pursued her many interests energetically, including her membership on the President's Foreign Intelligence Advisory Board, until her final illness.

Mrs. Luce was married to Henry R. Luce in November 1935. She served as a director of the Henry Luce Foundation from its founding in 1936 to December 1960.

Ken Haas

NANCY BRYAN LUCE was active in civic affairs and had wide-ranging international experience and interests. A graduate of Ashley Hall School in South Carolina, she attended Mills College in California. Married to Henry Luce III in 1975, she served as a director of the East Side Settlement House and as a member of the International Christian University's Women's Committee. She was, in addition, an accomplished horticulturist and a classical pianist. She died in 1987.

Ken Haas

CHARLES L. STILLMAN joined Time Inc. in 1928 as business manager of *Time* and held a variety of assignments before being elected executive vice-president and treasurer in 1949. Stillman was also founder of Eastex Inc., and chairman of its board from 1956 until 1970. Stillman was a member of the Board of Managers of the YMCA Vocational Service Branch in New York and a member of the Board of Trustees of Escuela Agricola Panamericana in Tegucigalpa, Honduras. In 1948 he headed a special ECA Mission to China. He was a member of the Alumni Board of Yale University and the advisory board of Chemical New York Trust Company and served the Henry Luce Foundation as a director, secretary-treasurer, and president. Stillman died in 1986.

Henry Luce III wrote in 1986:

> Charles Latimer Stillman served the Foundation for almost half a century and was my only predecessor as president. Charlie Stillman was Time Inc.'s early financial wizard who developed the company's forest products business. He was my boss when I supervised construction of the Time & Life building and, as host of my second wedding reception, he was, in effect, *in loco* father-in-law. His memory will be the stuff of legend.

Blackstone-Shelburne

MARTHA R. WALLACE was the executive director and a vice-president of the Henry Luce Foundation. A Phi Beta Kappa graduate of Wellesley College, with an M.A. from the Fletcher School of Law and Diplomacy, Wallace served as a member of the Board of Directors of the Council on Foundations, Inc., and of the Foundation Center. She was among the first group of women admitted to the Council on Foreign Relations, Inc., and in 1972 was elected to its Board of Directors. She also served on the board of the Association for Homemakers Service, Inc., the auxiliary of New York Orthopaedic Hospital, the Distribution Committee of the United Hospital Fund, and the Management Committee of the U.S.-South African Leadership Exchange Program. A former vice-president of the New York Junior League, she received the league's 1968 outstanding volunteer award. Wallace has been a trustee of the Bowery Savings Bank and a member of several boards of directors, including the New York Telephone Company, the Bristol-Myers Company, the Chemical Bank, and American Can Company.

Appendixes

When Wallace resigned in 1983, Henry Luce III wrote:

Mrs. Wallace's contributions to the Foundation are best summarized by the testimonial resolution adopted by the Board, which stated, in major part: "Mrs. Wallace was the catalyst for the development of a series of innovative programs ranging from the Henry R. Luce Professorship Program and the Luce Scholars Program to the Luce Fund for Asian Studies and the Chinese Scholars Program as well as the Luce Fund for Scholarship in American Art. In large measure, the enormous success of these and other unique Foundation programs is due to the clarity of her perceptions, her ability to give practical focus to abstract values, and the strength of her will to make a difference. Her profound influence is felt not only by her fellow Directors, but also by the hundreds of people who have participated in or have been touched by the broad range of Foundation programs.

"THEREFORE, BE IT RESOLVED that the Board of Directors of the Henry Luce Foundation, Inc. hereby records its deep appreciation for the tremendous contributions made to the development of the Foundation by Martha Redfield Wallace, whose intelligence, dynamism and determination have helped to assure the Foundation a respected place in American philanthropy."

The Faith of Henry Luce

Delivered at the Dedication of Luce Hall, Center of Theological Inquiry, Princeton, October 9, 1984, by Henry Luce III.

It is a great satisfaction, even a thrill, for me to have had a part in the creation of this building, which we are dedicating to the memory of my father. I'm delighted also to see here so many members of his family, who I know are equally proud of this memorial. And what a marvelous combination of events it is that after this ceremony we shall be having in Miller Chapel the Christening service of my father's first great-grandchild.

It is also a great honor for me to have had a part in the founding of The Center of Theological Inquiry, the new institution for which this building is headquarters. It is an institution whose purpose is to raise and pursue and elucidate and promulgate large questions. So its building is, as I hope to illustrate to you, a marvelously fitting memorial to my father.

Born as he was the son of an alumnus of Princeton Seminary, born in a mission compound populated by stern, bearded Calvinist educators, Henry R. Luce could not claim to have experienced, as most of us have, a theologically naive childhood. Referring to this, he liked to quote Matthew's "I thank Thee, O Father, Lord of Heaven and Earth, because Thou has hid these things from the wise and prudent, and hast revealed them unto babes."

In what may well have been his first sermon, addressed at the age of six or seven "to heathen people," Harry Luce preached, "Now I have no doubt that some of your friends have beautiful grounds and houses. Do they love one another or not? If they do, more beautiful than their earthly home will be their home in heaven. Now I hope every one of you understands love as well as those who are in near contact with God. Now if any of you do not understand, please ask questions."

At 16 from Hotchkiss, he wrote his father, "Mr. Ray, the elocution master, paid me a compliment unawares by telling one fellow that the only fellow who could sling the religious bull without appearing foolish was Luce." The oration in question was what Harry called a "hot" one on Christian Democracy as the foundation of America's leadership of the world at the close of the European War.

At 17 he was sending his father long distance advice on what to preach. "Will you not tell them of the strife and the factions of the big 'outside' world, and bid them to be of the same one mind that was and is Christ Jesus. For without are dogs wrangling over the dry bones of corruption. Within should be unity: one church, one faith, one Lord, one service, one aim, Jesus Christ." Perhaps as insurance against the advice not being taken, he went on to report his own agenda: "My next oration will, I think, be entitled 'Unity, One and Indissoluble', unity meaning strong individualities united in works and spirit greater than they."

As I was going through my father's scores of speeches, although I have read most of them before, I was astonished to see how many of them were on themes of the Faith, of Christianity, of God, and not just the ones given to church groups, but also ones given to university audiences, businessmen, lawyers and scientists. And this amidst speeches on practically every topic under Heaven, from foreign policy to journalism, to the arts and the art of making money. Neither did he lack courage in bearding the lion in his lair. For one day he marched to his church, the Madison Avenue Presbyterian Church, whose then pastor, a famous and stentorian preacher, was an uncompromising pacifist, and delivered a long and ardent lecture on the importance of maintaining a strong defense capability.

Harry Luce liked to allude to an early missionary named Paulinus who in the year 627 called at the court of Edwin, the pagan King of Northumbria. After hearing Paulinus' message, the king reflected on how little he and his people knew of why they were placed on this earth, and whither they might be heading from it. He decided that Paulinus' Christian message "tells us something more certain" than what they had heretofore perceived, and that, therefore, it deserved to be heeded.

The something more certain, as Harry Luce came to formulate it, was that "meaning was built into life, in the beginning, by the Creator" and with Tennyson that "through the ages one increasing purpose runs."

Luce saw his Presbyterianism as focusing on three precepts: First the doctrine of the sovereignty and majesty of God. "It is a blinding light," he said. He stressed the first commandment, "Thou shalt have no other gods before me." Time and again, his references affirmed this. "This is my Father's World." "Fear not, little flock. God will give you the victory."

Second, he saw Calvin's curious doctrine of predestination as imbuing Presbyterians with a sense of responsibility. Since all believers were either saved or damned from birth, no self-respecting Presbyterian wanted to contemplate that he might be damned, therefore he set out to prove that he had earned the right to be saved. Activism, the work ethic, responsibility.

I'm reminded of his telling me one day that he had brooded at length over the matter of to whom was he accountable for his great journalistic enterprise, Time Incorporated. In some detail, he explained that it could not be any of the obvious constituencies: not stockholders, who cared only for profit rather than journalistic quality and purpose; not advertisers with their self-evident conflicts of interest; not readers, who could not know what they wanted or needed to read until they read it; not the Board of Directors, a small group of well meaning but not necessarily wise gentlemen. No, he said, "I decided that my ultimate accountability had to be to my Creator." Responsibility.

Third, he said that "Presbyterianism is a theological religion. It is intensely concerned with truth. We have a duty to study, to think clearly, to express what we know and think candidly and precisely. The great truth is that the gulf between God and man was bridged. God became man in a mystery of love. That truth is known by faith. That faith must be held and elaborated in truth. That is the business of theology. Upon it all intellectual coherence depends. Without it, confusion reigns as it so nearly does in our day."

And that, I may say, can be taken as a charge to the Center of Theological Inquiry. For as God is the author of all truth, therefore that truth must be seen to be one and indivisible.

To Harry Luce, faith and reason, Jerusalem and Athens, church and state, were not dualities in opposition, but streams flowing in parallel, all toward the same purpose. On this he said, "When reason becomes humble and responsible, it discovers the need for Faith. Faith is the great word. For Faith is what men and nations live by, or by the want of it disintegrate and perish. Faith is the sum product of intellectual effort, of intuition, of experience and of the unmerited good fortune of the soul. Blind Faith? There never was such a thing. Faith is a continual dialectic between a man and whatever it is he believes in."

He quoted St. Anselm, Archbishop of Canterbury: "Just as the right order of going requires that we should believe the deep things of God before we presume to discuss them by reason, so it seems to me negligence if, after we have been confirmed in the faith, we do not study to understand what we believe."

"There is a hunger in the world," Harry Luce proclaimed in 1944, "and in America—which is not a hunger of the body. It is a hunger which the Church was commanded to assuage. In the grossly practical terms of the market, there is a pressing demand for a certain commodity. The name of that commodity is Truth. If it is now again truth which men deeply desire from the Church, it is a test which the angels themselves must welcome. For this hunger for truth presages the dawn of another Age of Faith. The essential characteristic of the great Ages of Faith was not that faith was one thing and reason another. The characteristic of an Age of Faith is that faith and reason march together—march together against doubt and evil and disunity, march together to attack the most terribly practical problems, march together toward the highest aspirations of the soul."

I come now to Harry Luce's conception of a triune God, which he called The Three Immanuels: God in history, God in nature and God in each person. In effect, God in time, God in space and God in the inner space of the soul.

It is a formulation perhaps not that different from the Trinity, if one sees God the Father as creator, God the Son as in history and the Holy Spirit as in each person. But it is a formulation whose vivid imagery is illuminating.

God in each person, no matter who (he mentioned the prodigal son, the man who fell among thieves). The Holy Spirit which is within us, each carrying some part of God's purpose. Meaning was built into life.

I remember one day my father had returned from visiting in the hospital an old friend who was connected to an array of tubes, terminally ill. I gather she was able to communicate by mumbling a few words, by bending a finger, by a twinkle in the eye. What he said to me was this: "I am overwhelmed by the enormous difference between the presence of life, however little, and its absence."

God in nature. "God," he said, "comes into his own creation to taste the beauty of the lilies and the music of the spheres, and, yes, to have a look at His tiger burning bright, and to speak with man, His co-worker in all this cosmic enterprise."

But he was not satisfied with God's conversations with His co-worker. "While we have got science and religion fairly well distinguished from one another, we have not got them cooperating with one another. Where there should be only distinction, there is separation. The two affairs go on unrelatedly, whereas they should go on unitedly. The result is a certain impoverishment of both the religious and the scientific enterprise. The man of faith fails to know the full truth about this terrestrial universe, which is the concern of religion." Unless these two come together, he said, "Man will lack the kind of picture of himself-within-the-universe that can unite his mind, place him at home in a harmonious universe of truth, and assure him that all his terrestrial tasks have their final consecration from the fact that they further a destiny that is not terrestrial."

In 1966, Harry Luce, in delivering the commencement address at Princeton Seminary, elaborated on this theme. "I will submit, as a prediction, that in the decade beginning now," he told the graduates, "you will have to cope with the conflict of science and religion more seriously and on a grander scale than ever before. It does indeed seem that, in recent years, the relation of science and religion has entered into a new phase of peaceful coexistence. Instead of conflict, there is felt to be reciprocity, a desire for accommodation and even for mutual support. There is very little overt attack on religion. Scientists are among those who tell you cheerfully that religion is a good thing."

But, he said, while "there exists a happy concordat between science and religion, that dialogue is not serious. I get the impression that religious leaders are not paying strict attention to what scientists are saying, and that scientists are making up their own versions of religion and even when they call themselves Christians, are politely ignoring all of the decisive propositions of the Christian faith."

Here, of course, is subject matter, a great pending agenda for the Center of Theological Inquiry.

To go on.

"God works in history. God is busy in the world he created." After unity of truth, this was Harry Luce's most cherished theological precept. God said to Joshua, "Fear not. Only be strong and very courageous. For the Lord thy God is with thee whithersoever thou goest."

Luce had enormous respect for the noted theologians of his day, including some who had attacked him, and he loved to quarrel with them. "I write all this only because of my admiration for Reinhold Niebuhr and my gratitude to him." And what was it that he wrote? "Niebuhr has got hold of a great message—that

Appendixes

God is in history; that not only is there a purpose in human life but it is God's purpose, and that God's purpose is going to be achieved even if most of us have to fry in hell for it. But Niebuhr has only just got hold of it; he sounds over and over again the overture. Niebuhr does not yet know how to write the opera."

God had to be in history, Luce thought, to place Calvin in Europe a century before the American colonization, thus to spread Calvinists across Europe in time for them to be the colonizers, with the result that two-thirds of the American population at the time of the Revolution were Calvinists. He saw America as the promised land, destined by Providence. Unlike the Old Testament Israelites, whom God had to rebuke, chastise, banish, America was organized by those responsible Calvinists. "One Nation Under God." He said, "The American proposition makes no political or social sense without God."

America was the product of Providence. But it was never perfect. "I was never disillusioned with or by America, but I was, from my earliest manhood, dissatisfied with America. America was not being as great and as good as I knew she could be, as I believed with every nerve and fiber God Himself had intended her to be." He exhorted America to be better. He coined the slogan "The Great Society" long before Lyndon Johnson borrowed it. He asked where were the American arches upon which he could inscribe "To the Greater Glory of God." As the Lord was in American history, Harry Luce was battling for the Lord.

Chancellor McCord, you were the first person to speak to the topic, "The Faith of Henry Luce," at the dedication in 1972 of the Henry R. Luce Tower of Faith of the National Presbyterian Church in Washington. I hope this has been an acceptable sequel. And I hope the Center of Theological Inquiry, under God's inspiration, will succeed in telling us something more certain.

The Foundation at Fifty

Parts of an address given at the Fiftieth Anniversary Dinner of the Henry Luce Foundation, Inc., at the Cotillion Room, Pierre Hotel, January 22, 1987, by Henry Luce III.

Good evening ladies and gentlemen. Welcome to The Henry Luce Foundation's Fiftieth Anniversary celebration.

I would like first to introduce my fellow directors of the foundation: Robert Eddy Armstrong, the executive director, John C. Evans, David V. Ragone, and Elisabeth Luce Moore. Beth Moore is one of the original directors, and therefore is having her golden jubilee after fifty years of service. The next person I have the honor of introducing was present at the creation—as the wife of the founder— the person for whom is named our newest program, The Clare Boothe Luce Visiting Professorships. It is a great pleasure for me to have with us tonight Marjorie Stillman, whose late husband Charlie Stillman was a director of the foundation for most of the half century and was my only predecessor as its president. Let me also present the lady who was present at the beginning of *Time*, my mother Lila Tyng.

In 1937 The Henry Luce Foundation made a grant of $250 to The Henry Street Settlement for its visiting nurse service.

In 1986 the foundation made a grant of $150,000 to The Henry Street Settlement to sponsor its Arts Program for Asian Immigrants.

The comparison between these two items well symbolizes in both scale and character, the changes which half a century have brought both to our foundation and to our world.

What is important for a foundation is that it have a coherent, focused program. All foundations together generate but a small fraction of all philanthropy, and represent an even tinier fraction of what government passes out in entitlements. And so all foundations, let alone one little one, cannot do everything.

They need to be focused, to pick a niche, so they will force themselves to find a need where they can make a difference, and be seen to be making a difference. They need an internal discipline in order to seek innovation and to take initiatives. They should innovate to make things happen which would not otherwise have happened and they should initiate so that limited resources will become more effective when the things they begin continue, grow and multiply under other auspices.

As all institutions need a constituency, this process has produced ours. It is a delight that ours is represented with such copiousness and distinction tonight.

The niche we have chosen is higher education, rather broadly defined in some respects, and rather narrowly constricted in others. Why, for example, did we not take on all of education? Well, it is already four decades or so that we have been wondering why Johnny can't read. Later we discovered that he can't count or spell, doesn't know who Abraham Lincoln was or where London is. Lately, the horrible truth has dawned on us that he can't even talk the national language, or in some cases, any other language, for that matter.

Let me say, those problems are just too much for me, or our foundation. I hope they don't continue to be too much for everybody else as well. On the other hand our concern is for what they imply for human aspirations at the cutting edge, and in fact, for human survival in the age of exploding population, rising expectations and growing resource scarcity. If Herbert George Wells was correct in saying that "Human history becomes more and more a race between education and catastrophe," then the effectiveness of education at its highest levels must hold top priority.

As the monastery was in the dark ages, today it is the university which must preserve the tradition, carry the flame, and spark the flowering of civilization. To do so it must search, challenge, innovate and demand. Judging by some proposals we receive, I'm not always sure that it does. For example, I have put my foot down when we have received university proposals to fund special remedial programs in English Composition. If the university cannot solve that problem out of routine resources, it doesn't deserve to be one.

We go with Friedrich Wilhelm Nietzsche when he said,

Dancing in all its forms cannot be excluded from the curriculum of all noble education: dancing with the feet, with ideas, with words, and, need I add that one must also be able to dance with the pen?

And so the particular things we do in the foundation, mostly through channels of higher education and scholarship, are to promote the faith and the moral order, to advance the knowledge of truth through integrative and interdisciplinary perceptions, to propagate international intercontinental cross-fertilization, particularly with east Asia, and to celebrate culture which is the most glorious epiphany of civilization.

I hope that sounds like quite a niche! So we don't do everything, but, if you ask me, we have a great deal on our plate.

We have thought of the foundation as a living memorial to my paternal grandparents, who were higher education missionaries in China. But one day when I discussed this with my father, worldly philosopher that he was, he said, "You know, if your grandparents were anything, they were invincibly curious, broadly learned and enthusiastically topical. If there's something which interests you or me now, it would probably have been interesting to them."

On the other hand, my father sometimes tried to use this formulation to destabilize the coherence I was trying to build in the foundation. That is to say he would ask me to have the foundation discharge some obligation of his which I regarded as irrelevant to our guide-lines. On the other hand the formulation has

Appendixes

come in handy as part of our rationale when we have branched out into new spheres. . . .

For me and my foundation colleagues it is a great stimulus and lots of fun to be partners with so many of you and many more of your counterparts at other institutions. We like to think that we are helping you stimulate the flow of ideas, propitiate the spirit of inquiry, and advance the edge of knowledge, and that in all of these the effort makes some small difference.

Distribution of Grants

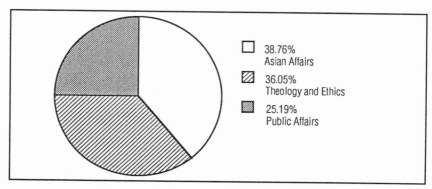

Luce Foundation Grants, 1936–1966

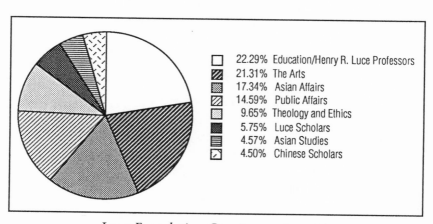

Luce Foundation Grants, 1976–1986

The Twenty Largest Grants Made by the Luce Foundation between 1936 and 1986

Metropolitan Museum of Art, New York, New York
Study Center for American Art, 1984 $2,500,000

Center of Theological Inquiry, Princeton, New Jersey
Henry R. Luce Hall, 1982   1,500,000

New Museum of Contemporary Art, New York, New York
Long-term Planning and Development Grant, 1985   1,000,000

Yale University, New Haven, Connecticut
President's Discretionary Fund, 1986   1,000,000

College of Wooster, Wooster, Ohio
Henry Luce III Fund for Distinguished Scholarship, 1980   500,000

Columbia University, New York, New York
Maurice T. Moore Professorship, 1986   500,000

Honolulu Academy of Arts, Honolulu, Hawaii
Clare Boothe Luce Wing, 1977   500,000

National Presbyterian Church and Center, Washington, D.C.
Henry R. Luce Tower of Faith, 1968   500,000

New Museum of Contemporary Art, New York, New York
Construction of new facilities, 1985   500,000

Princeton Theological Seminary, Princeton, New Jersey
Henry W. Luce Professorship of Ecumenics and Mission, 1964   500,000

Universidad Francisco Marroquin, Guatemala City, Guatemala
Charles L. Stillman Fund for Faculty Development, 1986   500,000

University of Kansas, Lawrence, Kansas
Christianity in China Project, 1985   500,000

Wellesley College, Wellesley, Massachusetts
President's Discretionary Fund, 1986   500,000

Appendixes

Yale University, New Haven, Connecticut
Program on Humanistic and Social Thought, 1981   500,000

Young Women's Christian Association, New York, New York
Fund for the Future, 1983   500,000

United Board for Christian Higher Education in Asia, New York,
New York
Chapel at Central Philippine University, 1986   480,000

St. Bernard's School, Gladstone, New Jersey
New classroom and library, 1969   440,000

Columbia University, New York, New York
Maurice T. Moore Professorship, 1967   400,000

Princeton Theological Seminary, Princeton, New Jersey
Asian-American Theological Center, 1986   400,000

Asia Foundation, San Francisco, California
Regional development in countries belonging to the Association of
Southeast Asian Nations, 1985   360,000

This list does not include the Henry R. Luce Professorships.

The Top Twenty Beneficiaries of Foundation Grants between 1936 and 1986

Yale University, New Haven, Connecticut	$3,764,300
Columbia University, New York, New York	2,958,000
Metropolitan Museum of Art, New York, New York	2,940,000
United Board for Christian Higher Education in Asia, New York, New York	2,496,450
Harvard University, Cambridge, Massachusetts	2,174,600
New Museum of Contemporary Art, New York, New York	1,720,000
Center of Theological Inquiry, Princeton, New Jersey	1,584,000
Princeton Theological Seminary, Princeton, New Jersey	1,425,000
Wellesley College, Wellesley, Massachusetts	1,402,500
China Institute in America, New York, New York	1,390,186
College of Wooster, Wooster, Ohio	1,297,500
The Asia Foundation, San Francisco, California*	1,267,500
Cornell University, Ithaca, New York	1,252,750
New York University, New York, New York	1,082,500
University of Chicago, Chicago, Illinois	961,400
Princeton University, Princeton, New Jersey	917,250
National Urban League, New York, New York	880,065
Young Women's Christian Association, New York, New York	827,000
Emory University, Atlanta, Georgia	797,000
The Johns Hopkins University, Baltimore, Maryland	785,600

*The Asia Foundation also received $1,700,000 for administration of the Luce Scholars Program.

The Henry R. Luce Professorships

The Luce professorships are granted for five years and are renewable for three years. The list below shows the date of the original grant.

University or College	Subject of the Chair	Holders of the Chairs (most recent occupant listed first)
Amherst College Amherst, Massachusetts	Comparative Religious Ethics (1978)	Lee Yearley Veena Das John P. Reeder Tara Tulku Khensur Rinpoche Yusuf K. Ibish Lal Mani Joshi Wande Abimbola David Little
Brown University Providence, Rhode Island	Comparative Study of Development (1978)	Morris D. Morris Gary R. Saxonhouse
California Institute of Technology Pasadena, California	Law and Social Change in the Technological Society (1971)	Michael E. Levine
Carleton College Northfield, Minnesota	Creative Arts (1974)	John F. Schott Frantisek Daniel
Case Western Reserve University Cleveland, Ohio	Aging, Health, and Society (1983)	Robert Binstock
Claremont-McKenna College Claremont, California	Information, Technology, and Society (1982)	Dean Gillette
College of the Holy Cross Worcester, Massachusetts	Religion, Economic Development, and Social Justice (1986)	Diane Bell

Appendixes

Columbia University New York, New York	International Political Economy (1984)	Richard R. Nelson
Cornell University Ithaca, New York	Science and Society (1968) The Social Implication of Biotechnology (1985)	Franklin A. Long Appointment pending
Dartmouth College Hanover, New Hampshire	Environmental Studies and Policy (1970)	Alan Taft Crane Weyman Lundquist Gordon J. F. MacDonald
Duke University Durham, North Carolina	Democracy, Liberty, and the Market Economy (1984)	Robert H. Bates
Emory University Atlanta, Georgia	Law and the Behavioral Sciences (1970) Humanities and Comparative Studies (1986)	Jonas Robitscher James Gustafson
Fletcher School of Law and Diplomacy Tufts University Medford, Massachusetts	Civilization and Foreign Affairs (1970)	John P. Roche
Hampshire College Amherst, Massachusetts	Law Studies (1969) Food, Resources, and International Policy (1986)	Lester Mazor Ben Wisner
Harvard University Cambridge, Massachusetts	Film Studies (1971) Business, Ethics, and Public Policy (1978	Vladimir Petric Standish D. Lawder Winthrop Knowlton
Haverford College Haverford, Pennsylvania	Ethics and the Professions (1976)	David Little William Ruddick Francis D. Fisher
The Johns Hopkins University Baltimore, Maryland	Science and Writing (1980)	Horace F. Judson
Kenyon College, Gambier, Ohio	Art and Politics (1987)	Lewis Hyde

Massachusetts Institute of Technology Cambridge, Massachusetts	Environment and Public Policy (1972)	Robert C. Seamans, Jr. Paul W. MacAvoy Pierre Raoul Aigrain
Mount Holyoke College South Hadley, Massachusetts	Cosmology (1972)	Norman F. Ramsey Abner Shimony Richard S. Westfall Preston Cloud Dennis W. Sciama Thomas Gold
New York University New York, New York	Urban Values (1968)	Irving Kristol Roger Starr
	Architecture, Urbanism, and History (1987)	Appointment pending
Northwestern University Evanston, Illinois	American Culture and Public Policy (1979)	Paul Boyer Garry Wills
Occidental College Los Angeles, California	Religion, Power, and the Political Process (1981)	Margaret E. Crahan
Princeton University Princeton, New Jersey	Politics, Law, and Society (1970)	Fred I. Greenstein
Rice University Houston, Texas	Engineering Psychology (1983)	Kenneth R. Laughery
Tufts University Medford, Massachusetts	Agricultural Production and Society (1982)	Stewart N. Smith
Tulane University New Orleans, Louisiana	Architecture and Society (1980)	David Scott Slovic Ligia Slovic-Rave'
University of Chicago Chicago, Illinois	Liberal Arts of Human Biology (1974)	Leon R. Kass
University of Rochester Rochester, New York	Cognitive Science (1979)	Patrick J. Hayes
Vanderbilt University Nashville, Tennessee	Public Policy and the Family (1976)	John C. Masters
Washington University St. Louis, Missouri	Law and Liberty (1981)	Douglass C. North

Appendixes

Wellesley College Wellesley, Massachusetts	Language, Mind, and Culture (1977)	M. N. Srinivas Virginia Valium Barbara von Eckardt Laura Nader Sheila Blumstein Alasdair MacIntyre Samuel J. Keyser Wallace L. Chafe
Wesleyan University Middletown, Connecticut	Democratic Institutions and the Social Order (1979)	Robert C. Wood
Wheaton College Norton, Massachusetts	Families, Change, and Society (1984)	Joseph H. Pleck
Yale University New Haven, Connecticut	History and the Environment (1985)	Appointment pending

The Advisory Committees

ADVISORY COMMITTEE TO THE HENRY R. LUCE PROFESSORSHIP PROGRAM

James M. Hester
 President
 The New York Botanical Garden
 New York, New York
 Former President of New York
 University and Rector of United
 Nations University

James A. Perkins
 Chairman
 International Council for
 Educational Development
 Princeton, New Jersey
 Former President of Cornell
 University

Theodore R. Sizer
 Chairman, Department of
 Education
 Brown University
 Providence, Rhode Island
 Former Headmaster of Phillips
 Academy, Andover

Howard R. Swearer
 President
 Brown University
 Providence, Rhode Island
 Former President of Carleton
 College

Paul Weiss
 Heffer Professor of Philosophy
 The Catholic University of America
 Washington, D.C.
 Former Professor, Yale University

ADVISERS TO THE LUCE FUND FOR SCHOLARSHIP IN AMERICAN ART

Charles C. Eldredge III
 Director
 National Museum of American Art
 Smithsonian Institution
 Washington, D.C.

William I. Homer
 H. Rodney Sharp Professor of
 Art History
 University of Delaware
 Newark, Delaware

Peter Plagens
 Artist, art writer
 New York, New York

Appendixes

MEMBERS OF THE SELECTION COMMITTEE
FOR LUCE SCHOLARS

Elie Abel
  Harry and Norman Chandler
  Professor of Communication
  Stanford University
  Stanford, California
Thomas N. Armstrong III
  Director
  Whitney Museum of American Art
  New York, New York
Edwin D. Dodd
  Chairman Emeritus and Director
  Owens-Illinois, Inc.
  Toledo, Ohio
Ulric Haynes, Jr.
  Consultant
  Former U.S. Ambassador to Algeria
  New York, New York
Margaret Hickey
  Public Affairs Editor
  Ladies' Home Journal
  Tucson, Arizona
Lucille (Mrs. George Frederick)
Jewett, Jr.
  Civic Leader
  San Francisco, California
Breene Mitchell Kerr
  President
  Kerr Consolidated
  Oklahoma City, Oklahoma
Peter F. Krogh
  Dean, School of Foreign Service
  Georgetown University
  Washington, D.C.
George R. Packard
  Dean, School of Advanced
  International Studies
  The Johns Hopkins University
  Washington, D.C.
Lynda Sharp Paine
  Associate Professor, School of
  Business Administration
  Georgetown University
  Washington, D.C.

Charles W. Parry
  Chairman and Chief Executive
  Officer
  Aluminum Company of America
  Pittsburgh, Pennsylvania
Lucian W. Pye
  Professor of Political Science
  Massachusetts Institute of
  Technology
  Cambridge, Massachusetts
David H. C. Read, D. D.
  Minister
  Madison Avenue Presbyterian
  Church
  New York, New York
Edward Rubenstein, M.D.
  Associate Dean of Postgraduate
  Medical Education
  Stanford University Medical Center
  Stanford, California
Donald B. Smiley
  Director and former Chairman
  R. H. Macy & Company
  New York, New York
Harmolyn (Mrs. Charls) Walker
  Educational Psychologist
  Potomac, Maryland
Charles Wright
  Judge, Court of Common Pleas
  Philadelphia, Pennsylvania
Robert B. Yegge
  Attorney, Nelson & Harding
  and Dean Emeritus, College of Law
  University of Denver
  Denver, Colorado
Former members, with affiliation at
time of service:
William S. Anderson
  Chairman
  NCR Corporation
  Dayton, Ohio

William W. Bradley, Jr.
  New York Knickerbockers
  New York, New York
  Later: U.S. Senate
  Washington, D.C.
John W. Dodds
  Professor of English (now Emeritus)
  Stanford University
  Stanford, California
Gaylord Donnelley
  Chairman of the Executive
  Committee
  R. R. Donnelley & Sons Co.
  Chicago, Illinois
Paul A. Freund
  Professor of Law
  Harvard University
  Cambridge, Massachusetts
Robert G. Gard, Jr.
  Lieutenant General, U.S. Army,
  Retired,
  President, National Defense
  University
  Later: School of Advanced
  International Studies
  The Johns Hopkins University at
  Bologna, Italy
W. H. Krome George
  Chairman
  Aluminum Company of America
  Pittsburgh, Pennsylvania
William Richard Goodwin
  President
  Johns-Manville Corporation
  Denver, Colorado
James P. Grant
  President, Overseas Development
  Council
  Later: Executive Director
  UNICEF
  New York, New York

Gordon Gray
  Attorney, former Secretary
  of the Army
  Washington, D.C.
Richard C. A. Holbrooke
  Vice President
  Public Strategies
  Former Assistant Secretary for East
  Asian and Pacific Affairs,
  U.S. Department of State
  Washington, D.C.
John Hughes
  Editor, *Christian Science
  Monitor*; later
  Assistant Secretary for Public
  Affairs
  U.S. Department of State
  Washington, D.C.
Vernon E. Jordan
  President, National Urban
  League
  Later: Attorney
  Akin, Gump, Strauss, Hauer & Feld
  Washington, D.C.
Michel Oksenberg
  Member, National Security Council
  Later: Professor of Political Science
  University of Michigan
  Ann Arbor, Michigan
Charles C. Tillinghast, Jr.
  Chairman of the Board
  Trans World Airlines, Inc.
  New York, New York
Robert Triffin
  Professor of Economics
  Yale University
  New Haven, Connecticut

Appendixes

1987 ADVISERS TO THE SOUTHEAST ASIA PROGRAM

David Dapice
  Professor of Economics
  Tufts University
Hildred Geertz
  Professor of Anthropology
  Princeton University
Hue-Tam Ho Tai
  Fairbank Center for East Asian
  Research
  Harvard University

Donald K. Swearer
  Professor of Religion
  Swarthmore College

APPENDIX I
Books Supported by the Luce Fund for Asian Studies

Anderson, Benedict, ed. and trans. *In the Mirror: Literature and Politics in Siam in the American Era*. Bangkok: Editions Duang Kamol, 1985.

Barker, Randolph, and Robert W. Herdt with Beth Rose. *The Rice Economy of Asia*. Washington, D.C.: Resources for the Future, Inc., 1985.

Barnett, Suzanne Wilson, and John King Fairbank, eds. *Christianity in China: Early Protestant Missionary Writings*. Cambridge, Mass.: Harvard University Press, 1985.

Borg, Dorothy, and Waldo Heinrichs. *Uncertain Years: Chinese-American Relations, 1947–1950*. New York: Columbia University Press, 1980.

Cumings, Bruce. *Child of Conflict: The Korean-American Relationship, 1943–1953*. Seattle: University of Washington Press, 1983.

Cumings, Bruce. *The Origins of the Korean War: Liberation and the Emergence of Separate Regimes, 1945–1947*. Princeton: Princeton University Press, 1981.

Edwards, R. Randle, Louis Henkin, and Andrew J. Nathan. *Human Rights in Contemporary China*. New York: Columbia University Press, 1986.

Iriye, Akira. *Power and Culture: The Japanese-American War, 1941–1945*. Cambridge, Mass.: Harvard University Press, 1981.

Kahin, George McT. *Intervention: How America Became Involved in Vietnam*. New York: Alfred A. Knopf, 1986.

Moskowitz, Karl, ed. *From Patron to Partner: The Development of U.S.-Korean Business and Trade Relations*. Lexington, Mass.: D. C. Heath, 1984.

Nathan, Andrew J. *Chinese Democracy*. New York: Alfred A. Knopf, 1985.

Scalapino, Robert A., and George T. Yu. *Modern China and Its Revolutionary Process: Recurrent Challenges to the Traditional Order, 1850–1920*. Berkeley and Los Angeles: University of California Press, 1985.

Stanley, Peter W., ed. *Reappraising an Empire: New Perspectives on Philippine-American History*. Cambridge, Mass.: Harvard University Press, 1984.

Tsou, Tang. *The Cultural Revolution and Post-Mao Reforms: A Historical Perspective*. Chicago: University of Chicago Press, 1986.

Museum Publications
Supported by the Luce Fund for
Scholarship in American Art

Name of Gallery or Museum	Name of Publication	Amount and Date of Grant
Albright-Knox Art Gallery	A catalog to accompany the exhibition *Abstract Expressionism: The Critical Development*	$100,000–1985
Amon Carter Museum of Western Art	A biography and a catalog raisonné of the work of the southwestern photographer Laura Gilpin	$125,000–1982
	Research on *American Frontier Life, Early Western Painting and Prints*	$100,000–1984
Art Institute of Chicago	A catalog of the institute's Universal Limited Art Edition's print collection	$100,000—1982
	A publication and exhibition drawn from the archival gift of architect Ludwig Hilberseimer's papers	$80,000—1983
Baltimore Museum of Art	A catalog of *American Furniture and Period Rooms in the Collection of the Baltimore Museum of Art*	$100,000—1983

	A catalog to accompany an exhibition on Benjamin West	$100,000—1986
Brooklyn Museum	A catalog of the museum's collection of historic American paintings	$150,000—1982
	Research and publication of a book to accompany the exhibition, *The New Path: Ruskin and the American Pre-Raphaelites*	$75,000—1983
	A catalog of the Stewart Culin Collection of North American art	$100,000—1985
Cincinnati Art Museum	A research project leading to publication of *The Creative Spark: American Sculpture, 1800–1900*	$60,000—1983
Sterling and Francine Clark Art Institute	A catalog of the American paintings and sculpture in the institute	$95,000—1986
Cleveland Museum of Art	A catalog of the museum's collection of American silver	$46,000—1982
Columbus Museum of Art	A catalog of the museum's collection of American art	$100,000—1985
Corcoran Gallery of Art	A study of the development of American landscape painting before 1825	$80,000—1982
	A study on James Peale	$70,000—1984

Dallas Museum of Art	A catalog of the museum's collection of pre–World War II American art	$49,000—1982
	A catalog to accompany the exhibition *African-American Art of the Twentieth Century*	$100,000—1985
	A catalog of the Faith P. and Charles L. Bybee Collection of American furniture	$100,000—1986
Denver Art Museum	A catalog of the L. D. Bax Collection of Plains and Plateau Indian art	$100,000—1984
	A catalog of the Herbert Bayer Archive	$100,000—1985
	A catalog to accompany the exhibition *Childe Hassam: An Island Garden Revisited*	$100,000—1986
Detroit Institute of Arts	*American Paintings in the Detroit Institute of Arts*, Volume 1	$110,000—1982 and 1984
	American Paintings in the Detroit Institute of Arts, Volume 2: *A Catalog of Works of Artists Born between 1816 and 1845*	100,000—1986
Fine Arts Museums of San Francisco	A catalog to accompany the exhibition *American Artists in Venice, 1860–1920*	$55,000—1982
	A catalog of the museums' collection of American paintings	$100,000—1984

	A catalog to accompany an exhibition of Winslow Homer's Civil War paintings	$90,000—1986
Hudson River Museum	Research, publication, and exhibition of *The Book of Nature: The Natural Sublime in American Painting from 1819 to 1918*	$20,000—1982
	A catalog to accompany the exhibition *Above the Clouds: Painters, Writers, and Tourists in the Catskills, 1820–1895*	$45,000—1985
Herbert F. Johnson Museum of Art	A study, leading to publication, of the impact of the William Macbeth Gallery on American art from 1892 to 1908	$40,000—1983
Los Angeles County Museum of Art	A catalog of the museum's collection of American art	$125,000—1982
	Research and publication of a catalog to accompany an exhibition on George Innes	$80,000—1983
	A catalog to accompany the exhibition *Chippendale Once Removed: Eighteenth-Century American Rococo Furniture*	$80,000—1985
Metropolitan Museum of Art	A catalog of the museum's collection of American sculpture	$180,000—1982

Munson-Williams-Proctor Institute	A catalog of key works of American art in the institute's permanent collection	$100,000—1985
Museum of Art, Carnegie Institute	A catalog to accompany an exhibition on John LaFarge	$80,000—1984
	A catalog of the museum's collection of American paintings and sculpture before 1945	$100,000—1985
	A catalog to accompany the exhibition *American Landscape Video, 1978–1988*	$65,000—1986
Museum of Art, Rhode Island School of Design	A catalog of *American Decorative Arts at the Museum of Art, Rhode Island School of Design*	$70,000—1982
	A catalog to accompany the exhibition *Views of the Rhode Island Landscape*	$30,000—1984
Museum of Fine Arts, Boston	A research project, leading to publication, on the Boston School	$150,000—1982
	A research project, leading to publication, on the work of Charles Sheeler	$125,000—1983
	A study on *The Art That Is Life: The Arts and Crafts Movement in America, 1875–1930*	$120,000—1984
Museum of Fine Arts of Houston	Catalog of the museum's Bayou Bend Collection of American art	$100,000—1984

Museum of Modern Art	A catalog, using computer format, of the museum's collection of American prints	$125,000—1982
	A catalog, using computer format, of the museum's collection of American drawings	$75,000—1983
	A catalog of Ludwig Mies van der Rohe's American work from 1939 to 1969	$100,000—1985
New Museum of Contemporary Art	Preparation and publication of a volume of essays, *The New Decade: Critical Essays on Contemporary Art and Ideas*	$60,000—1982
	An anthology of artists' writings of the past decade	$80,000—1984
	An anthology of interviews with leading artists of the past decade	$80,000—1985
New-York Historical Society	A catalog to accompany the exhibition *The Legacy of Luman Reed*	$135,000—1985
	A catalog to accompany the exhibition *Thomas Hiram Hotchkiss: Lost Romantic in Arcady*	$50,000—1986
Pennsylvania Academy of the Fine Arts	A catalog raisonné of the academy's collection of American paintings	$125,000—1983
	An annotated guide to the manuscripts of Charles Bregler's Thomas Eakins Collection	$53,700—1986

Philadelphia Museum of Art	A catalog of the museum's archive of material relating to Thomas Eakins	$27,800—1982
	Preparation of a reference book on the museum's collection of American silver and other metals	$100,000—1983
Phillips Collection	Preparation of the portion of the Phillips's permanent catalog devoted to American artists	$75,000—1983
St. Louis Art Museum	A research project on the architecture of Louis Sullivan	$125,000—1984
	A study, leading to publication, of the paintings and sculpture of Frederic Remington	$125,000—1985
San Francisco Museum of Modern Art	A research project, leading to publication, on the origins, history, and impact of surrealism in American art	$75,000—1982
	A research and publication project focusing on the figurative tradition in the painting and sculpture of northern California beginning in the 1950s	$85,000—1983
Seattle Art Museum	A catalog of the museum's collection of American art of the Pacific Northwest	$100,000—1985

Toledo Museum of Art	A catalog of the museum's collection of American glass	$100,000—1982
University Art Museum, Berkeley	Research toward the exhibition *Made in America: Art between the Cold War and Vietnam*	$80,000—1984
Wadsworth Atheneum	A research project, leading to publication, and an exhibition on the arts and culture of the Connecticut River Valley	$84,000—1982
	Research and publication of the Atheneum's collection of American paintings before 1945	$100,000—1983
	Research on the Atheneum's archives	$50,000—1984
Walker Art Center	A catalog of the center's permanent collection of American paintings, sculpture, and drawings	$125,000—1983
	A catalog of the center's Tyler Graphics print collection	$100,000—1984
Whitney Museum of American Art	A research project on contemporary American art in European collections	$125,000—1982
	A research study, leading to publication and a related exhibition on Charles Demuth	$100,000—1983

	A research project on the connoisseurship of twentieth century American art in Europe after World War II	$50,000—1985
Henry Francis du Pont Winterthur Museum	Research, preparation, and publication of *American Silver at Winterthur*	$120,000—1985
	Research, preparation, and publication of *New England Furniture at Winterthur: The Queen Anne and Chippendale Periods*	$125,000—1986
Worcester Art Museum	A catalog of the museum's collection of American watercolors	$70,000—1983
Yale University Art Gallery	A catalog for the exhibition *At Home in Manhattan: Modern Decorative Arts, 1925 to the Depression*	$30,000—1982
	A catalog of the gallery's American case furniture collection	$125,000—1983
	A catalog of the collection of American sculpture at Yale	$24,000—1985

Index

Page numbers in italics indicate illustrations.

Yates, Wilson, 181
Yearley, Lee, 226
Yegge, Robert B., 231
Yenching College for Women, 23
Yenching University, Peking, 22
Yeutter, Clayton, 188
Yonsei University, Korea, 28, 33
Young Men's Christian Association
  (YMCA), 23

Young Women's Christian Association
  (YWCA), 23, 24, 121, 223, 225
Youth Employment Program, NAACP,
  184

Zhang Mengbai, 109